Frommer's®

Budapest day BY day®

2nd Edition

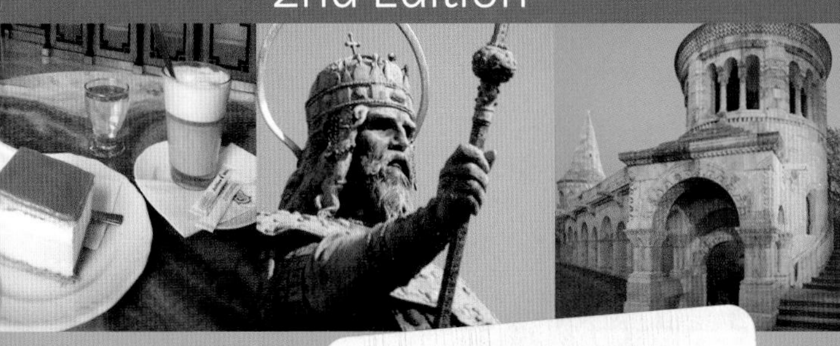

by Robert Smyth

John Wiley & Sons, Inc.

Contents

Copyright © 2012 John Wiley & Sons Inc, The Atrium, Southern Gate, Chichester, West Sussex PO19 8SQ, England
Telephone (+44) 1243 779777
Email (for orders and customer service enquiries): cs-books@wiley.co.uk. Visit our Home Page on www.wiley.com

Editorial Director: Kelly Regan
Production Manager: Daniel Mersey
Commissioning Editor: Fiona Quinn
Development Editor: Jill Emeny
Project Editor: Hannah Clement
Photo Research: Cherie Cincilla, Richard H. Fox, Jill Emeny
Cartography: Simonetta Giori

Wiley publishes in a variety of print and electronic formats and by print-on-demand. Some material included with standard print versions of this book may not be included in e-books or in print-on-demand. If this book refers to media such as a CD or DVD that is not included in the version you purchased, you may download this material at http://booksupport.wiley.com. For more information about Wiley products, visit www.wiley.com.

British Library Cataloguing in Publication Data

A catalogue record for this book is available from the British Library

ISBN 978-1-119-97003-3 (pbk), ISBN 978-1-119-97264-8 (ebk),
ISBN 978-1-119-97034-7 (ebk), ISBN 978-1-119-97035-4 (ebk)

Typeset by Wiley Indianapolis Composition Services
Printed and bound in China by RR Donnelley

5 4 3 2 1

A Note from the Editorial Director

Organizing your time. That's what this guide is all about.

Other guides give you long lists of things to see and do and then expect you to fit the pieces together. The Day by Day guides are different. These guides tell you the best of everything, and then they show you how to see it *in the smartest, most time-efficient way*. Our authors have designed detailed itineraries organized by time, neighborhood, or special interest. And each tour comes with a bulleted map that takes you from stop to stop.

Hoping to tour the best in Budapest's vibrant coffee and bath house culture, engage with its eclectic architecture, burgeoning restaurant scene and dynamic bar culture, or step back behind the iron curtain. Whatever your interest or schedule, the Day by Days give you the smartest routes to follow. Not only do we take you to the top attractions, hotels, and restaurants, but we also help you access those special moments that locals get to experience—those "finds" that turn tourists into travelers.

The Day by Days are also your top choice if you're looking for one complete guide for all your travel needs. The best hotels and restaurants for every budget, the greatest shopping values, the wildest nightlife—it's all here.

Why should you trust our judgment? Because our authors personally visit each place they write about. They're an independent lot who say what they think and would never include places they wouldn't recommend to their best friends. They're also open to suggestions from readers. If you'd like to contact them, please send your comments our way at feedback@frommers.com, and we'll pass them on.

Enjoy your Day by Day guide—the most helpful travel companion you can buy. And have the trip of a lifetime.

Warm regards,

Kelly Regan

Kelly Regan, Editorial Director
Frommer's Travel Guides

About the Author

Robert Smyth is a Budapest-based travel/wine writer who hails from the faded seaside resort of New Brighton, directly across the River Mersey from Liverpool, England. He has been living in Budapest for almost 18 years during which time he's seen certain aspects of the city change beyond recognition, but can still find enough old world and quirky charm to keep him there. He holds a degree in Economics from the U.K., which he followed up with an MBA at Budapest's former Karl Marx University only to find that writing holds more appeal than the world of business. He has written print and online guides respectively for the *Blue Guides* and *Whatsonwhen.com*; he also writes articles on wine tasting. He also still sometimes puts his qualifications to use in covering Hungary's hairaising economic woes.

Acknowledgments

For my partner Ágnes Molnár, our son Alex, my mother Sylvia and late father Robert James Smyth.

I'd like to give a big thanks to the people and city of Budapest for welcoming me to my adopted home and sharing with me the Garden of Budapest whose charms and appeal are growing by the year despite some tough times economically.

It was a pleasure to work once again with the team at Frommers.

Many thanks to all of you who have accompanied me on the great adventure that has been Budapest over the last two decades. From drinking in dive bars or *Kocsma* to devouring fois grois in the finest restaurants, you're too many to mention but you know who you are.

Star Ratings, Icons & Abbreviations

Every hotel, restaurant, and attraction listing in this guide has been ranked for quality, value, service, amenities, and special features using a **star-rating system.** Hotels, restaurants, attractions, shopping, and nightlife are rated on a scale of zero stars (recommended) to three stars (exceptional). In addition to the star-rating system, we also use a kids **icon** to point out the best bets for families. Within each tour, we recommend cafes, bars, or restaurants where you can take a break. Each of these stops appears in a shaded box marked with a coffee-cup-shaped bullet .

The following **abbreviations** are used for credit cards:

AE American Express
DC Diners Club
DISC Discover
MC MasterCard
V Visa

Travel Resources at Frommers.com

Frommer's travel resources don't end with this guide. Frommer's website, **www.frommers.com,** has travel information on more than 4,000 destinations. We update features regularly, giving you access to the most current trip-planning information and the best airfare, lodging, and car-rental bargains. You can also listen to podcasts, connect with other Frommers.com members through our active-reader forums, share your travel photos, read blogs from guidebook editors and fellow travelers, and much more.

Advisory & Disclaimer

Travel information can change quickly and unexpectedly, and we strongly advise you to confirm important details locally before traveling, including information on visas, health and safety, traffic and transport, accommodations, shopping, and eating out. We also encourage you to stay alert while traveling and to remain aware of your surroundings. Avoid civil disturbances, and keep a close eye on cameras, purses, wallets, and other valuables.

While we have endeavored to ensure that the information contained within this guide is accurate and up-to-date at the time of publication, we make no representations or warranties with respect to the accuracy or completeness of the contents of this work and specifically disclaim all warranties, including without limitation warranties of fitness for a particular purpose. We accept no responsibility or liability for any inaccuracy or errors or omissions, or for any inconvenience, loss, damage, costs or expenses of any nature whatsoever incurred or suffered by anyone as a result of any advice or information contained in this guide.

The inclusion of a company, organization or website in this guide as a service provider and/or potential source of further information does not mean that we endorse them or the information they provide. Be aware that information provided through some websites may be unreliable and can change without notice. Neither the publisher or author shall be liable for any damages arising herefrom.

How to Contact Us

In researching this book, we discovered many wonderful places—hotels, restaurants, shops, and more. We're sure you'll find others. Please tell us about them, so we can share the information with your fellow travelers in upcoming editions. If you were disappointed with a recommendation, we'd love to know that, too. Please e-mail: frommers@wiley.com or write to:

Frommer's Budapest Day by Day, 2nd Edition
John Wiley & Sons, Inc. • 111 River St. • Hoboken, NJ 07030-5774

MARKÓ

15 Favorite **Moments**

15 Favorite **Moments**

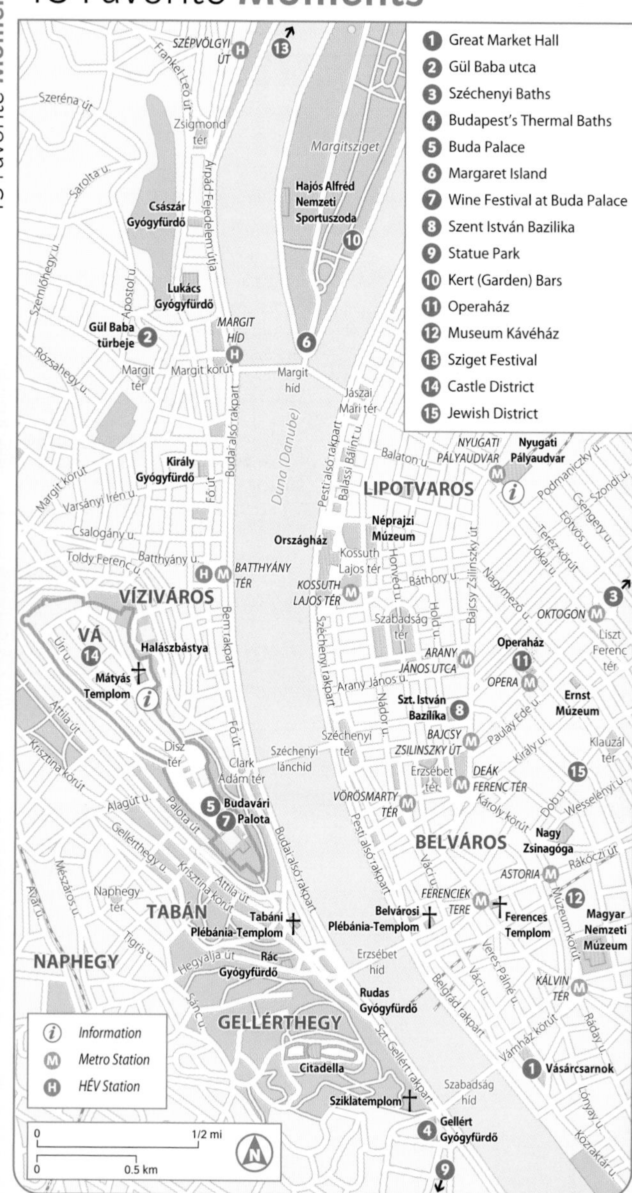

Previous page: View across the Dunube with Chain Bridge.

Budapest is a destination packed with impressive sights, including myriad buildings from the last great expansion phase of the Habsburg Empire; but many of my favorite moments are spent exploring the nooks and crannies that lie between the great edifices. From bathing in atmospheric thermal baths and drinking unique wines in funky bars in disused townhouse courtyards, to exploring the city's Communist past, Budapest has many magic moments to savor.

1 **Great Market Hall.** I never get bored of taking the no. 2 tram to buy "Hungaricums" (typically Hungarian foodstuffs) at the Great Market Hall. The tram winds past Parliament, along the impressive waterfront buildings and down the river with the Castle District and Gellért Hill directly opposite. *See p 17.*

2 **Gül Baba utca.** Be transported back to Turkish Budapest when climbing up the steep and narrow street, Gül Baba utca, named after the dervish who brought the rose to Buda. Pay your respects at his tomb. *See p 31.*

3 **Széchenyi Baths.** Take continental Europe's oldest metro that shunts under swish Andrássy út and then soak up the atmosphere at the neo-baroque Széchenyi Baths. *See p 13.*

4 **Relax in the waters at any one of Budapest's classic thermal baths,** switching between steaming hot and ice-cold pools, sauna, and steam and feel as good as new. It's the ideal way to clear the cobwebs of the city's nightlife excesses. *See p 26.*

5 **View Pest from Buda's Royal Palace.** Gaze down in awe at buzzing Pest from the relative tranquility—depending on how many tourists are accompanying you—of the Buda Palace across the river. It's best in the morning as the city rolls into work opposite or lit up at night when the city folk start to play. *See p 61.*

Relaxing in the neo-Baroque Széchenyi baths.

6 Stand in the middle of the River Danube on Margaret Island and look downstream to Parliament on one side and the Castle District on the other. Great for taking time out from the bustling city and enjoying a bit of green relief. *See p 88.*

7 Wine Festival at Buda Palace. For a touch of refined hedonism, enjoy mingling with the country's leading wine makers and drinking their fine wines in the splendor of Buda's Royal Palace—the best way to enjoy the castle. *See p 165.*

8 Look out to the epic Szent István (St. Stephen's) Bazilika, but from the alternative angle of the cool and contemporary DiVino Wine Bar, with a drink in hand. *See p 9.*

9 Contemplating the pillars of Communist society that once imposed themselves across the city but are now confined to the **Statue Park,** part of the Memento Park. I find the replica of Stalin's boots, left behind when his statue was torn down at Felvonulási tér (Hungary's answer to Red Square), particularly significant. *See p 46.*

The plush surroundings at the Operaház.

10 Budapest's Kert (Garden) Bars. Feel downright decadent—and very glad to be in Hungary after the winter is all but a memory—at one of the city's Kert Garden summer bars. *See p 121.*

11 Drink bubbly on the balcony of the Operaház during a break and marvel at the plush surroundings, wondering how the main chandelier can possibly stay up. *See p 10.*

12 Take in the tranquility of dawn and the power of the city's fin-de-siècle architecture from the terrace of the **Museum Kávéház** after a long night out. Have a last *Unicum* liqueur and some pastry as the city starts to wake up.

13 Sip a beer while taking a ferry down the Danube to rock till you drop at the Sziget Festival, and then hop back on the ferry well after sunrise. *See p 165.*

14 Explore the old cobbled narrow streets of the Castle District between Táncsics Mihály utca and Tóth Árpád sétány, which are off the beaten track. *See p 7.*

15 Feel the buzz and ambience of the Jewish District, which despite having seen a lot of adversity is still hanging on as buildings are bulldozed all around. *See p 54.*

1 The Best **Full-Day Tours**

The Best in One Day

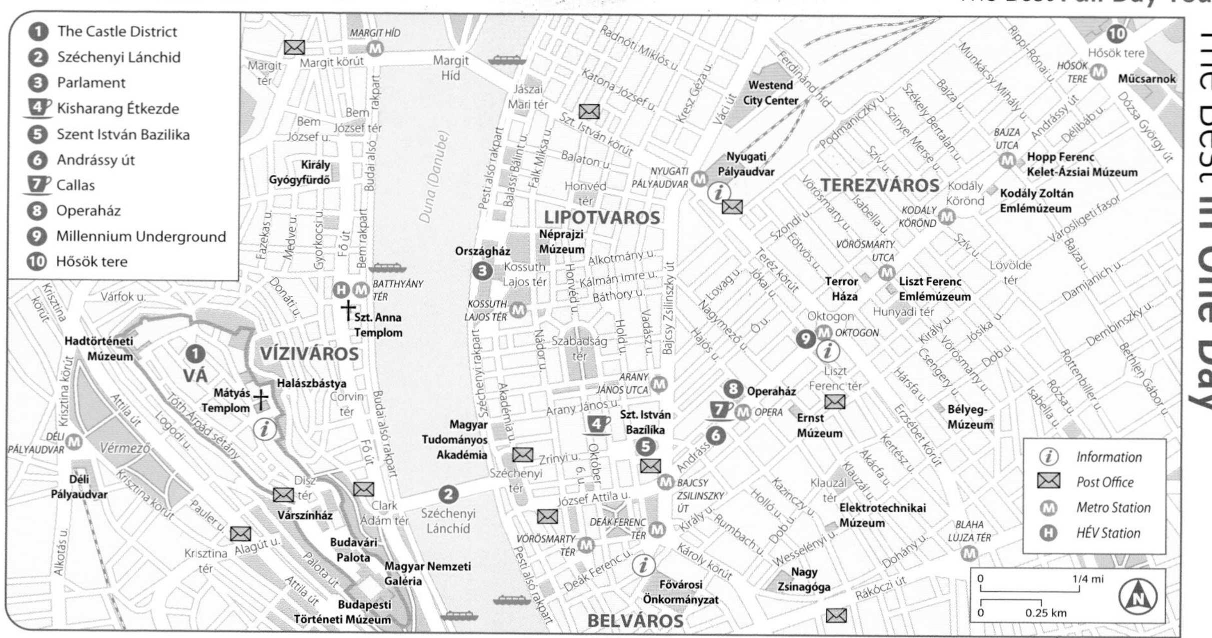

Previous page: The Gellért Baths.

This tour will introduce you to Budapest's architectural highlights in all their magnificence and magnitude. Particularly noteworthy is the architecture of the late 19th and early 20th centuries, when Hungary had finally found peace and prosperity. The stops on the tour can be navigated on foot, unless otherwise stated.

START: **Bus: 16/16A/116 to Dísz tér.**

Funicular in the Castle District.

1 ★★★ The Castle District. Bombed, burnt, battered, and rebuilt many times throughout the centuries, the **Royal Palace** and **St. Matthias Church** dramatically portray Hungary's trials and tribulations. I suggest you wander the district at your leisure to soak up the history of the place but return later for a more in-depth tour. ⌚ *2 hr. Bus 16/16A/116 to Dísz tér. See p 60.*

2 ★★★ kids Széchenyi Lánchíd (Chain Bridge). This, the pick of Budapest's varied bridges, isn't just an architectural marvel but is the first permanent bridge that linked Buda with Pest, setting in motion their eventual unification. It's also the most scenic way of traversing the Danube from Parliament and Pest's old town to the Castle District. The ornate bridge was the brainchild of István Széchenyi, an anglophile Hungarian count who sought to bring rural Hungary into the modern age. He employed two designers, both coincidently with the surname of Clark, although they came from opposite ends of Great Britain: William, an Englishman, and

The Chain Bridge.

The dome in architect Imre Steindl's Parlament.

Adam, a Scot. The structure opened in 1849 during Hungary's War of Independence with Austria and survived an immediate botched attempt to blow it up. The Germans later succeeded in causing serious damage to the bridge whilst in retreat from the city in 1945, although it was soon restored and re-opened on its centenary in the original style. The best time to see it is at night, when the Royal Palace and the bridge are brilliantly lit up together. ⏲ *20 min. Connects Clark Adám tér with Roosevelt tér. Bus 105/16 or Tram 2.*

3 ★★★ **Parlament.** Architect Imre Steindl's mostly neo-Gothic extravaganza dominates Pest's waterfront and bucks the Gothic trend with a 96m-high (315-ft.) dome at its center. It was the biggest parliament in the world when it opened for business in 1896, and even today the building still holds an air of opulence with its grandiose gold-plated details and red-carpeted staircases (which unfortunately do nothing to instill any form of collective unity between the polarized politicians). Although much like any parliament, should you happen to enter the chamber after a debate, to which the opposition actually shows up, you can almost feel the steam rising. Look out for the Hungarian crown, a gift from the Pope to King (now Saint) István (Stephen) in the year 1000 to thank him for signing up Hungary to Catholicism. ⏲ *1 hr for tour, 15 min viewing from outside; enquire ahead via Internet*

Off the Beaten Track

Although Budapest is blessed with many outstanding sights, I actively encourage you to step off the beaten path as and when the mood takes you. Budapest is visually impressive in virtually every direction. The charm of Budapest can be found in the architectural details, and so do take time to seek out the gargoyles or decorative motifs that adorn the plethora of striking late 19th- and early 20th-century buildings.

as Parlament is closed when in session. Kossuth tér 1–3. ☎ 1/441-4000. www.parlament.hu. Tour free for EU citizens, other nationalities 3,400 Ft adults, 1,700 Ft students & children. Buy tickets at gate X. English tours at 10am, 12noon, and 2pm daily. Turn up 15 min before the tour begins. Metro: M2 to Kossuth tér.

4 **Kisharang Étkezde.** Decked out in kitchen utensils, the enticing "Little Bell" serves tasty, no-nonsense Hungarian classics. It's fast and friendly, and the food is freshly prepared with half portions available for smaller appetites. If you're only after refreshment, try a delicious fruit cordial *(szörp)* such as *bodza* (elderberry) with soda. *Október 6 utca 17. ☎ 1/269-3861. www.kisharang.hu. Chicken paprika 1,590 Ft.*

5 ★★★ **Szent István Bazilika (St. Stephen's Basilica).** Building this Budapest landmark proved a job too far for the Hungarian architects József Hild and Miklós Ybl, who both died during the prolonged 54-year construction. The project literally hit rock bottom when the dome collapsed in 1868, a year after Hild's death. Fortunately, once the project's final architect József Kauser took over, Budapest's biggest church was finally accomplished in 1905. A massive restoration project was completed in 2003 and the gleaming marble is the result of the application of 200 kg (440 lb) of beeswax. Mathematically minded Hungarians love dealing in numbers and, like the Parlament's dome, Szent István's stands 96m (315 ft.) high, as a tribute to the Magyar settlement of Hungary in 896. Had they arrived a few years earlier, perhaps the roof wouldn't have fallen in! The almost 1,000-year-old withered hand of St. Stephen, Hungary's first king, is displayed in the **Szent Jobb Chapel.** Another great Hungarian hero Ferenc Puskás, the talisman of the Magical Magyars soccer team and Real Madrid goal machine, was laid to rest here in 2006. An elevator is on hand to whisk you up to near the top of the dome for sweeping views. ⌚ *1 hr. Szent István tér 1. ☎ 1/317-2859. www.basilica.hu (in Hungarian only). Free admission to Basilica; tower 500 Ft adults; 400 Ft children, students and seniors. Church open Mon–Fri 10am–5pm, Sat–Sun 10am–4pm. Tower open daily Oct–Jun 10am–5:30pm (exc. mid-Mar–end*

St. Stephen's Basilica.

Take a ride on continental Europe's oldest metro.

Apr closes 4:30pm); Jul–Sept 10am–7:30pm. Metro: M3 to Arany János utca.

6 Stroll up Andrássy út. This lower stretch of swanky tree-lined avenue is home to many of the high-end international designer labels. You can browse **Burberry** (no. 24), **D&G** (no. 33), **Emporio Armani/ Armani Jeans** (no. 9), **Gucci** (no. 23), Max Mara (no. 21), and **Louis Vuitton** (no. 24), to name a few. The **Párizsi Nagyáruház** (no. 39), a historic mall, has been beautifully restored and houses the attractive coffeehouse **Lotz terem** (p 35, 4). *10 min–1 hr.*

The Opera House.

7 ★★ Callas. This, the former ticket office of the neighboring Opera, which can be viewed through the large arched windows, has been superbly spruced up by the noted British designer David Collins in an engaging blend of fin-de-siècle and Art Deco. While Callas is a serious dining venue, it also serves up good-value lunch specials, homemade pastries, and cakes during the day. ***Andrássy út 20. ☎ 1/354-0954. www.callascafe.hu. Main courses from 3,450 Ft.***

8 ★★★ Operaház. The Miklós Ybl-designed Opera House provides the sumptuous veneer to classy Andrássy út. To really see the Opera House in all its glory, catch one of the performances (p 132), but be warned that the super-steep cheap seats are not for sufferers of vertigo. The neo-Renaissance exterior has semi-circular arches and columns, while statues of the two Hungarian musical greats, Liszt and Bartok, flank the main entrance. Step inside and the style changes dramatically to neoclassical with the walls and ceiling adorned by lavish works from leading artists of the day, including Gyula Benczúr and Bertalan Székely. *15 min, 45 min if you take the tour, but check ahead as tours may* *be cancelled due to rehearsals. Andrássy út 22. ☎ 1/332-7914 or 1/353-0170 for tickets, 1/332-8197 for tours. www.opera.hu/en. 1,900–2,900 Ft. Tours at 3pm and 4pm daily, performances vary. Metro: M1 to Opera.*

9 ★★ kids **Millennium Underground.** Take a ride on continental Europe's oldest metro, which opened in 1896 to coincide with the 1,000th anniversary of Magyar presence in Hungary. Board at the Opera or Oktogon stops and be whisked, just under street level, directly down the elegant Andrássy út. After London's underground system, this is the next oldest in the world and the stations in particular retain the fin-de-siècle feel. Whilst walking up to Oktogon to catch the underground, you pass one of Budapest's several centers where Andrássy út meets the Nagy körút (the Great Boulevard). ◷ *15 min. Entrances outside the Opera or at Oktogon. First metro 4:36am, last 11:20pm. www.bkv.hu/metro/metro1.html. Single journey ticket 330 Ft (260 Ft for less than 3 stops). Metro: M1 to Hősök tere.*

10 ★★★ kids **Hősök tere (Heroes' Square).** There's no better place to round off your first day than Heroes' Square. The key protagonists of Hungary's turbulent history are introduced as a series of imposing statues. The central column is guarded by the seven Magyar tribe leaders who, in A.D. 896, stormed into the Carpathian basin, comprising present-day Hungary and beyond. A statue of Árpád leads these seven heathen horsemen, and they appear to be kept in check by Archangel Gabriel, who presides over them from the top of the central column. The founding fathers are flanked by heroes including Szent (Saint) István, who converted Hungary to Christianity on Christmas Day in the year A.D. 1000, and all-conquering kings Bela IV and Mátyás Corvinus, as well as perennial thorns in Habsburg Austria's side like Rákóczi and Kossuth. Built in 1896 to celebrate a millennium of Magyar presence, nowadays Heroes' Square is a popular place with skateboarders—and with political right-wingers who use it as a backdrop for rallies. ◷ *30 min. Hősök tere at crossing of Andrássy út and Dózsa György út. Metro: M1 to Hősök tere.*

The central column in Heroes Square is guarded by seven Magyar tribe leaders.

The Best in Two Days

After a hard day of major sightseeing on Day 1, take the plunge and relax in one of Budapest's world-renowned thermal baths, while still admiring its architectural beauty. Afterwards, get out and about again to uncover some of the unique buildings that reflect the country's varied and troubled past. START: **Take the M1 or "Millennium Underground" to Széchenyi Fürdő.**

1 ★★★ kids Széchenyi Baths. The therapeutic waters of this neo-baroque bathing bonanza will revitalize tired joints and set you up for a fulfilling day. That's providing you don't spend all your time being slow cooked in the hot pools, which will leave you seriously sleepy. You can alternate between the pools of varying temperatures, saunas, and steam rooms, or just chill out on a deckchair. The most luxurious pool is the outdoor semi-circular one, from which steam dramatically rises in the cold of winter as locals play chess. The whirly pool is fun for youngsters. Come early to avoid the crowds, especially in summer. *2 hr.* *See p 27,* 2.

2 ★ kids Vajdahunyad Castle. Looking at it now, it's hard to believe that this fairly authentic-looking folly was once made out of cardboard and is barely a century old. The castle was erected as a temporary structure as part of the Magyar millennium celebrations in 1896, depicting the various Hungarian architectural styles over the centuries. By 1908, it had been transformed into a collection of stone replicas representing treasured creations from right across the Magyar realm. Particularly prominent are the ramparts facing the lake modeled on the original Vajdahunyad Castle and Sighişoara's clocktower, both in present-day Romania. The building now houses the **Museum of Hungarian Agriculture (Magyar Mezőgazdasági Múzeum)**, with information on Hungary's conservation, wine-making, and honey bees. *15 min–1 hr. City Park. ☎ 1/422-0765. www.mmgm.hu. 1,000 Ft adults, children & students aged 6–26 500 Ft. Tues–Sun*

Vajdahunyad Castle.

Take a dip in the therapeutic Széchenyi Baths.

10am–5pm. Metro: M1 to Hősök tere/Széchenyi Fürdő.

❸ ★★ **Szépmüvészeti Múzeum (Fine Arts Museum).** The mighty Habsburgs who once ruled as far as Spain and the Netherlands acquired an astonishing collection of art works, many of which found their way here. This is a tour de force in European art from the 13th to the late 18th centuries, with the Spanish masters forming the museum's strongest collection. Works by El Greco, Velázquez, Murillo, Ribera, Cano, Zurbarán, and Goya are represented. El Greco's *Annunciation,* painted in the late 16th century, is set to heavenly clouds and bright lights (it has a twin in Madrid's Prado museum with an architectural background), while Velázquez's early work *Peasants Around a Table,* dated around 1619, magically preserves the time-honored tradition of getting stuck into conversation over a few drinks. An hour can be enough to view the best pictures but you might want to come back another time to visit one of the temporary exhibitions. *1–1½ hr. Come early when major temporary exhibitions are running. Dózsa György út 41 (overlooking Heroes' Square). ☎ 1/469-7100. www.szepmuveszeti.hu. 1,600 Ft adults; 800 Ft children 6–14. Temporary exhibitions vary. Tues–Sun 10am–5:30pm. Metro: M1 Hősök tere.*

❹ **Walk up Andrássy út.** You are more than likely to have explored portions of this, the grandest of Budapest's boulevards on Day 1 when checking out the Opera House, but further examination is rewarding. Walking from **Heroes' Square** (p 11, ❿) the first stretch is lined with luxurious villas. Further up, Andrássy út is traversed by **Kodály körönd,** a striking square of faded but ornately painted townhouses. *30 min. See also p 10, ❻.*

❺ **Lukács Cukrázda.** Grab a coffee and snack at this tastefully restored coffeehouse that excels in freshly made cakes and pastries and is more laid back than most, set away from the madding crowd. *Andrássy út 70. ☎ 06/30-812-1525. www.lukacscukraszda.com. Coffee & pastry from 800 Ft.*

❻ ★★★ **Terror Háza (House of Terror).** An address that seems to be cursed, this visually impressive museum caused controversy with its highly politicized opening in 2002. Seen by many as an affront to the re-spun Hungarian Socialist Party, which

The cutting-edge museum at House of Terror.

The Great Synagogue.

once ruled Hungary with an iron fist but has since changed beyond recognition, on behalf of their archrivals Fidesz—it was even sponsored by the-then Fidesz Prime Minister Victor Orbán, who returned to power in 2010. There is fleeting coverage of Fascist Hungary and much denser coverage of the red terror. The fascist Hungarian Arrow Cross Party ran the country for only a year in 1944; but what a gruesome year that was, with the previously protected Jewish population being shipped off in droves to concentration camps. Politics aside, from the Russian tank that greets you to the pictures of victims and their jailors; the industrial and dark classical soundtrack; film footage and interviews; genuine exhibits including Hungarian Nazi Arrow Cross uniforms; and the trip to the cells and gallows, I can't help but feel indignation. ⌚ *1 hr. Andrássy út 60.* ☎ *1/374-2600. www.terrorhaza.hu. 1,800 Ft adults, 900 Ft for E.U. citizens, children and students 6–25. Tues–Sun 10am–6pm. Metro: M1 to Vörösmarty utca.*

7 ★★★ Nagy Zsinagóga (Great Synagogue). Budapest's great synagogue not only pioneered a new style of Jewish architecture, with its onion domes and Moorish and Byzantine influences, but also spawned the father of modern Zionism who was born here, Tivadar Herzl. ⌚ *15 min.* *See p 55, 1.*

8 ★★★ kids Iparművészeti Múzeum, IMM (Museum of Applied Arts). You might have encountered this remarkable-looking Art Nouveau masterpiece by architect Ödön Lechner (Budapest's answer to Barcelona's Gaudí) if you took the road in from the airport. Lechner, who also worked on the building's plans with secessionist sidekick Gyula Pártos, created a Hungarian take on the Art Nouveau movement, adding Hungarian folk touches and emphasizing certain eastern influences on Hungary. Accordingly, traces of architectural styles from as far afield as India can be detected, and the bright green and gold *Zsolnay* tiles that adorn the roof and dome are more Oriental than European. ⌚ *15 min. Üllői út 33–37.* ☎ *1/456-5100. www.imm.hu. Adults 1,000 Ft., children & students aged 6 to 26 500 Ft . Tues–Sun 10am–6pm. Metro: M3 to Ferenc körút.* *See also p 25, 13.*

The impressive entrance to the Museum of Applied Arts.

The Best in Three Days

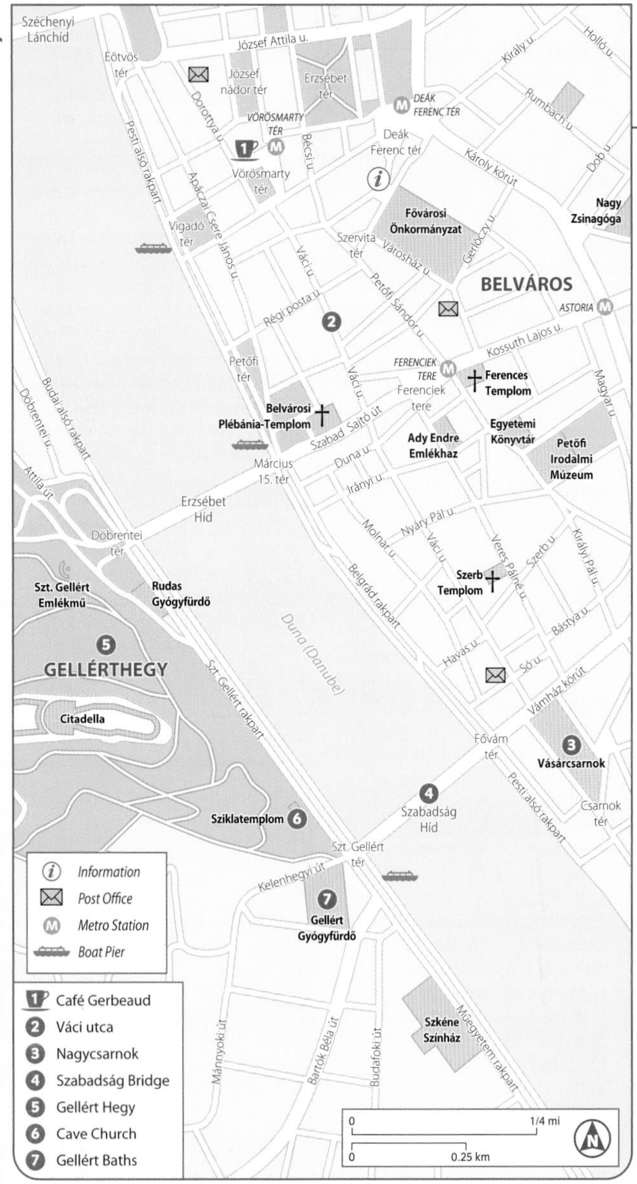

After pacing the streets in the first 2 days, start today with a coffee at one of Budapest's most luxurious coffeehouses, followed by a spot of shopping. This tour also gives you the option of ending the day with a thermal bathe to soothe the joints after scaling the dizzy heights of Gellért Hill. START: **M1 to Vörösmarty tér or Tram 2 to Vigadó tér.**

1 ★ **Café Gerbeaud.** Start your morning at the plushest of the city's illustrious coffeehouses. In summer, if the wealth of chandeliers, marble tables, fine wood paneling, and stucco ceilings gets a bit much, take to the terrace. Cafe culture here is now about reading papers and devouring Gerbeaud's renowned Esterházy and Dobos cakes, but in the past legend has it that young men indicated their availability to well-heeled ladies of pleasure by tipping an excessive amount of sugar into their coffee. *45 min. Vörösmarty tér 7. 1/429-9020. www.gerbeaud.hu/en. Metro: M1 to Vörösmarty tér. Coffee & croissant 950 Ft.*

2 ★★ kids **Váci utca.** Even those who aren't shopaholics can easily take in this relatively short shopping street and surrounding area, including **Fashion Street**—the new moniker for Deák Ferenc utca. Starting from the often lively Vörösmarty tér, you'll find most big international fashion brands from Zara to H&M, although most of them seem to offer a somewhat modest selection in comparison to other international cities. Keep an eye out on the side streets for high-end designer stores. Souvenir shops also abound, though with steep price tags, and if you are into embroidered tablecloths and folk art then you have come to the right place. The shopping street continues on the other side of Szabadsajtó út where the vibe is less frenetic. Before crossing or walking through the underpass that connects the two sides of Váci utca, take a left to the **Párizsi udvar** (at Ferenciek tere 10–11/Petőfi Sándor utca 2–8), which is a grandiose forerunner of the modern shopping mall. It seems to be lifted straight from turn-of-the-century Paris. **Ferenciek tere** (p 53, 13) itself is also a faded gem from the Belle Époque. *1 hr. Walk through the underpass that connects the two sides of Váci utca. From Vörösmarty tér to Vámház körút. Metro: M1 to Vörösmarty tér (starting point).*

3 ★★ **Nagycsarnok (Great Market Hall).** You may feel like you're walking through an Impressionist painting when the sunlight shines into this beautifully restored king of neighborhood markets. However, it's far from a museum piece; many locals come here to shop for fresh food and it's bustling with life

Café Gerbeaud.

Tinned paprika displayed in the Great Market Hall.

and color. The array of meat on sale shows just how thrifty Hungarians are, as they consider every part of the animal fair game for the pot. The carp and catfish crammed in tanks on fish "death row" downstairs are an uncomfortable sight for some, but on the positive—at least they're fresh. There are plenty of local foodstuffs from paprika to salami and goose liver. Upstairs look out for folklore and handicrafts hidden among the mountains of tourist goods. ⏱ *30 min–1 hr. Vámház körút 1–3.* ☎ *1/366-3300. Mon 6am–5pm, Tues–Fri 6am–6pm, Sat 6am–3pm. Metro: M3 to Kálvin tér. Tram: 47/49.*

4 Walk across Szabadság Bridge. Buda and Pest are seamlessly connected by this bright green piece of intricate ironwork that joins the Pest's Great Market Hall and its neighbor the **Budapest University of Economics** (formerly the Karl Marx University) with the **Gellért Hotel** and the dramatic Gellért Hill of Buda. On the day of its opening in 1896, Emperor Franz Joseph applied the finishing touch by knocking the final rivet into place. ⏱ *10 min. Starts where Pest's Vámház körút meets the Danube. Tram: 47/49 to Kálvin tér.*

5 ★★★ kids Gellért Hegy (Gellért Hill). This imposing hill that towers over the Pest waterfront of the Danube has been used to good effect to suppress forces for change. Italian missionary Szent Gellért was reportedly rolled down the hill in 1046 to his death by revolting pagans. The Austrians then built a Citadel from which to lord it over the Magyars.

The Gellért Hotel.

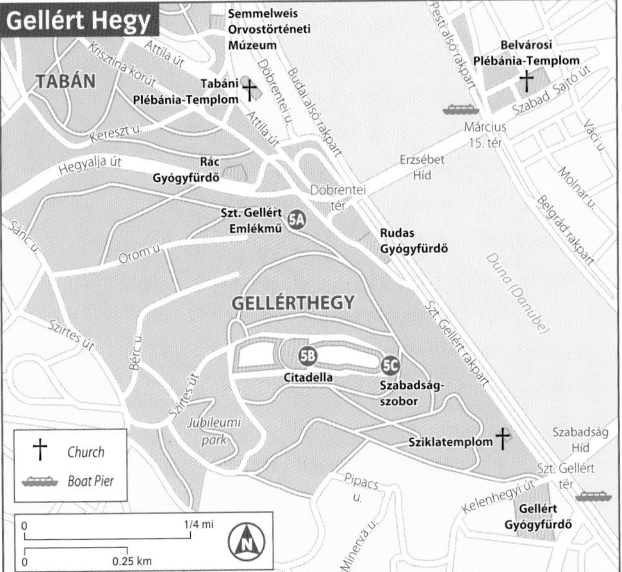

To find the 5A **Gellért Statue,** walk upstream toward the Erzsebet Bridge where you'll see the steps leading up. Gellért, who participated in spreading the gospel in 11th-century Hungary on King Stephen's request, met a grisly end being tumbled down the hill (that was subsequently named after him) in a barrel filled with nails. Ultimately, Christianity won through with Gellért being canonized in 1083. The statue, dating back to 1904 and the work of Hungarian sculptor Gyula Jankovits (1865–1920), captures the saint preaching defiantly but precariously on the edge of the hill. Follow the path up farther and you reach the 5B **Citadel,** built by the Austrians, soon after the Hungarian Revolution of 1848. There wasn't much use for it after they patched up their differences in 1867, although German occupying forces utilized it in World War II. The bunker inside the Citadel has waxworks and photos chronicling the Siege of Budapest. Close by and at the peak of the hill, Budapest's very own statue of liberty, the 5C **Freedom Statue,** ironically erected in 1947 as a tribute to the Soviet forces that liberated the city from the Nazis. Featuring a woman proffering the palm branch of triumph and not overtly Soviet-looking, it survived the cull of Communist statues from the capital. *1–2 hr.*

Relax in style at the Gellért thermal baths.

❻ **Cave Church.** On the way down, just before reaching the Gellért Hotel and Baths, look out for this spooky church—its eerie passages dig deep into the hill. Don't be alarmed if a priest appears from nowhere. ◷ *15 min.*

❼ ★★★ **Gellért Baths.** After another hard day of pounding the streets, the Art Nouveau architecture of these thermal baths allows you to relax in style. Inside, the central pool is surrounded by Romanesque columns and lions spitting water. At the end of the pool, the male and female thermal facilities are to the right and left respectively. This is where things start to get really colorful and heated, and I'm not just talking about the design or decoration, or the saunas and steam rooms. You can keep your bathing costume on, though many locals like to let it all hang out and dispense with their modesty cloths, although the authorities are said to be cracking down. The plunge pool is so icy you feel the chill right through your bones, but the thaw of the warm pools is always close at hand. While the waters are supposed to sort out arthritis, blood circulation, and the spine, I say just enjoy them and come out feeling squeaky clean and purified. In summer, be sure to check out the outdoor pools and garden, an area that's also more suitable for youngsters who can enjoy artificial waves in the main outdoor pool. ◷ *2 hr.* *See p 27,* ❶. ●

2 The Best Special-Interest Tours

The Best Art Nouveau

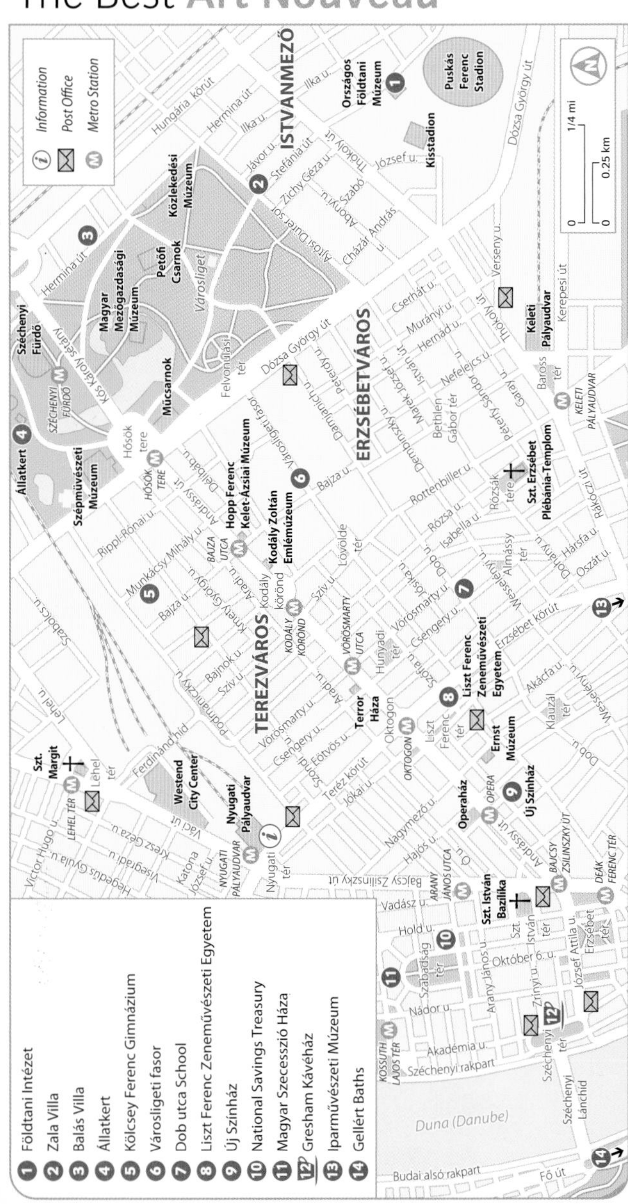

Sporting hero statue, Ferenc Puskás stadium.

Budapest is blessed with many buildings constructed using a unique take on the Art Nouveau movement known as *szecesszió*. Its figurehead is architect Ödön Lechner (1845–1914), often seen as Hungary's Gaudí. Much of this tour can be managed on foot, which is a great way to see lesser known but still impressive parts of the city. START: **M2 to Stadionak.**

1 ★★ kids **Földtani Intézet (Geological Institute).** Ödön Lechner incorporates geological elements such as fossils into his folk influenced, eye-catching purple and yellow facade. If you arrive on a nonvisitation day, a peek at the entrance hallway gives you an idea of the expressive interior. There's a small Lechner exhibition between floors. *30 min. Stefánia út 14.* ☎ *1/251-0999. www.mafi.hu/en. 500 Ft adults, 250 Ft children; free for children 5 and under. Thurs, Sat and Sun 10am–4pm. Metro: M2 to Stadionak.*

2 **Zala Villa.** A short walk from the Geological Institute, Lechner's 1901 castle-like structure, noteworthy for the elaborate sculptured motifs of human figures—the *Celebration of Venus*—that drape over the wavy arched window, now houses the Libyan Embassy. *5 min. Stefánia út 111 (corner of Ajtósi Dürer sor).*

3 ★★ **Balás Villa.** You may have heard of buildings resembling elaborate wedding cakes before, but this Ödön Lechner-designed building, with its various tones of brown, is more of a chocolate confection—and thanks to the angles, a Gothic one at that. It looks out onto the City Park, houses the Braille Institute, and is a short walk from the Zala Villa. *10 min. Hermina út 47.*

4 ★ **Állatkert (Zoo).** *Szecesszió* often draws on Indian and oriental elements and examples of this can be seen at the Zoo's elaborate entrance with its towers, sculptured elephants, and gruesome gorillas. *15 min.* *See p 84,* **4**.

5 ★ **Kölcsey Ferenc Gimnázium.** After seeing such an ornate zoo, I totally envy the local children. Just a few minutes' walk away, you will find the kind of epic and ornate school—designed in 1898 by Hungarian architect Körössy Albert Kálmán—that many of us would have loved to have gone to. *10 min. Munkácsy Mihály utca 26. www.kolcsey-bp.hu.*

6 ★ **Városligeti fasor.** The stretch of this elegant boulevard closest to the City Park is lined with some magnificent Art Nouveau mansions. *10 min.*

The elaborate entrance to the Zoo.

7 ★★ **Dob utca School.** I like the clever and subtle use of brown and blue paintwork that keeps the building subdued enough to be used as a seat of education, but still complements the building's wavy and wobbly Art Nouveau aspect. The school's coat of arms—murals of children playing hide and seek and marching soldiers—provides the perfect finish. ◷ ***10 min. Dob utca 85. www.dobsuli.hu. Tram: 4/6 to Király utca.***

8 **Liszt Ferenc Zeneművészeti Egyetem (Ferenc Liszt Music Academy).** The parallels between Budapest and Barcelona in terms of architectural modernism don't end with Gaudí and Lechner. Aside from the muscular sculptures holding up a seated statue of Liszt, and some handy ironwork, much like Barcelona's famed *Palau de la Musica,* the real beauty of this building is the awesome auditorium, which doesn't just look the part but sounds fantastic too. I suggest you get along to one of the Academy's great value concerts (p 131) or peek inside during term time. ◷ ***10 min. Liszt Ferenc tér 8. www.lfze.hu. Tram: 4/6 to Király utca.***

9 ★ **Új Színház.** Béla Lajta's compact and somewhat understated, but nonetheless striking, "New Theater" building is tucked into this narrow side street that runs adjacent to majestic Andrássy. Opened as the *Parisiana* nightclub in 1909, its charm can be found in the domineering sculptured monkeys and the gold-and-blue organ pipe-like trimmings at the top. ◷ ***10 min. Paulay Ede utca 35. Metro: M1 to Opera.***

10 ★★★ **National Savings Treasury.** Tucked away off the main drag, the facade is an engaging mix of wavy lines, light colors, Hungarian folk motifs, and Islamic pillars. Naturally, the bees making honey means money in Lechner-speak. However, the real drama comes with the roof, where Lechner deployed the wares of iconic Hungarian ceramics' manufacturer **Zsolnay** (p 72) to a more daring end than usual. Here the gentle curves of the facade give way to more stark angles in an eye-catching yellow and green layered finish. Opened in 1886 as the Royal Hungarian Postal Savings Bank, it now serves as the National Savings Treasury. Although it's closed to the public, you can step in the door for a peek of the interior. ◷ ***15 min. Hold utca 4. Metro: M3 to Arany János utca.***

National Savings Treasury.

The Art Nouveau Bedö Ház.

⑪ ★★ Magyar Szecesszió Háza (House of Hungarian Art Nouveau). The Art Nouveau **Bedő Ház** takes the interactive museum concept a step further. Although the objets d'art are inanimate—Art Nouveau furniture, beds, love chairs, and the like—you can actually sit on or stretch out on them should you desire. The museum stops short of letting you take the exhibits home, but have a word with them and they'll put you in touch with a carpenter who produces replicas. ⌚ *30 min. Honvéd utca 3.* ☎ *1/269-4622. www.magyarszecessziohaza.hu. 1,500 Ft adults, 1,000 Ft children, free for under-5s. Mon–Sat 10am–5pm. Metro: M2 to Kossuth Lajos tér.*

⑫ Gresham Kávéház. This suave coffeehouse-cum-bistro is housed in the stunningly restored Art Nouveau Four Seasons Gresham Palace Hotel [p 142] and offers up a noted deluxe burger from sirloin, exquisite sandwiches, and salads. *Széchenyi tér 5–6.* ☎ *1/268-5100. www.fourseasons.com/budapest/dining/. Burger 4,900 Ft.*

⑬ kids Iparművészeti Múzeum (Museum of Applied Arts). As you walk through the ornate entrance, the color of the facade gives way to a whitewashed interior. In 1920, the wishes of conservative critics were met and the daring design of the inside was painted over. This really shouldn't discourage you from entering though because, fortunately, they couldn't destroy the delightful essence of the place. The twisty curling shapes, wobbly staircases, and the immense conservatory remain true to their original design. Among the permanent Art Nouveau exhibits look out for the Frigyes Spiegel-designed Art Nouveau Tall Case Clock and lots of other marvelous furniture. ⌚ *1–1½hr.* *See p 15,* ❽.

⑭ ★★★ Gellért Baths. Although much of the Gellért Hotel was bombed to rubble in World War II, the side that houses the baths escaped the worst and remains close to its original Art Nouveau splendor. *See p 27,* ❶.

The Best Baths

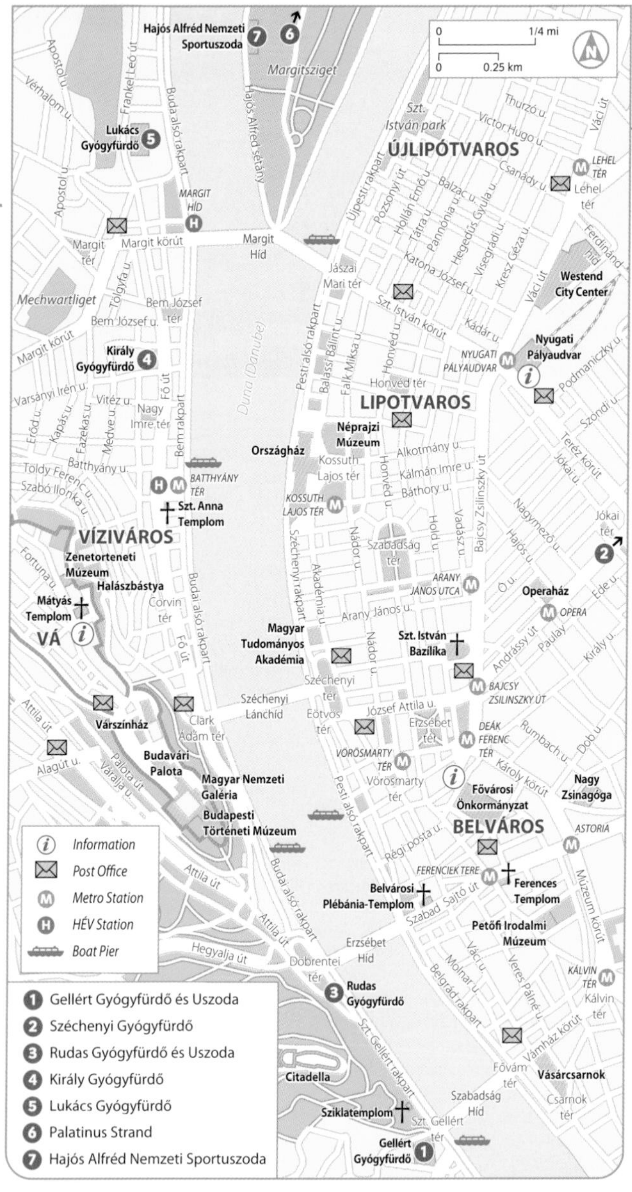

Budapest's thermal baths and lidos have helped people through many an icy winter and cooled them down in the heat of summer. Each has its own character, and although the thermal water itself is prescribed for treating all sorts of conditions many people go just to play chess in the steam or enjoy a swim in the waters. START: **Tram: 18/19/47/49. Bus: 7 to Gellért tér.**

1 ★★★ kids Gellért Gyógyfürdő és Uszoda (Gellért Baths). Although not the best place to come for a good swim, the Gellért offers outstanding, single-sex thermal bathing, with the men's side the most lavish. The cold plunge pool is so icy that you can feel your own bones, while the faded grandeur makes the garden a top place to take it very easy in the warmer months. For more information, see p 20, 7. *Kelenhegyi út 4. ☎ 1/452-4500. www.gellertbath.com. Mon–Fri. 3,800 Ft with locker, 4,100 Ft with cabin; Sat–Sun 4,000 Ft with locker, 4,300 Ft with cabin; 1,600 Ft children. Daily 6am–8pm (cashier closes at 7pm). Tram: 18/19/47/49. Bus: 7 to Gellért tér.*

2 ★★★ kids Széchenyi Gyógyfürdő (Széchenyi Bath). A magnificent neo-baroque bathing complex, but be warned it gets really busy on hot summer days. Go early like the locals do, or consider taking an evening dip. It's at its best in winter with snow on the ground while you're all snug and warm in the outdoor thermal pool. For more information see p 13, 1. *2 hr. Állatkerti körút 11. ☎ 1/363-3210. www.szechenyibath.com. 3,500 Ft (3,750 Ft at weekends) with cabin (partial refunds for finishing within 2 hr, 3 hr). Daily 6am–10pm. Metro: M1 to Széchenyi Fürdő.*

Neo-baroque bathing at Széchenyi.

3 ★★★ Rudas Gyógyfürdő és Uszoda (Rudas Baths). Plunge into the turquoise water, which is given an extra depth of beauty by the beams of light that penetrate through the holes in the domed ceiling. Relax in the main central pool and then dip in and out of the corner pools of varying temperatures. There's a really cold plunge pool around the corner on the way to the changing rooms. A welcome feature of the Rudas is the ward-like resting room and I heartily recommend a snooze after the extremes your body's just been through. Skip it and you might need an early night. The main bathing chamber features a large central pool and it's also open to women. The steamy thermal experience can be enjoyed all night long by both sexes at the weekends. *Döbrentei tér 9. ☎ 1/356-1322. www.rudasbaths.com. 2,800 Ft for the steam with cabin (400 Ft refund if you leave within 2 hr), 1,200 Ft (locker), 1,500 Ft (cabin), 1,000 Ft (children and pensioners) for the swimming pool. Swimming pool daily 6am–6pm. Thermal baths*

Beams of light penetrate the ceiling at Rudas Baths.

Mon–Thurs, Sun 6am–8pm (Fri–Sat 10pm–4am); thermal baths for men Mon, Wed, Thurs, Fri; for women Tues; for both sexes in swimming suits Sat, Sun. Tram: 18/19 to Döbrentei tér. Bus: 5/7/8/86.

④ ★★ **Király Gyógyfürdő (Király Baths).** Under Socialism, the Turkish domed "King" was a tolerated meeting point for gay men, including certain members of the ruling elite. This carried on post-1989 and I've heard this place referred to as "The Queens." It was so steamy in here that apparently most Budapest heterosexuals have only been once, but now, or so I'm told, overtly sexual behavior is no longer tolerated. Smaller than the Rudas, it also takes you back a long way in time. ***Fő utca 84.*** *☎ 1/202-3688. www.spasbudapest.com. 2,300 Ft for over 3 hr; 2,200 Ft within 2 hr. Women Mon, Wed, Fri 7am–6pm; Men 7am–6pm. Men Tues, Thurs, Sat 9am–8pm. Metro: M2 to Batthyány tér.*

⑤ ★ **Lukács Gyógyfürdő (Lukács Baths).** You see many regulars here where it's less touristy and has a mixed bathing option. I like to do a few lengths of one of the shortish open-air swimming pools before rewarding myself with the wonders of the interior. You can normally get a lane in the shorter of the two pools but it is cold, while in the longer pool you'll be competing for space with the leisurely swimmers. There's also a thermal pool with a fun whirlpool and once this switches off, many people head for the water massage. I love lying back, relaxing, and thinking of home as the water surges up to the blurry sound of people's voices. In summer, climb the stairs to the spacious sun terrace that looks out onto leafy Buda. Inside, the large pool is for taking it easy. Don't stay too long in the hot pool, tempting as it is, beautifully tucked into its own chamber. Brave the steam room, plop straight into the cold plunge pool immediately next to it, and feel purged of all

Lukács Gyógyfürdö.

Enjoy the Palatinus Strand.

impurities momentarily. It's nice to sit on a bench in the garden and let your pulse return to normal afterwards. It underwent an impressive and tasteful renewal in 2011. *Frankel Leó utca 25–29. ☎ 1/326-1695. www.lukacsbath.com. 2,900/2,500 Ft for over 3 hr with cabin/locker; 2,170/1,870 Ft for within 3 hr of closing time with cabin/locker. Mon–Fri, Sun 6am–7pm; Sat 6am–5pm. Tram: 4/6 to Margit híd Budai hídfő/18 to Lukács Gyógyfürdő.*

6 ★★★ kids **Palatinus Strand.** Located on Margaret Island, Palatinus Strand has a holiday camp atmosphere that you can check into every day in summer. There's a wide range of pools of varying temperatures including a long one for proper swimming, plenty of grass to camp out on, plus food stalls, bars, and fruit stands. Head here early on very hot days, at weekends, or in school holidays to avoid the crowds. *Margit Sziget. ☎ 1/340-4505. 2,200 Ft with locker, 2,500 Ft with locker at weekends. Mon–Wed 9am–7pm, Thurs–Sun 9am–8pm. Bus: 26 to Palatinus strand.*

7 ★ **Hajós Alfréd Nemzeti Sportuszoda.** Good for a proper swim with its Olympic-sized pool among others, but also an excellent place to catch some rays. The pools are warm enough for use in winter but you can also swim inside if you prefer. The big pool is sometimes devoted to training. *Margit Sziget. ☎ 1/340-4946. 1,700 Ft. May–Sept Mon–Fri 6am–5pm, Sat–Sun 6am–6pm; Oct–Apr Mon–Fri 6am–4pm, Sat–Sun 6am–6pm. Bus: 26 to Hajós Alfréd uszoda.*

Rave on at the Baths

The architecture and ambience of Budapest's thermal baths make for seriously unique party venues. The Cinetrip parties bring modern dance music and hard partying to these wonderful watery settings, ramping up the pleasure factor even further if that's your thing. Check out **www.cinetrip.hu** for details of latest parties, which are usually held at Széchenyi (see p 27, 2) in the summer and Rudas (see p 27, 3) in the winter, but at other sumptuous venues too.

Turkish Traces

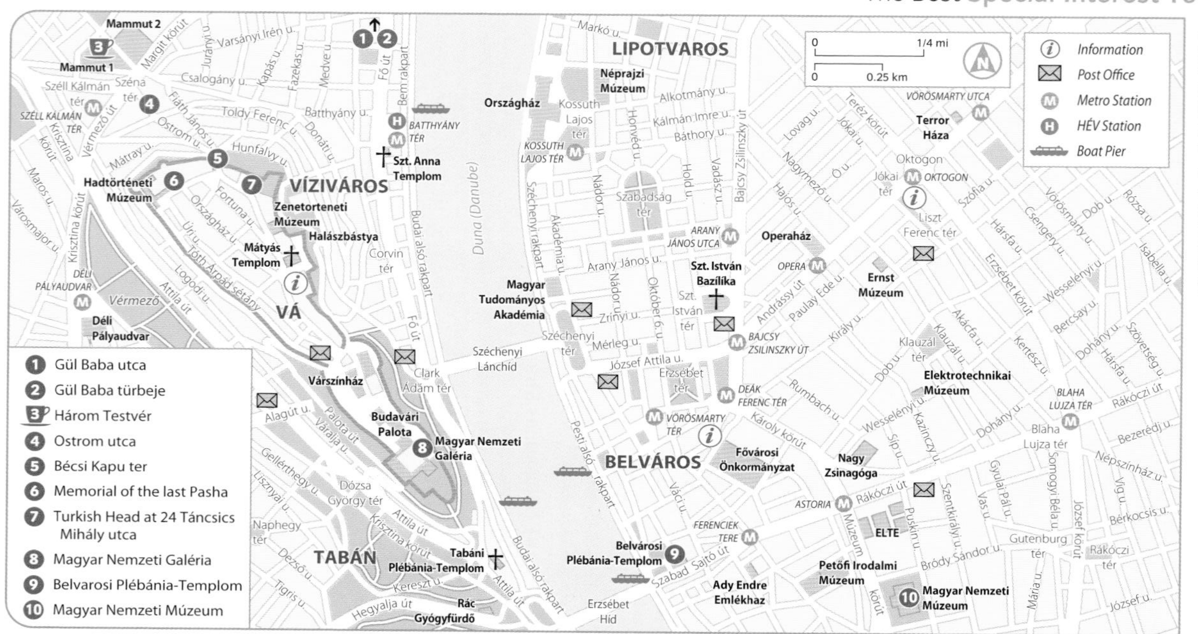

The Turks often ruled with an iron fist during their 140-year occupation, but they also left a unique cultural heritage. We start our tour on a street named after Gül Baba, an Ottoman fighter, preacher, poet, and influential consort of Suleiman the Magnificent. He's even said to have introduced the rose to "Budin", that is, Buda before falling in the otherwise successful Turkish invasion of the Castle in 1541. START: **Tram: 4/6 to Margit híd, Budai hídfő.**

1 ★★ **Gül Baba utca.** This steep and narrow cobbled Ottomanesque street could be straight out of a hilly Istanbul neighborhood. I find this a remarkable oasis of tranquility even though it's so close to **Margit Körút,** the noisy Buda thoroughfare. The preserved wooden bay window at no. 30 (unmarked) is directly opposite a very modern but tasteful take on wooden paneling at no. 23. *15 min. Tram: 4/6 to Margit híd, Budai hídfő.*

2 ★ kids **Gül Baba türbeje (Gül Baba tomb).** Hardly among the most frequented of sights these days, this was once the center of Islamic life in Buda. Gül Baba's pristinely restored mausoleum, which you can enter to view the colorfully decorated tomb and surrounding grounds, is a rare survivor from a period of history that has been all but wiped from Buda's visage. This Bektashi dervish is credited with introducing the rose to Buda and the plush surrounding neighborhood is known as Rózsadomb, literally "Rose Hill." *1/2 hr. Mecset utca 14/Türbe tér 1. ☎ 1/326-0062. 500 Ft adults, 250 Ft seniors and children aged 7 to 14. May–Sept Tues–Sun 10am–6pm, Oct–Apr Tues–Sun 10am–4pm. Bus: 91/191 to Apostol utca. Tram: 4/6 to Margit híd, Budai hídfő.*

3 kids **Három Testvér.** The "Three Brothers" is a chain of fast food Turkish joints dotted around the city, and this branch fits nicely in with the bustle of the food market above. Colorful carpets are strewn with cushions to stretch out on while you eat your meal. *Street level of Fény Utca Piac. Lövőház utca 12. ☎ 1/345-4125. Mains 800 Ft–1,000 Ft.*

Statue of Gül Baba.

Turkish Baths

On your way from the Castle District, you can wind down this tour early and take the weight off your feet at the once Turkish Rudas Baths (p 27, 3) and Király Baths (p 28, 4). The core of these stunning locations is identical in structure to those in Turkey, with the exception that the Turks don't bathe in the water, as it's considered unhygienic, and instead they sweat on slabs. These baths have long been converted to pools, but the old atmosphere is retained. Also look out for the disused mushroom-domed former bathhouse opposite the recently renovated Király Baths.

4 ★ **Walk up Ostrom utca (Siege Street).** Now suitably refueled, I recommend conquering the hill that is "Siege Street." You'll be following in the footsteps of the Christian international alliance as they headed toward the **Vienna Gate** (see below) where they overpowered the Turks. Look out for Turkish soldier figures carved into the Castle wall. *10 min. Metro: M2 to Széll Kálmán tér. Tram: 4/6 to Széna tér/Széll Kálmán tér.*

5 ★★ **Bécsi Kapu ter (Vienna Gate Square).** Here the Hungarians finally overpowered the Turks to enter and reclaim the Castle in 1686. Ironically, after being rebuilt in the years after the liberation of Buda, this historically important gate was taken down in 1896, the year of Hungary's millennium. The particular **Vienna Gate** (Bécsi kapu) that stands here today dates back to just 1936. As you pass under the gate look for the memorial dedicated to those who fell, not just Hungarians but also other European forces. *15 min. Bus: Várbusz 16/16A/116 to Bécsi Kapu ter.*

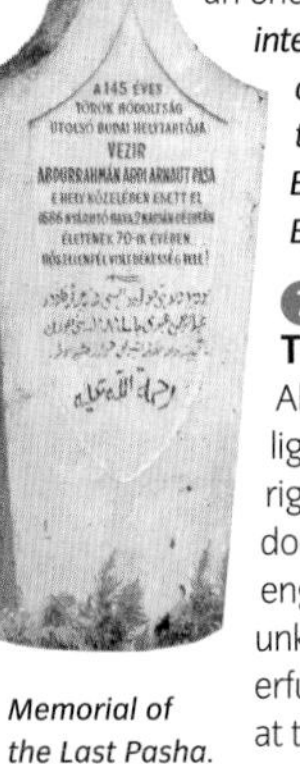

Memorial of the Last Pasha.

6 **Memorial of the Last Pasha.** It takes a bit of finding but it's there; a Muslim shrine in a typical design within the boundaries of the Castle District, albeit a little tucked away from the busiest parts. Near this spot in 1686, Abdurrahman was defeated and killed, bringing 145 years of Turkish rule of Buda to an end. He is apparently held in a certain amount of esteem according to the inscription that refers to him as both a hero and an enemy. *10 min. Close to the intersection of Anjou bástya and Országház utca, down the steps from the latter. Bus: Várbusz 16/16A/116 to Bécsi Kapu ter.*

7 **Turkish Head at 24 Táncsics Mihály utca.** Almost blending in with the light-colored stonework, and right above the Louis XVI doorway of no. 24, is the engraved head of an unknown but noble and powerful-looking Turk. Look inside at the remains of the original Gothic sedilla arches, which likely pre-date the Turkish influence in Budapest. *10 min. Bus: Várbusz 16/16A/116 to Bécsi Kapu ter.*

8 ★★ **Magyar Nemzeti Galéria (Hungarian National**

Turkish head at 24 Táncsics Mihály utca.

Gallery). I enjoy the dramatic paintings of Magyar battles with the Turks, particularly Benczúr Gyula's enormous canvas *The Recapture of Buda Castle 1686.* It makes you think about the history of the spot you're standing on, even if it was painted a couple of centuries later. *1 hr. Buda Royal Palace (see p 61, 1), Buildings A, B, C, D. Szent György tér 2. 0620/439-7325. www.mng.hu/en. 1,000 Ft adults, 500 Ft E.U. citizens aged 6–26 and 62–70. Tues–Sun 10am–6pm. Free guided tour Thurs 2pm and Sat 10am. Bus: Várbusz 16/16A/116 to Bécsi Kapu ter.*

9 ★★ Belvárosi Plébánia-Templom (Inner City Parish Church). Cross the Chain Bridge (p 7, 2) and walk downstream, or take Erszébet Bridge to go directly to the Inner City Parish Church. It was the only Christian church fully tolerated by the Turks, which perhaps has something to do with it being fitted out with a praying niche pointing toward Mecca. You can still see it to the right of the main altar. The surrounding restored Islamic paintwork contrasts sharply with the other more austere half that was destroyed in World War II. *15 min. Március 15 tér. 1/318-3108. Free admission. Mon–Sat 9am–5pm. Tram: 2 to Március 15 tér.*

10 ★★ kids Magyar Nemzeti Múzeum (Hungarian National Museum). Spend some time here admiring the Ottoman art, as well as military arms used by the Turk and Christian armies. The museum also has excellent attractions for youngsters, including a historical playhouse where for two hours they can dress up and play out the various eras of history. *45 min. Múzeum körút 14–16. 1/338-2122. www.hnm.hu. 1,100 adults Ft, 550 Ft children and students 6–26. Tues–Sun 10am–6pm. Metro: M3 to Kálvin tér.*

Inner City Parish Church.

The Best Coffeehouses

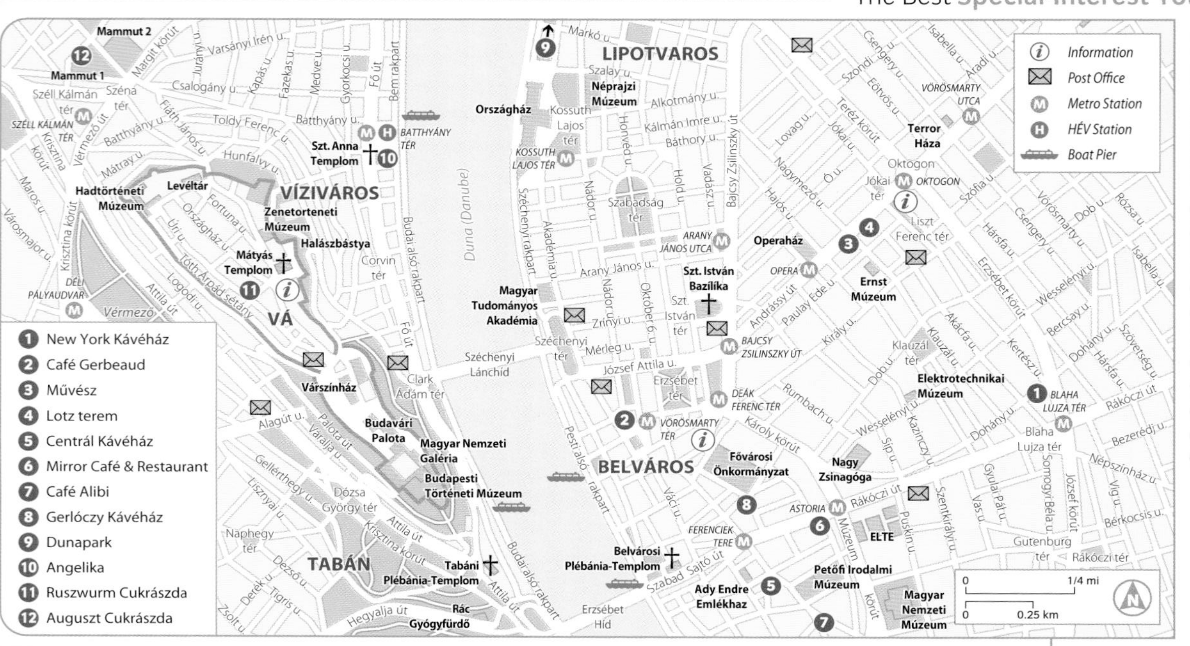

Budapest is legendary for its coffeehouse (*kávéház*) culture, which forms an integral part of the locals' lifestyle rather than being a cliché to attract tourist dollars. Look out for the *cukrászda,* basically cake shops, some of which are very appealing. I don't suggest visiting all these coffeehouses as a rigid tour; instead, drop in to one as and when you're passing.

1 ★★ **New York Kávéház.** This location is a former hangout of cash-strapped writers, poets, and future Hollywood legends back in the fin-de-siècle days. Today, however, fledgling and hard-up film school contemporaries of the likes of Hungarian-born movie mogul Alexander Korda are scared off by the corporate prices: There's no such thing as a preferential writers' menu these days. Before it closed for restoration in the late 1990s it had a faded grandeur, but now it's been immaculately restored to its neo-baroque splendor. Certainly worth a peek but not everyone's architectural cup of tea as it's almost overwhelming with a few too many cherubs for my liking. *Erzsébet körút 9–11.* ☎ *1/886-6111. Daily 9am–midnight. Metro: M2 to Blaha Luiza tér.*

2 ★ **Café Gerbeaud.** A neo-baroque bonanza with some of the best Esterházy and Dobos cakes in town. *See p 17,* 1.

3 ★ **Művész.** A simple but elegant coffeehouse, which may come across as old-fashioned with its arched windows, low-hanging chandeliers, and stripy wallpaper. The tables usually spill out onto the terrace on classy Andrássy út in summer, although the high ceilings keep it nice and cool inside. *Andrássy út 29.* ☎ *1/352-1337. Daily 9am–midnight. Metro: M1 to Opera.*

4 ★★★ **Lotz terem.** Painter, Károly Lotz, of Opera House fame, had fun here and let his mind, and brushes, run riot with epic and sometimes bawdy frescoes. Added to this the huge mirrors, arched windows,

Coffee and cake at Müvész.

leather armchairs, a good selection of Hungarian and international confections—including its own chocolate-marzipan inspired Book Café cake, soups, salads, and goose liver—and a piano player from 4pm make this place an absolute must. If you feel like you need a good book to keep you company, the Alexandra bookstore below has a substantial English language section. *Andrássy út 39.* ☎ *1/484-8000. Daily 10am–10pm. Metro: M1 to Opera/Oktogon.*

5 ★★★ Centrál Kávéház. Another famous institution from Budapest's heyday, Centrál is a bastion of old-world charm and service without overdoing the glitz. Once popular with city hacks, the salons of the coffeehouse were aptly named after the city's newspaper titles. Tastefully renovated in 1999, it has high ceilings, arched windows, and all the comfort you need. More than a mere coffeehouse, it also offers an extensive wine list and fine dining. *Károly Mihály utca 9.* ☎ *1/266-2110. www.centralkavehaz.hu. Daily 7am–midnight. Metro: M3 to Ferenciek tere.*

6 ★★★ Mirror Café & Restaurant. Formally the Astoria, this venue is faded 1920s' grandeur personified, with plenty of chandeliers, pillars, and red velvet. It's far from gloomy now they've opened the curtains, and with reasonably priced cafe lattes, it's just the kind of place you can relax in. *Kossuth Lajos utca 19–21.* ☎ *1/889-6002. Daily 7am–11pm. Metro: M2 to Astoria.*

7 ★ Café Alibi. A petite modern take on the grand coffeehouse of old, borrowing something of a French bistro feel. Located in the quaint University District, Alibi gives you an excuse to take time to chill out. The food menu is available all day. *Egyetem tér 4.* ☎ *1/317-4209. www.cafealibi.hu. Mon–Wed 8am–9pm, Thurs–Fri 8am–10pm, Sat 9am–9pm, Sun 9am–5pm. Metro: M3 to Kálvin tér.*

8 ★★★ Gerlóczy Kávéház. Look out through the high arched windows from this excellent bistro-cum-coffeehouse onto a charming small square named after the first mayor of Budapest, Károly Kamermayer. The interior is simple and tasteful with a long marble-topped bar and a relaxed French feel. Expect homemade pastries for breakfast and creative lunch and dinner options. With its free Wi-Fi, many make this their office. *Gerlóczy*

Relax with a good view of the Danube at Dunapark.

Angelika.

utca 1. ☎ 1/501-4000. www.gerloczy.hu. Daily 7am–11pm. Metro: M1/M2/M3 to Deák tér.

9 ★ Dunapark. Part modern, part 1930s, Dunapark is housed in a Bauhaus housing block and has plenty of cool Art Deco touches. Big windows provide views to the Danube and the attractive Szent István Park, while the cakes are exquisitely and temptingly presented. *Pozsonyi utca 38. ☎ 1/786-1009. www.dunaparkkavehaz.hu. Mon–Fri 8am–midnight, Sat 10am–midnight, Sun 10am–10pm. Tram: 2/4/6 to Jaszai Mária tér.*

10 Angelika. With views of Batthyány tér and across to Parliament, this is a very special and relaxing place to sit outside in summer. Unfortunately, the eclectic neo-baroque and 1970s' retro decor is gone, although you can still use your imagination to picture the interior chambers as a one-time crypt. *Batthyány tér 7. ☎ 1/201-0668. www.angelikacafe.hu. Daily 10am–10pm. Metro: M2 to Batthyány tér.*

11 ★★★ Ruszwurm Cukrászda. This bijou and cozy cake joint with low-arched walls dates back to 1827 and retains plenty old baroque charm despite its location in the tourist epicenter of Budapest. It looks a little like a medieval pharmacy but, behind the curtain, confectionery from classic recipes by Hungarian cake guru Illés Tóth are created. Cream pastries, Tirol strudels, buttered dough, and many more are presented enticingly above the charming wooden counter—it's easy just to point to the ones you want. If you fancy something savory try the scone-like pogácsa. *Szentháromság utca 7. ☎ 1/375-5284. www.ruszwurm.hu. Daily 9am–8pm, closes 7pm off season. Várbusz 16/16A/116 to Szentháromság tér.*

12 ★★ Auguszt Cukrászda. Run by the same family for five generations, this charming confectionery shop now has three branches. It is famous for the E80 cake—made originally for the 80th birthday of founder Elemér Auguszt, it's a mix of his favorite cakes including both coffee and chocolate cream. *Fény utca 8. ☎ 1/316-3817. www.augusztcukraszda.hu. Tues–Fri 10am–6pm, Sat 9am–6pm. Metro: M2 to Széll Kálmán tér.*

Budapest with Kids

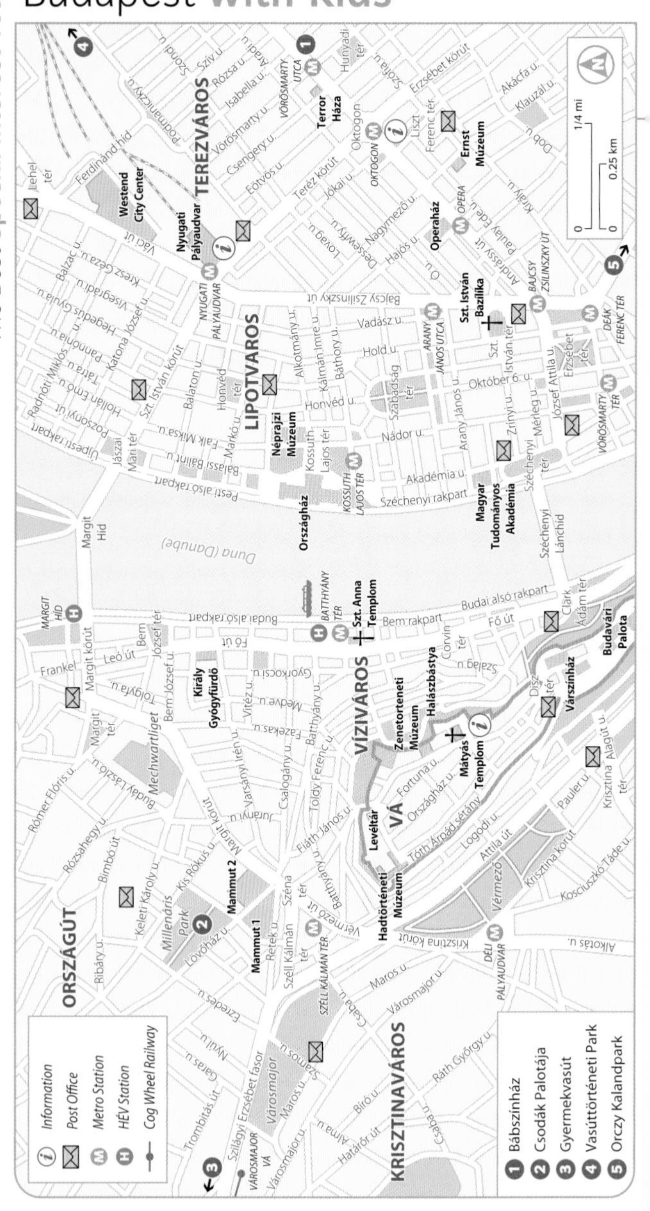

Budapest is extremely child-friendly, with playgrounds strewn across the city. Aside from the green areas of City Park and Margaret Island, there are a number of other outstanding family attractions, ranging from good old-fashioned fun to the modern and interactive. START: **M1 to Vörösmarty utca.**

1 ★★ Bábszínház (Puppet Theater). Traditional fairy tales and acclaimed modern adaptations of ballet, opera, and pantomime classics are performed here daily. Look out for *The Wooden Prince* from local legend Béla Bartók. *40 min–2 hr. Andrássy út 69. 1/322-5051. www.budapest-babszinhaz.hu (in Hungarian only). 800–3,000 Ft depending on the performance. Metro: M1 to Vörösmarty utca.*

2 ★★★ Csodák Palotája (Palace of Wonders). Inside, interactive exhibitions keep the children entertained and absorbed, but also teach them scientific principles without them even realizing it. Part of the Millenáris arts complex, the outdoors area is great for relaxing with the youngsters. *1 hr. Millenáris, Building D. Fény utca 20–22. 1/336-4044. www.millenaris.hu. 1,400 Ft adults, 1,100 Ft children, 3,900 Ft family. Sept–mid-June Mon–Sun 10am–5pm; mid-June–late Aug Mon–Fri 9am-5pm, Sat–Sun 10am–6pm. Closed 2 weeks late Aug. Metro: M2 to Széll Kálmán tér. Tram: 4/6 to Széna tér.*

3 ★ Gyermekvasút (Children's Railway). A bizarre but delightful hangover from the former system in which youngsters, or "pioneers" as they were referred to, were handed the responsibility of running this railway that snakes through the scenic Buda Hills. A packed lunch is a good idea. *1 hr. www.gyermekvasut.hu. Fogaskerekű (Cog Wheel Railway) to Széchenyi hegy. Daily 8:45am–7pm.*

Take a packed lunch aboard the children's train.

4 ★★★ Vasúttörténeti Park (Railway Museum). Drive a steam engine, operate a hand wagon, or ride on a horse-pulled tram at Europe's first interactive railway museum, which is home to Hungary's 50-strong operation steam fleet. A vintage diesel shuttle runs to the museum from Nyugati Station from April 3 to October 24. *2 hr. 06/70-313-4957. www.mavnosztalgia.hu/en. Apr–Sep Tues–Sun 10am–6pm; 2 Nov–5 Dec 10am–3pm. Closed Oct, Jan–Mar. 1,100 Ft adults, 400 Ft children 4–18, 2,200 Ft family, free for children 3 and under. Interactive rides by appointment only. Bus: 30 to Rokolya utca. Tram: 14 to Rokolya utca.*

5 ★★ Orczy Kalandpark (Adventure Park). Attached to a safety cable, youngsters and adrenalin-seeking adults can crawl, climb, and slide their way past the assault courses obstacles in this green oasis. *2 hr. Orzcy út 1. 06/20-/236-1214. www.orczykalandpark.hu. 2,000 Ft adults, 1,700 Ft children aged up to 14, 6,800 Ft family. Daily 10 am–7pm in summer. Metro: M3 to Klinikák.*

Revolutionary Budapest

Start at Bem tér (Square), the meeting point of protestors on October 23, 1956, from where the revolution against the Soviet-backed government was initiated. Partially successful demonstrations in Poland earlier that year against Soviet influence made people believe change could come to Hungary. START: **Tram: 4/6 to Margit híd, Budai hídfő. Bus: 86 to Bem József tér.**

1 Bem Statue, Bem József tér. This is the spot where the spark that triggered the 1956 Revolution was ignited. Rewind to October 23, 1956: in the wake of a promisingly tolerated rebellion in Poland, groups of protestors, starting with students and soon spreading to the masses, met here to stand united against hardcore Communist rule. The Hungarian Revolution was ultimately ill-fated but nevertheless saw many Hungarians escape the tyranny. It also led to a gradual softening of the regime through reforms that saw the implementation of so-called "goulash Communism." Bem himself was a swashbuckling Polish general who fought with Hungary against Austria in the 1848–9 Revolution. *15 min. Bem tér. Metro: M2 to Batthyány tér. Tram: 4/6 to Margit híd, Budai hídfő. Bus: 86 to Bem József tér.*

2 ★★★ Kossuth Lajos tér (Parlament). After the meeting of minds in front of the Bem Statue in 1956, the crowd that was growing in size and revolutionary fervor marched onto Parliament demanding change. The bullet holes in the walls of the Agricultural Ministry opposite testify to the point where a peaceful demonstration turned violent as Russian tanks and troops fired into the crowd after being shot at from the roof of the Ministry. *30 min. Kossuth Lajos tér. Metro: M2 to Kossuth Lajos tér.* *See also p 8, 3.*

3 kids Imre Nagy Bridge Statue. Imre Nagy was Hungary's ill-fated hero of the 1956 Revolution, a reform-minded Communist Party politician and former leader who sought a new, less strict brand of Socialism for Hungary. He is captured here looking back at Parliament as if thinking about what might have been had the West supported his country in its revolution against Soviet-backed rule. *15 min. Vértanúk tere. Corner of Báthory utca, Nádor utca and Vécsey utca. Metro: M2 to Kossuth Lajos tér.*

Hungary's ill-fated hero Imre Nagy.

4 ★★ **Radio Building.** After things turned nasty at Parliament, the battle was on for control of the airwaves. There may not be many battle scars to see except for a bombed-out wall from the original Radio Building, but wander the streets of this atmospheric neighborhood behind the National Museum and soak up the past. Look out for the beautifully restored palaces either side of the Radio Building's modern entrance. ⌚ *15 min. Bródy Sándor utca 5–7. Metro: M2 to Astoria or M3 to Kálvin tér.*

5 ★ **Corvin Mozi.** This cinema complex, with its key strategic position next to Pest entry and exit thoroughfare Üllői út, was the site of intense fighting against the Soviets. You won't find any rubble, mortar marks, or bullet holes here, however, as Corvin has been restored to its former glory and function, although you will find a statue of a boy with a rifle that pays tribute to those who fell in the name of the Revolution. ⌚ *15 min. Corvin Köz 1. (Close to corner of József körút and Ullői út.)* ☎ *1/459-5050. Metro: M3 to Ferenc körút. Tram: 4/6 to Ferenc korut.*

6 **Blaha Lujza tér.** After being pulled down with only his boots remaining in place, the Stalin statue was dragged here and smashed up. The square bears the marks of the Communist period. The roof of Socialist superstore Corvin is given over to a fabulous expansive rooftop bar in summer. ⌚ *30 min. Blaha Luiza tér. Metro: M2 to Blaha Luiza tér.*

Statue of a boy soldier at Corvin Mozi.

7 **Lanzhou.** The Chinese poured into Budapest to study and work in the former Communist system. This restaurant may look really simple, but plenty of Chinese are among the patrons and the food is very authentic. A bowl of chicken noodle soup appears in no time and really tides you over to a bigger meal later. *Luther utca 1/b.* ☎ *1/314-1080. Noodle soup 900 Ft.*

8 ★ **János Pál Pápa tér.** A short walk from Blaha Lujza tér, this is the site where revolutionaries committed brutal executions of the wrong people. At the Communist Party headquarters (no. 26) on October 30, 1956, an angry crowd turned on surrendering army officials who they thought were members of the despised secret police. The Socialist Party headquarters was controversially housed here until relatively recently. ⌚ *5 min. János Pál Pápa tér 26.*

9 ★ **Serbian Embassy.** Imre Nagy, who led Hungary's uprising against the Soviet Union in 1956, sought refuge here at the Yugoslavian Embassy overlooking **Heroes' Square** (p 11, 10). Yugoslavia managed to pursue its own path of market-oriented Socialism, keeping clear of the restraints imposed by the Soviet control organ of the Warsaw Pact. Yugoslav Socialism could have provided an economic and political model something akin to what Imre Nagy, himself a reform-minded Socialist, might have envisaged for Hungary. Thus, the then Yugoslavian Embassy seemed a safe haven for Nagy as the Revolution became a crushed rebellion. Eventually he was seized

Stalin's boots, Memento Park.

by Soviet agents and shipped off to eventual but certain death, despite assurances to the contrary by his successor János Kádár. Often seen as a pawn of Soviet wishes, Kádár is nevertheless credited with reforming the economy along free-market lines, thus making Hungary the so-called happiest barrack in the Communist camp. Opposite at Heroes' Square, in 1989, with the winds of change in the air, Nagy was laid to rest once more with full state honors in front of a huge crowd. Kádár, who relinquished the leadership due to ill health and a struggling economy in 1988, passed away just weeks later on July 6, ironically on the same day as Nagy was acquitted of treason by the Supreme Court. *5 min. Dózsa György út 92/b. Metro: M1 to Hősök tere.*

⑩ **Felvonulási tér.** This was the Hungarian Communist equivalent of Moscow's Red Square, where the annual show parade of Communist might took place. Party dignitaries watched from a podium over which a statue of Stalin stood. For a replica of the podium, replete with Stalin's boots, head to **Memento Park** (p 46, ❶). *5 min. Next to Heroes' Square. Metro: M1 to Hősök tere.*

The Name Game

Some 22 years after the end of Communism, the Hungarian government decided to change the name of the busy transport hub of Moszkva tér (Moscow Square) back to its pre-Communism name of **Széll Kálmán tér.** It seems, however, that people had got used to the name regardless of the political connotations for this was the least popular of some 27 changes of name for streets and squares that came into effect in May 2011. Be prepared for people to still say Moszkva tér for a while. Republic Square, the site of brutal executions in the 1956 Revolution, is now **János Pál Pápa tér** (the Hungarian name of Pope John Paul II). In the same piece of legislation, an unnamed piece of grassland next to Margit híd on the Buda side was given the totally non-Magyar moniker of **Elvis Presley Park.** Someone in the city council must be a fan. In a separate move, also in 2011, Budapest's airport took on the name of composer **Ferenc Liszt,** ditching its former name of Ferihegy.

Behind the **Iron Curtain**

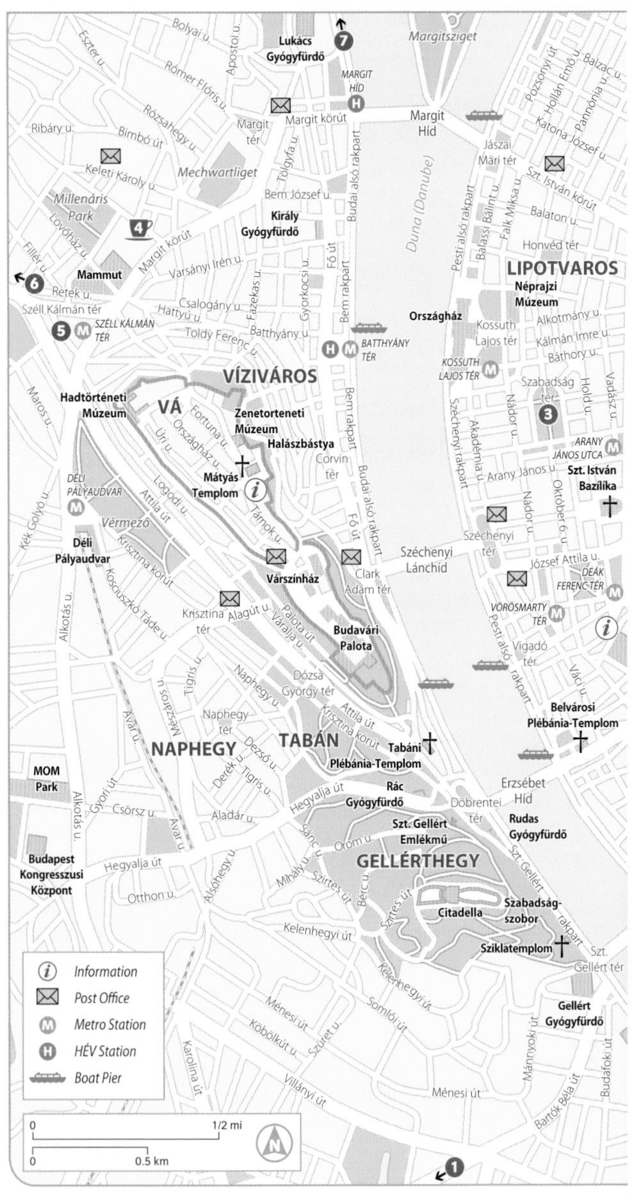

TEREZVÁROS
ERZSÉBETVÁROS
JÓZSEFVÁROS
FERENCVÁROS
Városliget
Duna (Danube)
Széchenyi Fürdő
Szépművészeti Múzeum
Magyar Mezőgazdasági Múzeum
Hősök tere
Műcsarnok
Felvonulási tér
Westend City Center
Nyugati Pályaudvar
Lehel tér
Hopp Ferenc Kelet-Ázsiai Múzeum
Kodály Zoltán Emlémúzeum
Terror Háza
Lövölde tér
Hunyadi tér
Oktogon
Liszt Ferenc tér
Operaház
Ernst Múzeum
Klauzál tér
Almássy tér
Rózsák tere
Keleti Pályaudvar
Baross tér
Blaha Lujza tér
János Pál Pápa tér
Kerepesi temető
Nagy Zsinagóga
Fővárosi Önkormányzat
Astoria
Ferenciek tere
Rákóczi tér
Teleki László tér
Mátyás tér
Magyar Nemzeti Múzeum
Petőfi Irodalmi Múzeum
Józsefvárosi Plébánia-Templom
Horváth Mihály tér
Kálvin tér
Kálvária tér
Vásárcsarnok
Fővám tér
Iparművészeti Múzeum
Corvin-negyed
Ferenc tér
Boráros tér
Szkéne Színház
Petőfi Híd
Goldmann György tér
1 Memento Park (includes Statue Park)
2 Terror Háza
3 Soviet War Memorial
4 Marxim
5 Széll Kálmán tér
6 Gyermekvasút
7 Flórián tér, Óbuda
8 PECSA
9 Pántlika Bisztró
10 Sporting hero statues

Aside from ugly Soviet-era buildings next to fin-de-siècle masterpieces, traces of the past regime are not immediately apparent and so this tour requires some traveling. Most of the Communist statues were dragged off to Memento Park on the outskirts of Budapest, which is where we start our tour. START: **Bus: 150 from Kosztolányi Dezső tér to Memento Park.**

1 ★★★ Memento Park (includes Statue Park). Hungarians are reflective about their history. Instead of destroying all traces of the past, the despised statues of the former regime were dragged here to stare at each other. You're greeted by an imposing statue of Lenin and a funky Cubist one of the Communist Manifesto authors **Marx and Engels.** My favorite has to be the Herculean worker figure of the **Republic of Councils Monument** (statue no. 33) in full flight, sprinting for the Communist cause. The statues still get the emotions going and it's easy to get indignant at the statue commemorating Soviet/Hungarian cooperation where a worker shakes hands with a beefy Soviet soldier (statue no. 4), almost visually suggesting "don't mess with me and you'll be fine." ⌚ *1 hr. Corner of Balatoni út and Szabadkai utca.* ☎ *1/424-7500. www.mementopark.hu. 1,500 Ft adults, 300 Ft children; 2,000 Ft family. Daily 10am–dusk. Bus: 150 from Kosztolányi Dezső tér to Memento Park (25 min). Dedicated bus: 4,500 Ft including return trip via direct bus from Deák tér (bus departs 11am all year, plus 3pm in July and Aug).*

Statue at Memento Park.

2 ★★★ Terror Háza. A cutting-edge museum detailing the horrors of oppressive regimes that occurred on this site. ⌚ *1 hr.* *See p 14, 6*

3 ★ Soviet War Memorial. This war memorial is a notable survivor of the purge of the Socialist-era statues that found their way to Memento Park. Controversial, thanks to the

The Soviet War Memorial.

Óbuda—Traces of "Old Buda" Behind the Socialist Facade

Communist town planners really took to consigning Óbuda's one-time beauty to the history books; however, nearby pockets of charm thankfully remain. Baroque Fő tér has survived intact and still looks striking despite the ugliness of huge tower blocks bearing down on it. In addition to charming old houses, Roman ruins are also spattered around the "prefab paradise." The **Amphitheater** off Pacsirtamező (Intersection of Viador utca) is said to have been as big as the Coliseum, while the densest collection of Roman ruins can be found at Acquincum. Entry costs 1,500 Ft (850 Ft in winter) and the site is a stop on the HÉV suburban railway. **Hercules Villa** (Meggyfa utca 21) and its impressive mythological floor mosaics can be viewed with a minimum group of six for 6,000 Ft by calling ☎ 1/ 250-1650. The museum itself is very retro and blends in well with the Socialist-era housing blocks of the area.

Soviet "liberators" who overstayed their welcome by more than 40 years, the memorial still stands proud, although unsurprisingly there's a movement underway to tear it down. It was severely vandalized during the anti-government riots of 2006. Interestingly, the final touches to its refurbishment were applied when the then Socialist Prime Minister, Ferenc Gyurcsány, was in Moscow. The memorial is directly opposite the U.S. Embassy, where Cardinal Mindszenty sought refuge in 1956 as the Soviets extinguished the fire of the uprising. 🕘 *10 min. Szabadság tér. Metro: M2 to Kossuth Lajos tér or M3 to Bajcsy-Zsilinsky út.*

4 ★★ **Marxim.** Communist-themed pizzeria and pub with barbed/chicken wire separating the booths, decked out with plenty of Socialist-period memorabilia. The "Master Comrade and Margarita" pizza is topped with tasty smoked cheese. Feel free to write your messages on the walls. *Kis Rókus utca 23. ☎ 1/316-0231. Pizza from 790 Ft.*

5 **Széll Kálmán tér.** This charming old square, formerly known until recently as Moskvá tér (Moscow Square), is surrounded by dramatic buildings, including the castle-like **Post Office** admin building. The masterpiece, however, is the surge of Socialist-Realism that emerges from the center in the form of the

Communist-themed bar Marxim.

Sporting hero statues at Ferenc Puskás stadium.

space-age metro station. On top, a rooftop bar awaits all year round. 15 min. *Széll Kálmán tér. Metro: M2 to Széll Kálmán tér.*

6 ★★ **Gyermekvasút (Children's Railway).** A delightful hangover of the previous political system, the Children's Railway was run by the Communist "pioneer" youth movement that delivered organizational skills and an understanding of responsibility to future Party members. *1 hr.* *See p 39,* **3**.

7 ★★ **Prefab housing overlooking Flórián tér, Óbuda.** A bizarre sight that bears the architectural stamp of two contrasting empires: Roman and Soviet. The prefab housing block was among the city's drabbest until some recent paintwork broke up the monotony somewhat, and it's supposedly Eastern Europe's longest connected estate. It's a far cry from what's left of the classical columns that make up the ruins of a Roman settlement in the square it overlooks. Tucked under the flyover you'll find the remains of Roman baths. *30 min. HÉV to Arpád híd.*

8 ★ **PECSA.** This Socialist-era music venue replete with a funky exterior is still going strong and you can see some big names here, both on the indoor and outdoor stage. On weekend mornings it's the place to buy Socialist bric-à-brac (see p 76). *Zichy Mihály utca.* ☎ *1/363-3730. Metro: M1 to Széchenyi fürdő.*

9 ★★ **Pántlika Bisztró.** Funky but authentic retro bar-cum-diner, decked out in Socialist era knick-knacks, replete with red seats and chairs. Choose from hamburgers, goulash, plus a quality selection of Pálinka (fruit brandy) and Traubisoda, a tasty brand of grape soda that thankfully survived the end of Communism. *Opposite Hermina út 47, in the City Park (Városliget).* ☎ *1/222-2949. Usually closed in winter. Goulash 850 Ft.*

10 ★★ kids **Sporting hero statues.** I've always found these statues of Socialist sporting titans inspiring. They almost seem to transcend political ideology, although sport was used to express the supposed superiority of the political left. Nevertheless, they stand as tributes to an impressive sporting past. The statues are part of the Ferenc Puskás stadium, which has many interesting Socialist design elements. *30 min. Ifjúság út 1–3. 100m (320 ft.) on right from entrance. Free admission. Metro: M2 to Stadionak.*

3 The Best Neighborhood Walks

Belváros

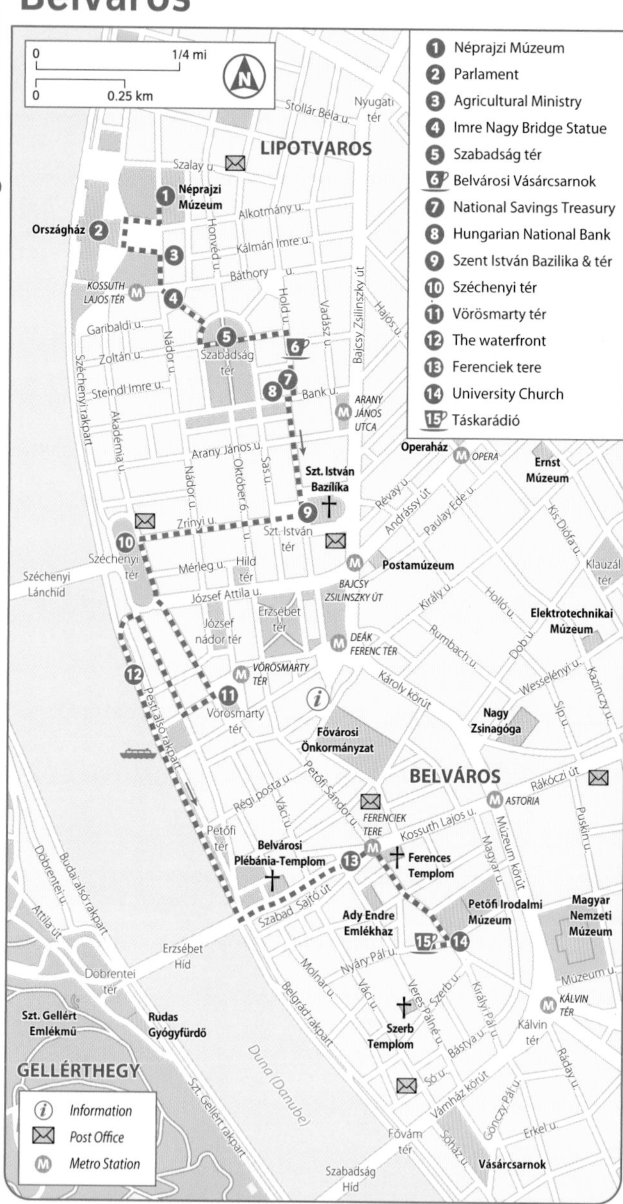

Previous page: National Savings Treasury.

You won't miss the size and extravagance of Hungary's neo-Gothic Parliament that looks built for a superpower—which in fact the country was when it was completed in 1904. However, this is just the start of epic central Pest and on this tour you'll see other landmark buildings from Budapest's heyday and experience a distinct air of faded grandeur. START: **Metro: M2 to Kossuth Lajos tér/Tram: 2 to Szalay utca. TIME: 4 hr.**

1 Néprajzi Múzeum (Museum of Ethnography). This impressive neoclassical building helps counterbalance the power of the Parlament opposite and is situated in yet another beautiful Budapest square. On the inside, its permanent exhibitions help give a perspective on the maverick Magyars. *15 min–1 hr (depending on whether you visit the exhibition). Kossuth Lajos tér 12. www.neprajz.hu. 1,000 Ft adults, 500 Ft children and students 6–26. Tues–Sun 10am–6pm. Closed Mon. Metro: M2 to Kossuth Lajos tér/ Tram: 2 to Szalay utca.*

2 ★★★ Parlament. Sprawling in size and style, Hungary's giant parliament building signifies the country's pre-Trianon might. The Trianon Treaty of 1920 might have seen Hungary lose two-thirds of its territory and around the same in population, but this building is still there to be savored in all its glory. *1 hr for tour; 15 min view from outside.* *See p 8, 3.*

3 kids Agricultural Ministry. Make a beeline for the arches of the Agricultural Ministry and walk along the covered passage. Look out for the marked bullet holes from the 1956 uprising-cum-revolution against the Soviets. *Kossuth Lajos tér 11.*

4 kids Imre Nagy Bridge Statue. Hungary's ill-fated leader is captured here in a moving forlorn pose. *See p 41, 3.*

5 ★ kids Szabadság tér. Grab a coffee at **Café Farger** at Zoltán utca 18 or **Hütte Café** bang in the middle of Szabadság tér, sit outside, and contemplate this grand and spacious square's contradictions. The controversial **Soviet War Memorial** (p 46, 3) pays thanks to the Soviet forces for liberating Hungary from the Nazis, though ironically they then effectively stayed for more than 40 years. The memorial faces the old Cold War foe in the form of the **American Embassy,** which was severely vandalized in the 2006 riots for its association with the Socialist-led government. The then Prime Minister, Ferenc Gyurcsány, was caught on tape at a supposed closed party convention admitting that his government had screwed it up and done nothing for the country. At the same time, in perhaps the most drastic

Imre Nagy looks over to the parliament building.

action of the 2006 anti-government insurrection, the building that houses the **Hungarian State Television** (MTV) was stormed by right-wing protestors and curious members of the onlooking crowd. The vast structure was built by Ignác Alpár, also of National Bank fame, and once housed the stock exchange. *Szabadság tér.*

6 **Belvárosi Vásárcsarnok.** Head to the far end of this inner-city food market for a Hungarian version of fish 'n' chips, next to which there's a hole-in-the-wall eatery serving hearty Hungarian classics. Also here are stalls selling deep-fried dough *(lángos)*, sausages galore, and cheap Chinese and Thai. *Hold utca.* ☎ *1/332-3976. Lángos from 400 Ft.*

7 ★★★ **National Savings Treasury.** The depictions of bees making honey, symbolizing money-making, can be seen on the exterior walls of this Art Nouveau masterpiece from architect Ödön Lechner. *See p 24, 10.*

8 **Hungarian National Bank.** Like the epic Parliament building, the stature of Hungary's Central Bank is reflected in the size and drama of the building. It was originally constructed as the headquarters for the Budapest network of the Austro-Hungarian Bank in 1905. An eclectic and empowering palatial structure, it was designed by the financial institution architect supremo Ignác Alpár. *Szabadság tér 8–9.*

9 ★★★ **Szent István Bazilika & tér.** My first memory of St. Stephen's Basilica is from the early 1990s when it was a neglected, blackened structure—a far cry from its gleaming condition now. The square itself is also looking good these days and appears to have been hand-polished. *Szent István tér. See p 9, 5.*

10 ★★ **Széchenyi tér.** This area comprises the opulent **Academy of Sciences,** on the left-hand side as you face Pest from the no. 2 tram stop, and the stunningly restored Art Nouveau Four Seasons Gresham Palace Hotel (p 142) opposite. The southern side, however, is the realm of the big hotels built to Socialist-Realist specifications. *Széchenyi tér.*

11 ★ **Vörösmarty tér.** This is one of the many mini-centers of Pest. Toward Christmas an atmospheric

Bees making honey on the facade of the National Savings Treasury.

Szent István Bazilika.

Christmas market pops up on the square where shoppers keep the cold off by imbibing mulled wine (*forralt bor*). ***Vörösmarty tér.***

⓬ ★ kids **Walk the waterfront.** The highlight of this stretch of the hotel-lined promenade is pretty Vigádo tér, which is named after the arch-windowed and pillared concert hall. The views over the river to the Buda Castle and Gellért Hill are impressive and so no wonder that this area is heaving with tourists. ***Vigádo tér.***

⓭ ★★★ **Ferenciek tere.** This square is most notable for the ornate Habsburg-period and neo-Renaissance towers Klondit and Matilda. These old girls, whose decaying beauty could be enhanced by a facelift, lie directly opposite each other, either side of the busy Szabadsajtó út. They form an impressive exit gate from Pest over **Erszébet Bridge.** The view looking between the buildings to the more modern bridge and to Gellért Hill is striking. A major renovation of Ferenciek tere is expected in 2012. Meanwhile, the under-utilized shopping arcade **Párizsi udvar** (at Ferenciek tere 10–11/Petőfi Sándor utca 2–8), is finished in polished dark colors that resemble the interior of a cathedral and is topped off by intricate and sumptuously colored glasswork. It was built on the eve of World War I during the last phase of Budapest's epic Austro-Hungarian construction frenzy.

⓮ ★★ **University Church.** A baroque beauty tucked away in this less frequented but atmospheric corner of District V. Famous Hungarian saints and mythical Magyars feature in the side chapels, while fading baroque brushwork makes this the kind of church I like. ⏱ ***15 min. Free admission. Egyetem tér.***

15 **Táskarádió**. This lively and colorful Communist retro-themed hangout serves everything from snacks such as Retró *melegszendvics* (toasted sandwiches) to heartier meals. ***Papnövelde utca 8.*** ☎ ***1/266-0413. www.taskaradioeszpresszo.hu. Toasted sandwich 550 Ft.***

Locals rest on the steps at Vörösmarty tér.

The Jewish Quarter

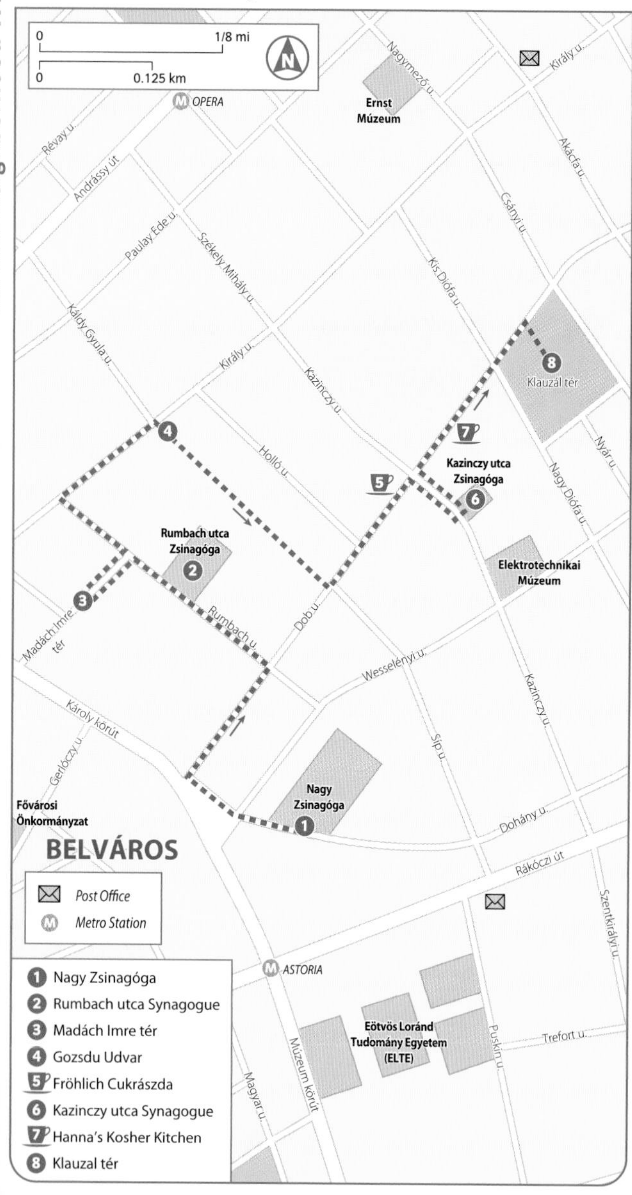

Budapest is home to Central and Eastern Europe's largest Jewish community and this neighborhood in District VII is its core. This popular bar quarter is also steeped in atmosphere by day, with magnificent synagogues and faded grandeur defining this former ghetto. START: **M2 to Astoria then walk a couple of minutes to the Great Synagogue at Dohány utca 2 on the corner of Wesselényi utca. TIME: 3 hr.**

1 ★★★ Nagy Zsinagóga (Great Synagogue). Somewhat tucked away off the main drag, the Great Synagogue has been beautifully restored and reopened in 1995. It also houses the **Hungarian Jewish Museum.** For me the real drama of the building, which is the world's second largest synagogue after New York's, is in the Moorish and Byzantine exterior. Some Gothic touches, like the arched windows and trefoil ledge, are also apparent, although the interior is suitably lavish. The twin onion-domed towers crown the building's oldest part, designed by Viennese Ludwig Förster, while the wing that houses the museum to the left side was added in 1931. After its consecration in 1859, the revolutionary form influenced synagogue design internationally. However, it's not just the architecture of this Neolog house of worship that changed the course of history: Tivadar Herzl, the father of modern Zionism, who sought the establishment of a Jewish country in the Middle East, was born within its grounds in 1860. A central part of the ghetto in World War II, the back courtyard has a cemetery where around two thousand Jews, who perished in atrocious conditions, are buried. The leaves of Imre Varga's moving metallic weeping willow contain names of those who died in the holocaust. 🕘 *1 hr. Go early at 10am on weekdays before crowds in summer. Dohány utca 2 (corner of Wesselényi utca). 2,250 Ft adults, 1,100 Ft children. Guided tour 2,650 Ft adults, 1,900 Ft children. Summer Mon–Thurs, Sun 10am–6pm, Fri 10am–4:30pm; Winter Mon–Thurs, Sun 10am–4pm, Fri 10am–2pm. Metro: M2 to Astoria.*

2 Rumbach utca Synagogue. A symbol of compromise between squabbling factions of the local

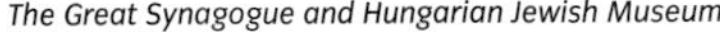

The Great Synagogue and Hungarian Jewish Museum.

Jewish community, Viennese Otto Wagner built the so-called "status quo" synagogue in 1872 using bright Moorish colors and topping the structure with a pair of classic mosque-like towers. Although it no longer functions as a synagogue, visitors are sometimes allowed in to view the colorful turquoise-dominated interior for a small fee. ***Rumbach utca. No phone.***

3 Arch between buildings at Madách Imre tér. The huge archway that connects the towering bright red-brick townhouses that look out onto the central boulevard of Károly körút was to have been the entry point to a new grand boulevard that would have graced Jewish Budapest. However, the tragic events of World War II put paid to that idea. The view back through the archway to Gellért Hill is spectacular, but the boulevard peters out quickly when a modern banking center crosses its path. ***Madách Imre tér.***

Rambach utca Synagogue can sometimes be entered for a small fee.

4 ★★★ Gozsdu Udvar. Continue down Rumbach utca and walk up Király utca to no. 13. This stunning tunnel-like courtyard network, which has been used in numerous films, connects the upcoming and trendy Király utca with the still ghetto-like Dob utca. Now it's gone a bit upmarket, with high-end boutiques, cafe-bars, and a fancy gym as tenants, compared to its state of decayed beauty of just a few years back, when it was home to one solitary obstinate tenant who resisted the developers. The developers got their way, of course, but, fortunately, much of the old atmosphere remains. ***Enter from Király utca 13 or Dob utca 16. www.gozsduudvar.hu.***

5 ★ Fröhlich Cukrászda. The place to come for flavorsome *flódni* (a triple whammy of apple, poppy seeds, and walnuts, encased in crispy pastry), which is Hungary's contribution to Jewish confectionery. Kosher Fröhlich has been home-baking since 1953 and has a real neighborhood cafe feel. ***Dob utca 22. ☎ 1/266-1733. Flódni 370 Ft.***

6 Kazinczy utca Synagogue. Half hidden down a narrow street, this synagogue boasts an awesome Art Nouveau facade, which is all the more remarkable when you think that this was commissioned by orthodox traditionalists. ***30 min. Kazinczy utca 29–31. Adults & children 800 Ft. Mon–Thurs 10am–3:30pm, Fri and Sun 10am–12:30pm.***

7 ★ Hanna's Kosher Kitchen. Hungarian classics gone Kosher, such as the simple but crispy and succulent kosher chicken fried in breadcrumbs, are served in this atmospheric, no-frills 1970s' style dining room. Roast duck, beef

The stunning tunnel-like courtyard Gozsdu Udvar.

goulash, and stuffed cabbage also feature. *Dob utca 35.* ☎ *1/342-1072. Fried chicken 2,600 Ft.*

8 kids **Klauzal tér.** This large, ambient square has quite a history. The ironwork doorway into the indoor market hall retains some pre-war charm, although there's a lack of market stalls with the space mainly taken up by a supermarket. For atmosphere head a few doors down to the **Kádár Étkezde** (p 100). Forget retro, this is the genuine article with pictures of past celebrities, soda siphons to dilute raspberry cordial *(málna szörp)*, and patchwork tablecloths. And you still pay the man on the door on the way out for what you've had. *Klauzal tér.*

Best of the Rest of Jewish Budapest

The functioning synagogue at Frankel Leó út 49 is a bizarre sight. Passing from the Danube side, onto which the back juts between two large townhouses, it appears to be bricked up. However, from the Frankel Leó side there's a fully functioning synagogue amazingly tucked inside a courtyard. The main Budapest Jewish cemetery at Kozma utca 3 in District X (☎ 1/262-4687) contains some stunning Art Nouveau tombs, especially that of the Schmidl family, which is the work of Hungary's secessionist kings Lechner and Lajta who used Zsolnay ceramics in the design. The **Holocaust Memorial Center** at Páva utca 39 in District IX (☎ 1/455-3333) charts the tragic path from deprivation of rights to genocide for local Jews and Roma. Another chilling reminder of many of the local Jewish population's terrible fate comes from the permanent ***Shoes on the Danube Promenade*** memorial, a few hundred yards from Parliament in the direction of the Chain Bridge. This 40m (130-ft) row of sculpted iron shoes, created in 2005 by Gyula Pauer and Can Togay, stands as a memorial to victims of Nazi atrocities.

The Watertown (Víziváros)

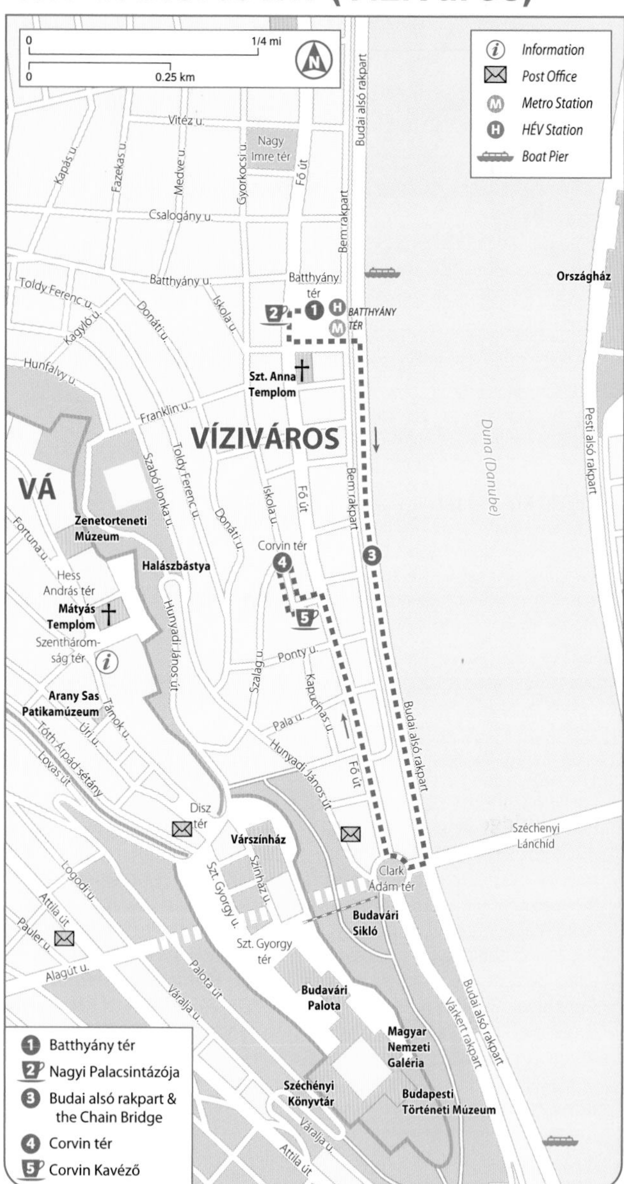

I love wandering this gem-packed area wedged between the Castle District and the Danube, especially at the weekend when all's peaceful. The main sights are down toward the river but I also recommend climbing the steep picturesque streets, particularly Ponty utca (Carp Street) that starts down on Fő utca. START: **M2 to Batthyány tér. TIME: 1 hr.**

❶ ★★★ **Batthyány tér.** Strikingly situated directly opposite **Parlament** (p 8, ❸), which effectively makes up the fourth corner of the square despite being on the other side of the Danube, Batthyány tér is a haven of baroque beauty in this busy part of Buda. The baroque attractions include **St. Anne's Church** and a number of colorful houses, including one sunk below street level. Sip a coffee in the famous cafe **Angelika** (p 37, ❿) and you'll be sitting in the church's former crypt. The impressive market hall is a more recent addition. *Batthyány tér.*

❷ **Nagyi Palacsintázója.** Fast food Hungarian style with sweet and savory pancakes, plus salads and filled jacket potatoes. *Batthyány tér 5. ☎ 1/212-4897. Pancakes from 130 Ft.*

❸ **Budai alsó rakpart & the Chain Bridge.** Stroll along next to the tree-lined tramline overlooking the Danube to the Chain Bridge. Budapest's most famous bridge features two arched neoclassical buttresses that rise high above the water. Often compared to a pair of imperious "silent" lions, they were sculpted by János Marschalkó who curiously didn't give them tongues. There's also plenty of both solid and intricate ironwork hanging from the buttresses. *See p 7, ❷.*

❹ ★ **Corvin tér.** Here you'll find another haven of baroque buildings clustered either side of the square, as well as the eclectic-looking turn-of-the-century **Budai Vigadó** at no. 8, which is home to the Hungarian National Folk Ensemble. It's worth peeking inside for the Art Nouveau interior decoration and grand staircases. I find the square at its best on weekends when the traffic is sparse.

❺ **Corvin Kavézó.** This bijou cafe right on pretty Corvin tér enables you to refuel while admiring the baroque houses and the view up to Castle Hill. *Corvin tér. ☎ 06/20-982-1402.*

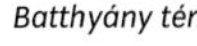

Batthyány tér.

The Castle **District**

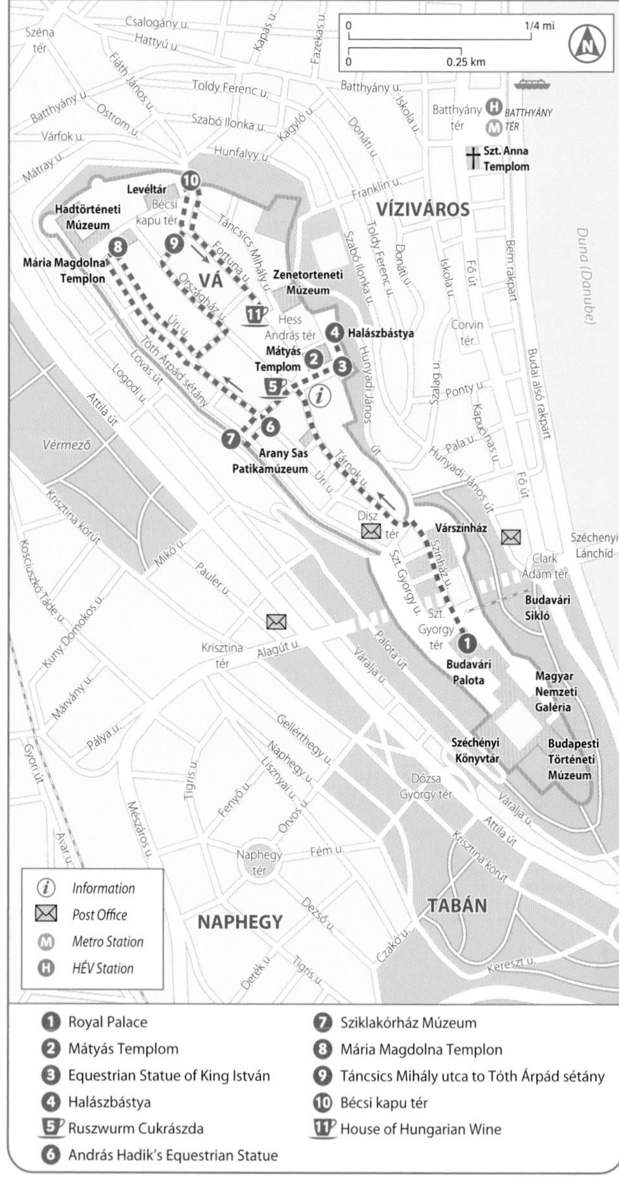

The opulence of the repeatedly razed and rebuilt Royal Palace and St. Matthias Church dramatically portrays Hungary's trials and tribulations. However, these buildings are only the beginning of this historic and richly bequeathed district. START: **Bus: 16/16A/116 to Dísz tér. There is also the more expensive Sikló (funicular) for 800 Ft to the Castle gate from Clark Ádám tér. TIME: 4 hr.**

1 ★★★ Royal Palace. The imposing and multi-faceted Royal Palace may have become a Royal Residence in the 14th century but it dates back further to the 13th-century Mongol invasion of Hungary. The Palace took a serious battering when the Turks were evicted in 1686, and the first attempts at rebuilding it were much more austere than the opulence you see today. Its grand design was literally created to be fit for a King—Austria's Franz Josef I—by leading local architects after the Austro-Hungarian Compromise of 1867. If you alight from the funicular right next to the entrance you're greeted by a statue of the mythical Magyar bird, the Turul, which looks like it's about to fly away from all the tourists. The sweeping views down the Danube and over to Pest from the Castle Gardens, which you enter through an ornamental gate, help put much of the Budapest jigsaw into place. The main attraction on the inside of the Royal Palace is the **Hungarian National Gallery** (p 32, 8). In the outer courtyard, Alajos Stróbl's **King Matthias's Fountain** dates back to 1904 and fits perfectly in the niche in the Palace wall. The ramparts are much older, and the stretch south of Szent György tér dates back to Sigismund of Luxembourg's rule in the early 15th century. *1–2 hr. Várbusz 16/16A-116 to Dísz tér. For Hungarian National Gallery, see p 32, 8.*

2 ★★★ Mátyás Templom (St. Matthias Church). Just a stone's throw away from the Fisherman's Bastion (4) is the mainly neo-Gothic St. Matthias Church, which is topped off by an extraordinarily multi-colored tiled roof. Although King Matthias Corvinus didn't build the church from scratch, he did extend and repair the then 200-year-old Gothic structure in the 15th century. He also made good use of it, having two of

The imposing and multi-faceted Royal Palace.

his three marriages there. Charles Robert was the first to be crowned here in 1308, while Charles IV was the last in 1916 (and indeed the last Habsburg monarch). In preparations for the millennium celebrations in 1896, Frigyes Schulek hacked away some of the 15th-century additions in a rather impressive bid to restore the church's original look. Nineteenth-century artists Károly Lotz and Bertalan Székely bring Hungarian legends and history to life inside. I love the calm and soft tones of the interior, which is also one of the few places where the din of tourist chatter dies down, and the color of the roof gives something modern (well, it was cutting edge in 1896) to the neo-Gothic visage. *30 min. Szentháromság tér 2. 1/489-0716. 990 Ft adults, 650 Ft children, 2,500 Ft family. Free to pray. Mon–Fri 9am–5pm, 9am–1pm Sat, 1–5pm Sun. 16/16A/116 to Dísz tér.*

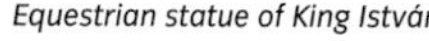

Equestrian statue of King István.

3 Equestrian Statue of King István. Popping up right between Matthias Church and the Fisherman's Bastion, Hungary's first monarch reminds everyone who was the boss in Hungary's story. He even stole King Matthias's thunder by putting the first church up here in A.D. 1015. The statue itself is the work of master sculptor Alajos Stróbl, but the altarpiece on which the statue rests is from Frigyes Schulek's design, hence the smooth integration with its two surrounding sights.

4 ★★★ kids Halászbástya (Fisherman's Bastion). The seven Disney-like mini towers might look custom-built for Snow White's troupe, but the fact that there are seven refers rather to the seven leaders of the Magyar tribes who galloped in to claim Hungary in A.D. 896. This fairytale blend of neo-Gothic and neo-Romanesque, conjured up by Frigyes Schulek, affords stunning views over to Parliament and sprawling Pest. The steps that run down beside it were poorly guarded when the invading Turks piled in to seize the Castle. *30 min. Adults & children 450 Ft. Admission is for*

Ornate altar in St. Matthias Church.

The fairytale towers of the Fisherman's Bastion.

entrance to towers—you can explore lower areas free. Metro: Moszkva Tér, then castlebus (VÁRBUSZ).

5 ★★★ kids **Ruszwurm Cukrászda.** Refuel over coffee with a green marzipan-topped Mátyás cake at this cozy, family-run Budapest institution. *See p 37,* 11. *Coffee & cake from 1,200 Ft.*

6 **András Hadik's Equestrian Statue.** It is a mystery as to why students from the nearby Engineering University consider it good luck before exams to rub the big brassy testicles of this Huszár's horse, but it's one of the few remaining activities that are free in the Castle District. Hadik, incidentally, was a Slovak who rose to the high rank of commander in the Austrian army serving in the Seven Years War, even taking Berlin and serving as the protector of Buda Castle.

7 kids **Sziklakórház Múzeum (Hospital in the Rock Museum).** The fascinating subterranean complex of 2,000 sq m (6,560 sq ft) runs underneath the Castle and served as a World War II hospital and Cold War nuclear shelter. Subterranean fans should also check out the labyrinth of the dense cellar network of the Buda Castle at Úri utca 9. *Lovas út 4c. www.sziklakorhaz.hu. Adults 3,000 Ft, Children & students 6–26 1,500 Ft; 7,000 Ft family; free for children 5 and under. Tues–Sun 10am–6pm; closed Mon.*

8 kids **Mária Magdolna Templom (Mary Magdalene Tower).** The large 13th-century Franciscan church was almost consigned to the history books by allied bombing in World War II, but the tower and a Gothic vaulted window obstinately rise out of the ghostly ruins thanks to reconstruction completed in 1997. In the early days of the Ottoman occupation, the Turks allowed Christians to use the church, bringing both Protestants and Catholics to worship here, but in different parts of the church of course. Later it was converted into a mosque, returning to its former use after the Turks were expelled. You can wander free through the ruined nave and admire the tower next to the car park. *Kapisztrán tér.*

9 ★★★ **Explore the old cobbled streets between Táncsics Mihály utca and Tóth Árpád sétány.** These streets, slightly away from the madding tourist crowd, hold more fascination for me than the more famous sights. Here, you realize that the Castle District isn't just a museum-piece and that people do actually live in these houses, many of which date back to the 19th and 18th centuries, some earlier. On Táncsics Mihály utca, which was once part of the Jewish quarter, look out for the elaborate courtyard of former **Erődy mansion** at no. 7, which is now home to the Music History Institute. Steeped in history itself, Beethoven once stayed here. On the same street, you can see houses that have been built on the original medieval

Great views from the Castle District.

foundations, such as no. 10 with its upper niche containing a vase and shell. Fortuna utca features charming neoclassical and baroque houses, while the triangle of houses on Országház utca at nos 20, 22, and 5, directly opposite, feature a Gothic ledge with arch, a fabulous bay window, and a stunning gate, respectively. At 32 Úri utca, check out the partly preserved Gothic sedilia next to the gate. Tóth Árpád sétány skirts around the perimeter of the inner Castle District and is great for a walk with a view. *30 min–1 hr.*

10 ★★ **Bécsi kapu tér.** The "Vienna Gate" is where the Hungarians finally overpowered the Turks to re-enter and reclaim the Castle in 1686, though the Vienna Gate that stands here today dates back to just 1936. At the square's center, the fountain, which features a girl protecting a sacred light, is a tribute to writer Ferenc Kazinczy and his efforts to develop the Hungarian language in the 18th century when its usage was far from universal. Kazinczy was sentenced to death for his role as a Jacobin along with the movement's leader Ignác Martinovics, priest of the Magdalene Church. Like the Hungarian language, but unlike Martinovics, Kazinczy survived. It seems fitting that the domineering National Archives building, with its colorfully tiled roof, overlooks the square. Substantially less imposing is the tiny **Lutheran church** on the opposite side of the square. Noted Greek and Roman guru József Grigely once lived at 7 Bécsi kapu tér, which accounts for the relief featuring Pallas Athena and classical authors including the likes of Virgil and Socrates. ***Bécsi kapu tér.***

11 **House of Hungarian Wine.** Wind down your tour with a flight of fine Hungarian wine and a selection of handmade local cheese, as you learn about the country's wine regions and unique grape varieties via the informative visual display set up by region. *Szentháromság tér 6. ☎ 1/201-4062. Cheese and wine from 4,500 Ft.* ●

4 The Best **Shopping**

Shopping Best Bets

Best **American Mall Experience**
★★ Arena Plaza, *Kerepesi út 9 (p 78)*

Best **Art Auction House**
★★★ Kieselbach Gallery & Auction House, *Szent István körút 5 (p 71)*

Best **Beijing-style Market**
★ Józsefvárosi Piac, *Kőbányai út 21–23 (p 76)*

Best **Budapest Gift**
★★ Printa, *Rumbach Sebestyén utca 10 (p 78)*

Best **Ceramics**
★★★ Herend, *József Nádor tér 11 (p 72)*

Best for **Firewater**
★ Magyar Pálinka Háza (House of Hungarian Pálinka), *Rákóczi út 17 (p 80)*

Best **Flea Market**
★★★ Ecseri Piac, *Nagykörösi út 156 (p 76)*

Best **Food Market**
★★★ Great Market Hall, *Vámház körút 1–3 (p 78)*

Best for **Funky Gifts**
★ Forma Bolt, *Ferenciek tere 4 (p 78)*

Best **Handmade Shoes**
★★ Vass Shoes, *Harris köz 2 (p 76)*

Best **Hats**
★★ V50 Design Art Studio, *Váci utca 50 (p 73)*

Best **Hungarian Designer**
★★★ Katti Zoób, *Szent István körút 17 (p 74)*

Best **Jewelry**
★★★ Wladis Galéria és Muterem, *Falk Miksa utca 13 (p 75)*

Best for **Retro Magyar Sneakers**
★ Tisza Cipo, *Károly körút 1 (p 76)*

Best **Salami**
★★ Pick Márkaáruház, *Kossuth Lajos tér 9 (p 79)*

Best for **Sweet Teeth**
★★★ Sugar, *Paulay Ede utca 48 (p 80)*

Best **Wine Shop**
★★★ Bortársaság, *Vécsey utca 5 (next to Imre Nagy statue opposite Parliament; p 80)*

Handmade footwear at Vass Shoes. Previous page: Retrock Deluxe.

Buda Shopping

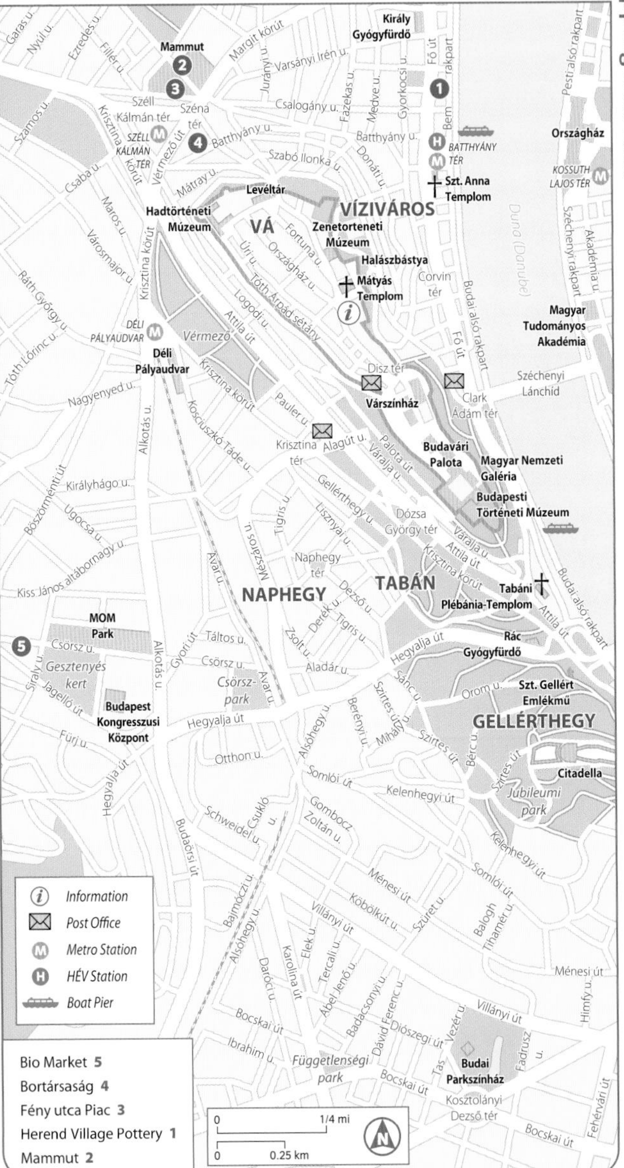

Bio Market 5
Bortársaság 4
Fény utca Piac 3
Herend Village Pottery 1
Mammut 2

Central Pest Shopping

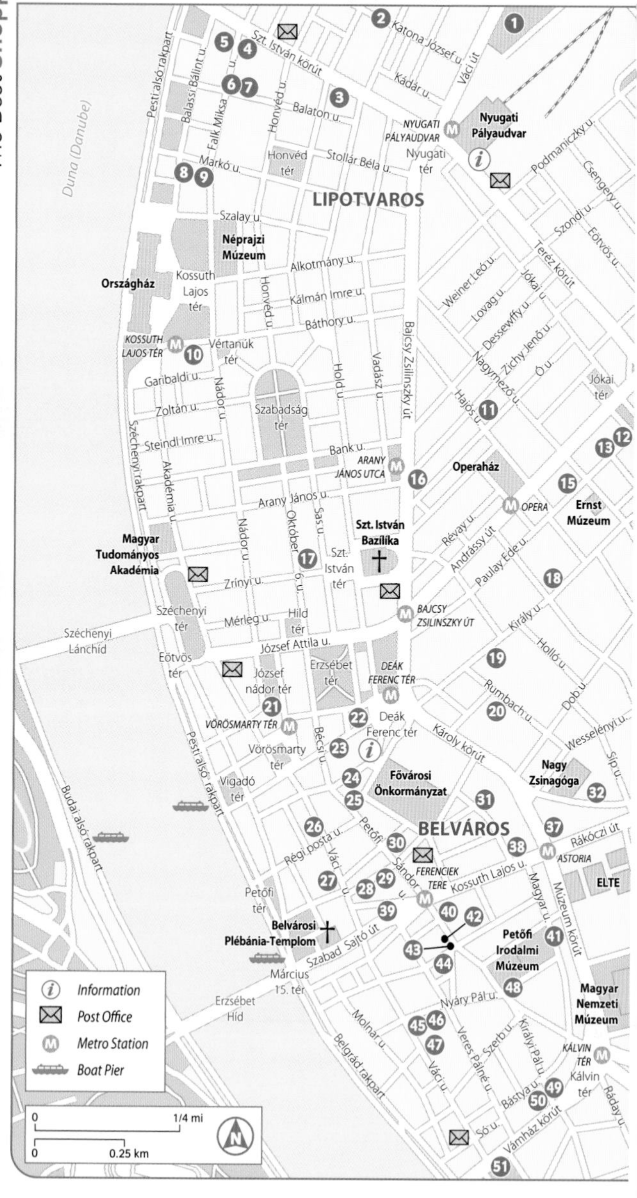

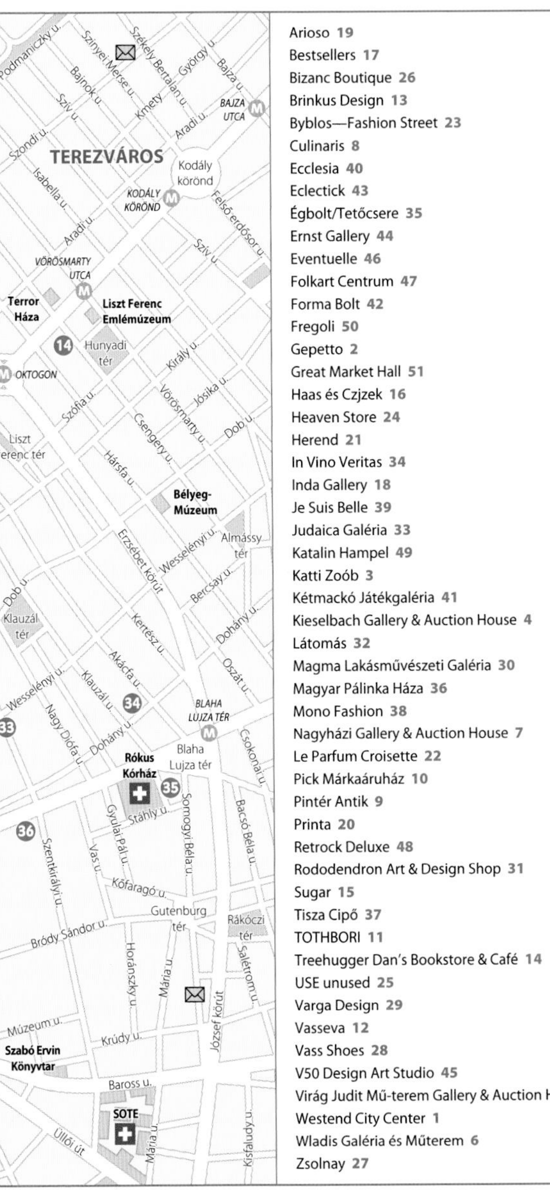

Arioso **19**
Bestsellers **17**
Bizanc Boutique **26**
Brinkus Design **13**
Byblos—Fashion Street **23**
Culinaris **8**
Ecclesia **40**
Eclectick **43**
Égbolt/Tetőcsere **35**
Ernst Gallery **44**
Eventuelle **46**
Folkart Centrum **47**
Forma Bolt **42**
Fregoli **50**
Gepetto **2**
Great Market Hall **51**
Haas és Czjzek **16**
Heaven Store **24**
Herend **21**
In Vino Veritas **34**
Inda Gallery **18**
Je Suis Belle **39**
Judaica Galéria **33**
Katalin Hampel **49**
Katti Zoób **3**
Kétmackó Játékgaléria **41**
Kieselbach Gallery & Auction House **4**
Látomás **32**
Magma Lakásművészeti Galéria **30**
Magyar Pálinka Háza **36**
Mono Fashion **38**
Nagyházi Gallery & Auction House **7**
Le Parfum Croisette **22**
Pick Márkaáruház **10**
Pintér Antik **9**
Printa **20**
Retrock Deluxe **48**
Rododendron Art & Design Shop **31**
Sugar **15**
Tisza Cipő **37**
TOTHBORI **11**
Treehugger Dan's Bookstore & Café **14**
USE unused **25**
Varga Design **29**
Vasseva **12**
Vass Shoes **28**
V50 Design Art Studio **45**
Virág Judit Mű-terem Gallery & Auction House **5**
Westend City Center **1**
Wladis Galéria és Műterem **6**
Zsolnay **27**

Outer Pest Shopping

Budapest Shopping A to Z

Art & Antiques

★★ Ernst Gallery CENTRAL PEST This charming gallery sells work by en vogue "neglected" local artists; decorative and applied arts, plus baroque, Biedermeier, Art Nouveau, and Art Deco furniture. *Irányi utca 27 (corner of Cukor utca). ☎ 1/266-4016. www.ernstgaleria.hu. AE, MC, V. Metro: M3 to Ferenciek tere. Map p 68.*

★ Inda Gallery CENTRAL PEST Located on arty Király utca but hidden away in a townhouse, Inda offers paintings, installations, and sculptures from talented young creatives. *Király utca 34 2/4 (corner of Székely Mihály utca). ☎ 1/413-1960. www.indagaleria.hu. MC, V. Metro: M1/M2/M3 to Deák tér. Tram: 4/6 to Király utca. Map p 68.*

★★★ Kieselbach Gallery & Auction House CENTRAL PEST This prestigious auction house, which marks the start of Pest's gallery-rich Falk Miksa utca, holds the world record for the auction of a Hungarian painting at US$1.42 million for a Csontváry, who Picasso referred to as the other great painter of the 20th century. *Szent István körút 5 (corner of Falk Miksa utca). ☎ 1/269-3148 or 1/269-3149. www.kieselbach.hu. AE, DC, MC, V. Tram: 2/4/6 to Jászai Mari tér. Map p 68.*

★★ Nagyházi Gallery & Auction House CENTRAL PEST Prominent auction house offering everything from paintings and sculpture to furniture, carpets, objets d'art, jewelry, folk art, and antiquities. *Balaton utca 8 (corner of Falk Miksa utca). ☎ 1/475-6000 or 1/475-2090. www.nagyhazi.hu. AE, DC, MC, V. Tram: 2/4/6 to Jászai Mari tér. Map p 68.*

★ Pintér Antik CENTRAL PEST Huge selection of antiques, traditional and modern paintings, chandeliers, clocks, and sculpture for sale. They also hold regular auctions here. *Falk Miksa utca 10 (corner of Markó utca). ☎ 1/311-3030.*

Ernst Gallery for Art Deco furniture and other treasures.

www.pinterantik.hu. MC,V. Tram: 2/4/6 to Jászai Mari tér. Map p 68.

★★★ **Virág Judit Mű-terem Gallery & Auction House** CENTRAL PEST Here you can buy and bid on 19th and 20th-century Hungarian paintings from big names in local art, including Munkácsy, Csontváry, and Rippl-Rónai, along with Art Nouveau ceramics from Zsolnay. *Falk Miksa utca 30 (between Szent István körút and Balaton utca). ☎ 1/312-2071. www.mu-terem.hu. MC, V. Metro: M2 to Kossuth tér. Tram: 2/4/6 to Jászai Mari tér. Map p 68.*

Books (English Language)

★ **Bestsellers** CENTRAL PEST Although this store has plenty of healthy competition these days, its multi-genre selection of new English language books is hard to beat. Try here for your newspapers and magazines too. *Október 6. utca 11. ☎ 1/312-1295. www.bestsellers.hu. AE, DC, MC, V. Metro: M3 to Arany János utca. Map p 68.*

★ **Treehugger Dan's Bookstore & Café** CENTRAL PEST Grab a used paperback with a cup of Fairtrade coffee at this branch of American environmental activist Dan Swartz's ever expanding used bookstore empire. Regular readings, gigs, stand-up comedians, and wine tastings are also hosted here. *Lázár utca 6 ☎ 1/269-3843. www.treehugger.hu. No credit cards. Metro: M1 to Opera. Tram: 4/6 to Oktogon. Map p 68.*

Treehugger Dan's Bookstore branches.

Ceramics

★ **Haas és Czjzek** CENTRAL PEST Look out for Hollóháza with its funky "Four Seasons" design featuring a woman's face in each season, as well as plates from Alföldi (that serve many restaurants) plus Herend, Zsolnay, and Swarowski crystal. *Bajcsy Zsilinszky út 23 (corner of Zichy Jenő utca). ☎ 1/311-4094. AE, MC, V. Metro: M3 to Arany János utca. Map p 68.*

★★★ **Herend** CENTRAL PEST From tasteful and intricate traditional items to light and breezy, Herend's legendary porcelain is always classy, and Queen Victoria was among its fans. A national treasure, albeit a pricey one. *József Nádor tér 11. ☎ 1/317-2622. www.herend.com. AE, DC, MC, V. Metro: M1 to Vörösmarty tér. Map p 68.*

Herend Village Pottery BUDA More charming and colorful, easy-going, country-style designs from Hungary's renowned ceramics producer—still handmade—without breaking the bank. *Bem rakpart 37 (between Vitéz utca and Csalogány utca). ☎ 1/356-7899. www.herendmajolika.hu. AE, MC, V. Metro: M2 to Batthyány tér. Map p 67.*

★★★ **Zsolnay** CENTRAL PEST Zsolnay's colorful and super-durable pyrogranite tiles adorn the roofs of some of Budapest's most spectacular buildings. Its iridescent eosin (from the Greek word 'eos') technology also makes unique ceramics. *Váci utca 19–21 (corner of Párizsi*

Unique ceramics from Zsolnay.

utca). ☎ 1/266-6305. www. zsolnay.hu. MC, V. Metro: M3 to Ferenciek tere. Map p 68.

Design

★★ Brinkus Design CENTRAL PEST Textile designer Kata Brinkus became known for her anthropomorphic and zoomorphic pillows, and then started doing all sorts of crazy things with carpet, such as building in wood, metal, mirrors, and even LED-lights. *Paulay Ede utca 56. ☎ 1/321-2138. www. brinkusdesign.com. No credit cards. Metro: M1 to Opera. Map p 68.*

★ Eventuelle CENTRAL PEST This friendly shop that originally only featured works of Hungarian textile designers, now also has a selection of jewelry and clothes. *Nyári Pál utca 7. ☎ 1/318-6926. www.eventuelle.hu. MC,V. Metro: M3 to Ferenciek tere. Map p 68.*

★★ Gepetto CENTRAL PEST International award-winning, sleek minimalist interior design encompassing sofas and shelves to kitchen furniture, lamps, and some smaller household objects. *Katona József utca 15. ☎ 1/270-0107. www. gepetto.hu. No credit cards. Metro: M3 to Nyugati pályaudvar. Map p 68.*

★ Magma Lakásművészeti Galéria CENTRAL PEST Among the neighborhood's folk art offerings, this central shop displays a striking selection of handmade works by Hungarian artisans made from glass, ceramics, leather, jewelry, textile, and woodwork. *Petőfi Sándor utca 11. ☎ 1/235-0277. www.magma.hu. AM, MC, V. Metro: M3 to Ferenciek tere. Map p 68.*

★ Rododendron Art & Design Shop CENTRAL PEST A small art and design heaven, displaying works of young and upcoming Hungarian artists. Find shoes, bags, jewelry, beautifully illustrated books for children, as well as some unique souvenirs, such as Buda/Pest earrings. *Semmelweis utca 19. ☎ 06/70-419-5329. www. rododendronart.com/ hu. AE, MC, V. Metro: M2 to Astoria. Map p 68.*

Fashion—Accessories

★★ Anh Tuan CENTRAL PEST Vietnamese-born Anh Tuan became known for his beautiful leather bags and belts, before getting his hand into designing clothes. By appointment only, but you can find some of his designs at Retrock Deluxe and Mono Fashion. *Rózsa utca 74. ☎ 06/20-444-4704. www.anh-tuan. com. No credit cards. Metro: M1 to Vörösmarty utca. Map p 70.*

★★ V50 Design Art Studio CENTRAL PEST Internationally renowned hat and fashion designer Valeria Fazekas promotes her headwear as unique, wearable art objects. Whether sporty, trendy, or elegant, they're beautiful to look at and to put on. Expect a friendly service. *Váci utca 50. ☎ 1/337-5320. No credit cards. Metro: M3 to Ferenciek tere. Map p 68.*

Fashion—Hungarian Designers

★★ Eclectick CENTRAL PEST Edina Gyovai-Farkas's funky, colorful streetwear and accessories attract all ages. Her designs featuring a wild grinning dog and girl in glasses have been popular ever since the shop opened 10 years ago. Other Hungarian designers are also stocked.

Hungarian design at Eclectick.

Irányi utca 20 (corner of Károlyi Mihály utca). ☎ 1/266-3341. www.eclectick.hu. MC, V. Metro: M3 to Ferenciek tere. Map p 68.

Je Suis Belle CENTRAL PEST Establishing their label in 2005, fashion designer duo Dalma Dévényi and Tibi Kiss shot to fame with great speed. Feminine elegance combined with casual, playful, innovative ideas and good quality, wearable clothing. *Ferenciek tere 11. 4th floor. ☎ 06/70-220-1044. www.jesuisbelle.hu. No credit cards. Metro: M3 to Ferenciek tere. Bus: 7/178. Map p 68.*

★★★ **Katti Zoób** CENTRAL PEST Internationally acclaimed Katti Zoób creates flowing and classy feminine designs from top Italian fabrics, as well as distinctive jewelry and accessories using Zsolnay ceramics. *Szent István körút 17. ☎ 1/312-1865. www.kattizoob.hu. MC, V. Metro: M3 to Nyugati pu. Tram: 2/4/6 to Jászai Mari tér. Map p 68.*

★ **Mono Fashion** CENTRAL PEST Currently holds the best selection of top young Hungarian designers. Beside the shop's own Nubu brand, for women, men, and babies, check out the amazing Suck Right accessories, Anh Tuan's beautiful bags, and Artista's clothing. *Kossuth Lajos utca 20. ☎ 1/317-7789. www.monofashion.hu. MC, V. Metro: M3 to Ferenciek tere. Map p 68.*

★ **Retrock Deluxe** CENTRAL PEST A turn-of-the-century salon turned into a madhouse of crazy works by young Hungarian designers. Find a range of brands here including Nanushka, Use Unused, Tamara Barnuff, Je Suis Belle, and Anh Tuan. *Henszlmann Imre utca 1. ☎ 06/30-556-2814. No credit cards. Metro: M3 to Ferenciek tere. Map p 68.*

★★ **TOTHBORI** CENTRAL PEST Local designer Bóri Tóth works for the modern woman, creating wearable, elegant, business-style collections. Beside the high quality prêt-a-porter, her Haute Couture collections comprise wedding dresses and cocktail gowns. *Hajós utca 25. (corner of Ó utca). ☎ 1/354-1588. www.tothbori.com. MC, V. Metro: M1 to Opera. Map p 68.*

USE unused CENTRAL PEST This designer trio makes amazingly chic, prêt-a-porter clothes for women and men. Come here for superb tailoring and timeless designs. *Szervita tér 5. ☎ 1/215-8445. www.use.co.hu. Credit DC, V. Metro: M1/M2/M3 to Deák Ferenc tér. Map p 68.*

★★ **Vasseva** CENTRAL PEST A compact shop on a side street off Liszt Ferenc tér selling Éva Vass' creations and interior decor items. Original ideas are combined with interesting materials, which results in wearable clothes but with a unique, quirky edge. *Paulay Ede utca. 67. ☎ 1/342-8159. AE, MC, V. Metro: M1 to Oktogon. Tram: 4/6. Map p 68.*

Fashion—International Designers

★★ Byblos—Fashion Street CENTRAL PEST Hungarian Hollywood movie producer Andy Vajna opened this exclusive boutique in 2007 selling Byblos, Byblos Blu, and some Rocco Barocco clothes and accessories. *Deák Ferenc utca 17 (corner of Bécsi utca). ☎ 1/337-1908. AE, MC,V. Metro: M1/M2/M3 to Deák tér. Map p 68.*

★★★ Heaven Store CENTRAL PEST The first high-flying multi-brand store in Budapest offering personal appointments and a wide selection of brands including Patrizia Pepe, Replay, Chloé, G-Star Raw, and Stella McCartney among others. *Fehérhajó utca 12–14. ☎ 1/266-8335. www.heavenstore.hu. AE, DC, MC, V. Metro: M1/M2/M3 to Deák tér. Map p 68.*

Látomás CENTRAL PEST A great selection of international labels limitedly available elsewhere in Budapest can be found here, many at affordable prices. Látomás has three shops, each showcasing different styles. The oldest and biggest boutique specializes in jeans and floaty, floral outfits. *Dohány utca 16–18. ☎ 1/266-5052. www.latomas.hu. MC, V. Metro: M2 to Astoria. Tram: 47/49. (Branches at Király utca 39 and Párizsi utca 4.) Map p 68.*

Fashion—Jewelry

★★ Varga Design CENTRAL PEST Handmade jewelry based on Miklós Varga's patented approach to imitate the image of sun reflecting on dewdrops collecting on a cobweb. Like a spider's web, each item is unique. *Haris Köz 6. ☎ 1/318-4089. www.vargadesign.hu. AE, DC, MC, V. Metro: M3 to Ferenciek tere. Map p 68.*

★★★ Wladis Galéria és Műterem CENTRAL PEST Peter Vladimir's original jewelry reflects traditional and ancient designs. Chunky but classy these sculpted pieces are made from quality silver. *Falk Miksa utca 13 (corner of Balaton utca). ☎ 1/354-0834. www.wladisgaleria.hu. MC, V. Tram: 2/4/6 to Jászai Mari tér. Map p 68.*

Fashion—Secondhand

Égbolt/Tetőcsere CENTRAL PEST Situated in Corvintető, one half of this shop (Égbolt) offers clothes from upcoming Hungarian designers, while the other (Tetőcsere) specializes in clothes swapping. Open from 8pm until club closing time. *Corvintető, Blaha Lujza tér 1–2. 4th floor of Corvin Áruház. ☎ 06/20-398-1956. http://corvinteto.hu/hu/egbolt. No credit cards. Metro: M1 to Blaha Lujza tér or. Tram: 4/6. Map p 68.*

Iguana CENTRAL PEST If it's a Jesus or Elvis T-shirt you're missing, pop in to Iguana. Vintage fans will enjoy delving through the clothes, shoes, and retro accessories. Another branch can be found at Tompa utca 1. *Krúdy Gyula utca 9. ☎ 1/317-1627. www.iguanaretro.hu. No credit cards. Metro: M3 to Kálvin tér. Tram: 4/6. Map p 70.*

Drop by Iguana for secondhand clothes and accessories.

Bric-a-brac at Ecseri Piac flea market.

Fashion—Shoes

★★ Bizanc Boutique CENTRAL PEST The best assortment of the season's designer shoes for men and women, from Jimmy Choo, John Richmond, Moschino, Anna Sui, Giuseppe Zanotti, GML, and more, with handbags to match. *Váci utca 9. ☎ 1/317-8368. AE, MC, V. Metro: M1 to Vörösmarty tér. M2/M3 to Deák tér. Map p 68.*

★ Tisza Cipő CENTRAL PEST Retro sneakers with the trademark "T" on each design from Hungary's very own casual shoemaker. Also, look out for funky tops and jackets. There's another store in the West-end shopping mall (p 79). *Károly körút 1 (corner of Rákóczi út). ☎ 1/266-3055. www.tiszacipo.hu. AE, MC, V. Metro: M2 to Astoria. Tram: 47/49 to Astoria. Map p 68.*

★★ Vass Shoes CENTRAL PEST Handmade shoes that fit perfectly, boast amazing quality of material and precise craftsmanship. László Vass has managed to turn the old traditional shoemaking profession into a modern business. *Harris köz 2. ☎ 1/318-2375. www.vass-cipo.hu. AE, DC, MC, V. Metro: M3 to Ferenciek tere. Map p 68.*

Flea Markets

★★★ Ecseri Piac OUTER PEST Remarkable flea market packed with some quality antiques and no end of Socialist-era bric-à-brac. Paintings, furniture, soda siphons, rocking horses, Zsolnay ceramics, old motorbikes, even antique BMW bubble cars—it's all there. *Nagykörösi út 156. ☎ 1/348-3200. No credit cards. Bus: 54 to Alvinc utca. Map p 70.*

★ Józsefvárosi Piac OUTER PEST While the bottom is likely to fall out of the jeans you buy quicker than it takes you to walk around this sprawling Chinese market, it feels pretty close to being in China. Good oriental food available too. *Kőbányai út 21–23. ☎ 1/313-8890. No credit cards. Tram: 28 to Orczy tér. Map p 70.*

★ PECSA Flea Market OUTER PEST With the abundance of fake brands, chunky transistor radios,

Russian dolls, medals, and so on, I feel momentarily transported back to pre-1989 Budapest when I visit this market. Open Saturday mornings. *Zichy Mihály utca.* ☎ *1/363-3730. No credit cards. Metro: M1 to Széchenyi fürdő. Map p 70.*

Flowers

★★ Arioso CENTRAL PEST Creative arrangements verging on designer, and just the ticket if you've been invited to dinner. Much more than flowers, Arioso is also an interior designer. *Király utca.* ☎ *1/266-3555. www.arioso.hu. Closed first 3 weeks of Aug. AE, MC, V. Metro: M1/M2/M3 to Deák tér. Map p 68.*

Folk Art

★ Folkart Centrum CENTRAL PEST Folk art products including embroidered tablecloths, painted dolls, and ceramics for those who don't want to haggle in return for guaranteed quality from serious artisans. *Váci utca 58.* ☎ *1/318-4697. AE, DC, MC, V. Metro: M3 to Ferenciek tere. Map p 68.*

Folkart Centrum.

Katalin Hampel CENTRAL PEST Hungarian and European folk costumes adapted "for the modern woman," although some outfits, as well as the menswear, are more the preserve of period ball-goers. *Váci utca 8.* ☎ *1/318-9741. www.hampelkati.com. AM, MC, V. Metro: M1 to Vörösmarty tér. Map p 68.*

Food Markets

★ Bio Market (Ökopiac) BUDA Taste just how fresh Hungarian fruit and veg can be at this Saturday morning organic produce extravaganza that runs from 6am to noon. The fruit juices are sublime. *Csörsz utca 18.* ☎ *1/214-7005. No credit cards. Tram: 61 to Csörsz utca. Map p 67.*

★ Fény utca Piac BUDA Made from 1970s'-style iron and girders, this neighborhood market lacks the fin-de-siècle charm of some of its

Fresh Hungarian fruit at the Bio Market.

Jewish gifts and art at Judaica Galéria.

peers, but makes up for it in the range of Hungarian agricultural produce. For fine cheese, hams, and salami head to the top level. *Lövőház utca 12. ☎ 1/345-4101. No credit cards. Tram: 4/6 to Széna tér. Map p 67.*

★★★ Great Market Hall CENTRAL PEST Aside from the interesting architecture, this is a great place to pick up powdered paprika, tubes of paprika paste, tins of chestnut puree, and goose liver. Plenty of painted folk art and tablecloths, too. *Vámház körút 1–3. ☎ 1/366-3300. Credit cards not widely used. Tram: 2/47/49 to Fővám tér. Map p 68.*

Funky Gifts

★ Forma Bolt CENTRAL PEST You never know when a plastic duck or frog-shaped bottle opener will come in handy. Come here for fun gift ideas and other wacky items. *Ferenciek tere 4. ☎ 1/266-5053. www.forma.co.hu. AE, MC, V. Metro: M3 to Ferenciek tere. Map p 68.*

Fregoli CENTRAL PEST An original shop embracing designs such as bicycle tire bags and T-shirts featuring famous Hungarian moustaches. Beside the bike rubber bracelets, rubber belts, and bags by Balkantango you can find some inspired, locally themed gifts by Instant Hungary. *Bástya utca 12. ☎ 06/70-521-0474. www.fregolishop.com. MC, V. Metro: M3 to Kálvin tér. Map p 68.*

★★ Printa CENTRAL PEST A shop, cafe, gallery, workshop, silkscreen studio—all in one. The shop offers groovy clothes for all ages, along with books, magazines, and its own postcards. The "Hungaricum"- and Budapest-inspired collection by Bolt is only available here and makes an ideal souvenir. *Rumbach Sebestyén utca 10. No phone. www.printa.hu. No credit cards. Metro: M1/M2/M3 to Deák tér. Map p 68.*

Malls

★★ kids Arena Plaza OUTER PEST Just when Budapest seemed to reach saturation point with mega malls, along came Arena Plaza with more space and brands than anybody else, plus the first IMAX cinema in Hungary, replete with VIP booths. *Kerepesi út 9. ☎ 1/880-7000. www.arenaplaza.hu. Credit cards vary. Metro: M2 to Keleti Pu or Stadionok. Map p 70.*

★ kids Mammut BUDA Divided into two main parts: Mammut 1 and 2, Mammut (meaning mammoth), never gets too overwhelming in proportions and is more easy-going than Westend (p 79) but still packed with shops. *Lövőház utca 2–6.*

☎ 1/345-8020. www.mammut.hu. Credit cards vary. Metro: M2 to Széll Kálmán tér. Tram: 4/6 to Széna tér. Map p 67.

★★ kids **Westend City Center** CENTRAL PEST You could be fooled into thinking you're in a big American mall here. It is certainly busy and popular, with a huge number of Hungarian and international brands to choose from. *Váci út 1–3. ☎ 1/238-7777. www.westend.hu. Credit cards vary. Metro: M3 to Nyugati pályaudvar. Tram: 4/6 to Nyugati pu. Map p 68.*

Perfumes

★★ **Le Parfum Croisette** CENTRAL PEST Custom-made fragrances from the philosophical and talented French-educated perfumer Zsolt Zólyomi. You can also purchase limited edition, high-end perfumes from the likes of Burberry, Bottega Veneta, and Clive Christian. *Hotel Le Méridien, Deák Ferenc utca 18. ☎ 06/304-050-668. www.leparfum.hu. AE, MC, V. Metro: M1/M2/M3 to Deák tér. Map p 68.*

Religious

Ecclesia CENTRAL PEST This is the place to come for religious objects including hand-painted icons from Hungary and further east. *Városház utca 1. ☎ 1/317-3754. www.ecclesia.cc. MC, V. Metro: M3 to Ferenciek tere. Map 68.*

★★ **Judaica Galéria** CENTRAL PEST Teddy bears wearing *kippas* (skullcaps), Dead Sea beauty treatments, and recipe books feature among the eclectic Jewish gift items here. It also serves as a serious arts gallery and auction house. *Wesselényi utca 13. ☎ 1/267-8502. MC, V. Metro: M2 to Astoria. Map p 68.*

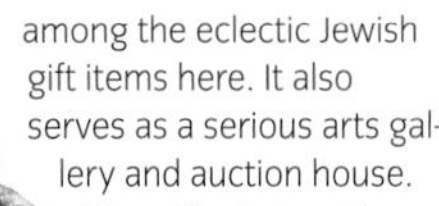

Pálinka fruit brandy bottles.

Specialty Foods

★★ **Culinaris** CENTRAL PEST Packed out with hungry expats relishing the range of international foodstuffs that they take for granted back home. *Balassi Bálint utca 7. ☎ 1/373-0028. www.culinaris.hu. AE, MC, V. Tram: 2/4/6 to Jászai Mari tér. Branches: Hunyadi tér 3 and Perc utca 8. Map p 68.*

★★ **Pick Márkaáruház** CENTRAL PEST Although you'll see Pick's definitive *téliszalámi* "winter" salami all over town, this shop stocks many other delicious variations, some spicy, others smooth, alongside other meat products. There's a cafeteria upstairs. *Kossuth Lajos tér 9. ☎ 1/331-7783. No credit cards. Metro: M2 to Kossuth Lajos tér 9. Tram: 2. Map p 68.*

Culinaris for International foodstuffs.

★★★ **Sugar** CENTRAL PEST You can buy designer confectionery, colorful candy, a remarkable range of jelly beans available by the gram, and milk rice to tease your taste buds here. Also sells toys and accessories. ***Paulay Ede utca 48.* ☎ *1/321-6672. www.sugarshop.hu. AE, MC, V. Metro: M1 to Opera. Map p 68.***

Toys

★★★ **Fakopáncs** CENTRAL PEST Creative Hungarian-made wooden toys to make youngsters think beyond the realm of the X-box and Barbie doll. Excellent for gifts and with a flawless safety record, too. ***József körút 50.* ☎ *1/333-1866. www.fakopancs.com. No credit cards. Tram: 4/6 to Baross utca. Map p 70.***

★★ **Kétmackó Játékgaléria** CENTRAL PEST Old-fashioned puppets and dolls, wooden toys, and game-themed paintings are on sale along with skill-enhancing activity and board games at the "Two Bears Toy Gallery." ***Magyar utca 18.* ☎ *1/266-0928. www.ketmacko.hu. No credit cards. Metro: M2 to Astoria. Map p 68.***

Wine & Spirits

★★★ **Bortársaság (Wine Society)** BUDA Superb selection of wines from across Hungary and the globe with highly knowledgeable staff on hand. *Vécsey utca 5 (next to Imre Nagy statue opposite Parliament).* ☎ ***1/212-2569. www.bortarsasag.hu. AE, MC, V. Metro: M2 to Kossuth tér. Tram: 4/6 to Széna tér. Map p 67.***

★ **In Vino Veritas** CENTRAL PEST More old-fashioned looking than the slick Bortársaság (above), Veritas also represents an impressive batch of quality-driven Hungarian winemakers. ***Dohány utca 58–62.* ☎ *1/341-3174 or 1/341-0646. www.borkereskedes.hu. MC, V. Metro: M2 to Astoria. Tram: 47/49 to Astoria. Map p 68.***

★ **Magyar Pálinka Háza (House of Hungarian Pálinka)** CENTRAL PEST Comprehensive collection of Hungary's fruit brandy known as *Pálinka,* now an EU-protected name. Variations range from the seriously fiery to the soft and fruity. ***Rákóczi út 17.* ☎ *1/338-4219. MC, V. Metro: M2 to Blaha Lujza tér. Map p 68.***

★★ **Zwack Shop** OUTER PEST Zwack makes the ubiquitous bitter Hungarian liqueur *Unicum* that you'll either love or hate. You may prefer the deliciously fruity *Nemes Pálinka* (fruit brandy) range and its boutique wines. ***Soroksári út 26.* ☎ *1/476-2383. www.zwack.hu. AE, MC, V. Tram: 2 to Haller utca. Map p 70.***

5 The Best of the Outdoors

City **Park**

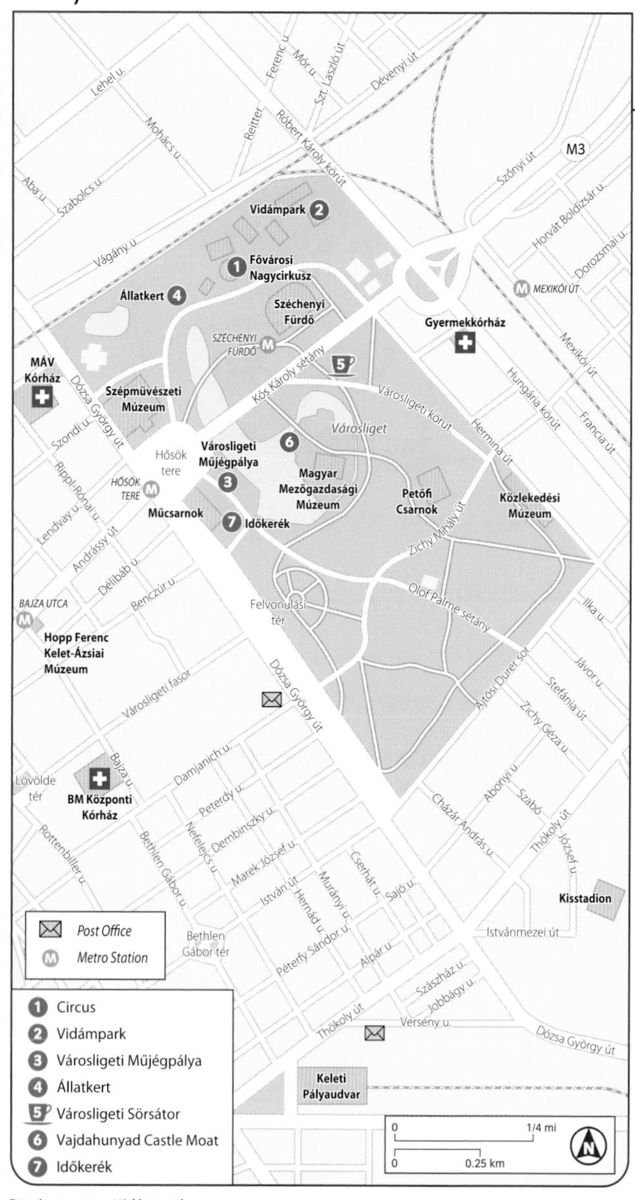

Previous page: Vidámpark.

This oasis of green is flanked by a multitude of old-fashioned attractions including a classic circus, a zoo, an atmospheric ice rink, and the popular amusement park, which features Europe's longest wooden rollercoaster alongside more up-to-date laser dodgems and go-karts. START: **M1 to Széchenyi Fürdő.**

1 ★★★ kids **Circus.** Lions, tigers, bears, and elephants, too, although this Budapest institution that dates back to 1889 seeks to embrace the age of animal rights with an increasing reliance on its talented human performers. Three different troupes feature classic circus performances from clowns, acrobats, trapeze artists, and tightrope walkers. *1½ hr. Állatkerti Körút 12/a. ☎ 1/343-8300. www.maciva.hu. 2,400 Ft–3,100 Ft adults, 2,000 Ft–2,400 Ft children 4–14, free for children under 4 if sitting on parent's lap. Performances Wed–Sun (excluding Sept). More performances at weekends.*

2 ★★★ kids **Vidámpark (Amusement Park).** Passing by, it looks a sorry excuse for an amusement park but step in and you're transported back to a charming, old-fashioned world of well-kept and restored attractions. Among the star rides is the centegenarian wooden merry-go-round, which churns out swirlingly authentic Wurlitzer music—you have to ride the horses to keep the old girl moving. Budapest's "Happy Park" boasts the longest wooden rollercoaster in Europe—a fairly pleasant ride compared to most up-to-date versions. The laser dodgems show that the park isn't entirely stuck in the past. Go-karting costs an extra 500 Ft a go. Take toddlers of 3 and under to the mini amusement park that's attached. You'll find playgrounds for younger infants within the surrounding City Park. It also has an interesting pay-according-to-height entry policy. *2–3 hr. Állatkerti Körút 14–16. ☎ 1/363-8310. www.vidampark.hu. 4,700 Ft for people over 140cm (nighttime 2,900 Ft for everybody), 90cm–140cm 3,300 Ft, free for under 90cm. Jun and Aug Mon–Thurs, Sun 10am–8pm, Fri–Sat 10am–1am; May and Sept daily 11am–7pm; mid-Mar–Apr and Oct daily noon–6pm. Winter closure Nov–mid-Mar.*

The old-style Vidámpark.

Hidden City Squares—Pest

The peaceful park—bar youngsters playing—at Honvéd tér with its trimmed lawn and neat flowerbeds is tucked away close to the busy thoroughfare of Szent István Körut. Here you'll find concrete ping-pong tables with iron nets that are an unglamorous hangover from Communism. **Szabadság tér,** literally Freedom Square, may be synonymous with the violence after the riots of 2006 (p 51, 5) and repression in the form of the Soviet War Memorial, but this big open space—surrounded by colossal buildings that serve to block out the bustle—is a superbly relaxing place. **Károly kert** also belies its central location, transcending metropolitan modernity and transporting you to Budapest's early 20th-century heyday. Step through the wrought-iron gate and feel at the center of a living bastion of old-world charm.

3 ★★★ kids **Városligeti Műjégpálya (Ice Rink).** As the chill of winter hits, the fairytale atmosphere of the ice rink, with a pavilion on one side and the **Vajdahunyad Castle** (p 13, 2) on the other, keeps the locals coming to the City Park. At the time of writing the rink was being extensively renovated. *2 hr. Olof Palme sétány 5. 1/364-0013. www.mujegpalya.hu. Metro: M1 to Hősök tere.*

4 ★★ kids **Állatkert (Zoo).** The first time I came here in the 1990s I felt indignant when I saw the cramped conditions and the sorry-looking, stir-crazy elephants. However, credit where credit's due, this place has become much more animal-friendly and is a nice place to bring the family. I'm fascinated with the big rock that looks just like the one out of Spielberg's *Close Encounters* movie and is the domain of gorillas and orangutans. The Art Nouveau entrance, with its Oriental and Indian aspects and fine animal carvings and sculptures, is a suitably impressive teaser for what's inside. *2 hr. Állatkerti Körút 6–12. 1/273-4900. www.zoobudapest.com. 2,100 Ft adults, 1,500 Ft children, 6,100 Ft family. Summer daily 9am–7pm; winter daily 9am–4pm. Metro: M1 to Széchenyi fürdő.*

Monkey about at the zoo.

5 **Városligeti Sörsátor.** An old-fashioned beer tent ideally located in the middle of the park. Perfect for a sausage (*kolbász*), pretzels (*perec*), or the savory scone known as *pogácsa*. *Városligeti Sétány. 1/363-1904. www.sorsator.hu. Beer and sausage from 1,400 Ft.*

Rowing on Vajdahunyad Castle Moat.

6 kids Row in the Vajdahunyad Castle Moat. It may be a folly and an eclectic mix of Hungarian architectural styles across the ages, but the Vajdahunyad Castle (p 13) sure makes an attractive backdrop for a spot of easy rowing in summer. Pick up a boat opposite the Castle entrance. *30 min–1 hr. No phone. 1,000 Ft for 30 min, 1,300 Ft for 1 hr. Summer only.*

7 kids Időkerék (Time Wheel). Unveiled as Hungary entered a new epoch in joining the EU on May 1, 2004, public interest in this, one of the world's largest hourglasses, has dwindled. However, this clock isn't built for short-term hype. It doesn't actually tell the time but it is an impressive fusion of ancient techniques and state-of-the-art technology that's built to last the ravages of time. *5 min. Behind the Műcsarnok.*

Classic Courtyards—Behind the City's Grand Facades

As you're walking around the downtown areas, do look out for open doorways of the magnificent buildings and have a peek in. Each of Budapest's stunning Habsburg-era townhouses, and there are many, tell their own story on the inside where they really come to life. If you get stuck, there's always a button to press that lets you out.

Buda **Hills**

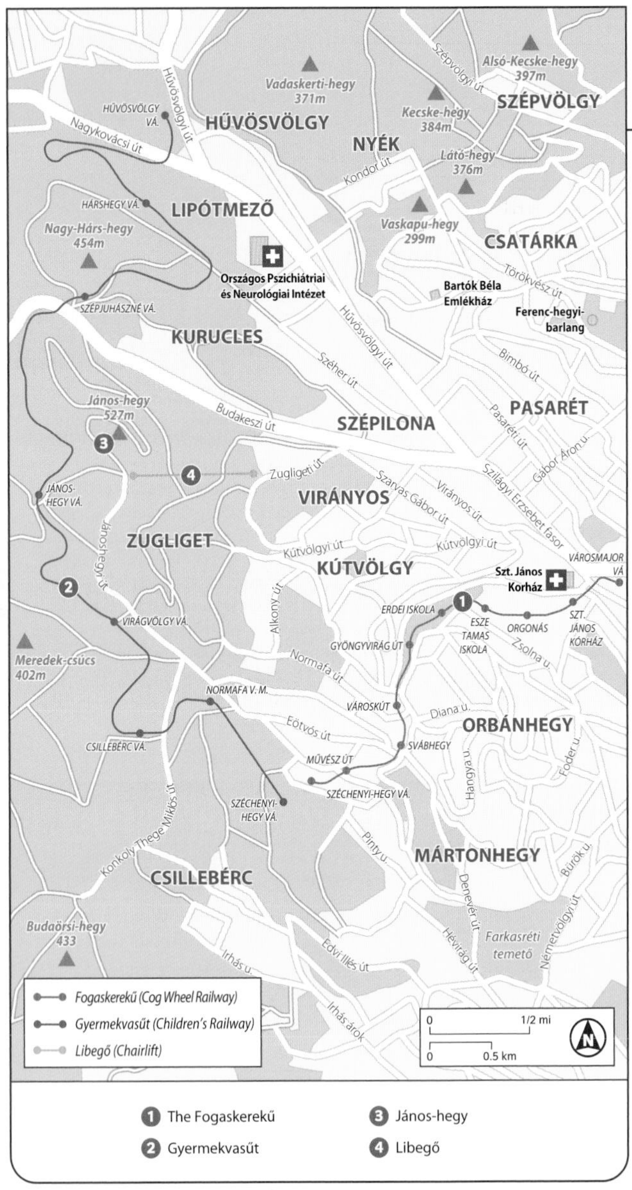

1. The Fogaskerekű
2. Gyermekvasút
3. János-hegy
4. Libegő

Budapest is hardly a small city, with its population of around 2 million. However, I love the fact that you can get out into the fresh air of the hills within minutes. This "best of the hills" route provides a sampler but I encourage you to jump off wherever the mood takes you. START: **Tram 56 to Városmajor to connect with the Cog Wheel Railway to start your ascent.**

1 kids **Ride the Fogaskerekű (Cog Wheel Railway).** The route to the Buda Hills is gradual but the feeling of being dragged up at an angle as the city starts to give way to more and more green certainly sets the tone. Take the cog to Széchenyi-hegy where you can connect with the Children's Railway (below) by walking along Golfpálya utca. *13 min. The Cog Wheel Railway now runs under the no. 60 according to the Budapest Public Transport Company. Daily 5am–11:10pm. Tram: 59/61 to Városmajor.*

2 ★★★ kids **Gyermekvasút (Children's Railway).** There's nothing like running a railway for instilling discipline, and that was the philosophy behind the founding of this narrow gauge railway, once run by "pioneers," a kind of Communist youth initiative. Today children still run the show although, like in the past, I'm relieved to know that adults actually drive the trains and do the signaling. However, I do find it reassuring how seriously these youngsters take their jobs. It's a great way of traversing the Buda Hills and I recommend you just jump off wherever takes your fancy; otherwise continue to János hegy. Be warned, don't mess with these children, they're stricter than adults—who knows what they'll do if you don't buy a ticket! A steam engine runs at weekends (p 39, 3). *17 min to János hegy. Széchenyi hegy. www.gyermekvasut.hu/english/. Tues–Sun 9am–7pm summer; Tues–Sun 9am–5pm winter. Adults 500 Ft one way; children 300 Ft one way, free children 5 and under. Tram: 59/61 to Városmajor, then take Cog Wheel 1 to Szechenyi-hegy.*

Ride the Cog Wheel Railway.

3 ★★ kids **János-hegy (János Hill).** Budapest's highest point is topped off by the **Erszebet Kilátó** (lookout) tower. It's the work of that man Schulek again, he of Fisherman's Bastion (p 62, 5) fame and renovator of St. Matthias (p 61, 3), and you'll certainly see his signatory dreaminess here. *30 min.*

4 ★★ **Libegő (Chairlift).** Hang on and be whisked down 262m (860 ft) from János hegy through the forest by this clunky but cool chairlift. Although it's not specifically a ski lift, locals will take their skis up to the top on it when there's snow. Alternatively, you can also ascend this way to reach János-hegy from the terminus at Zugligeti út 97. *15 min. ☎ 1/391-0352. Mon–Fri 9am–5:30pm, Sat–Sun 9am–6pm. Adults 750 Ft one way; children 350 Ft one way. Bus: 155 to Zugligeti út.*

Margitsziget (Margaret Island)

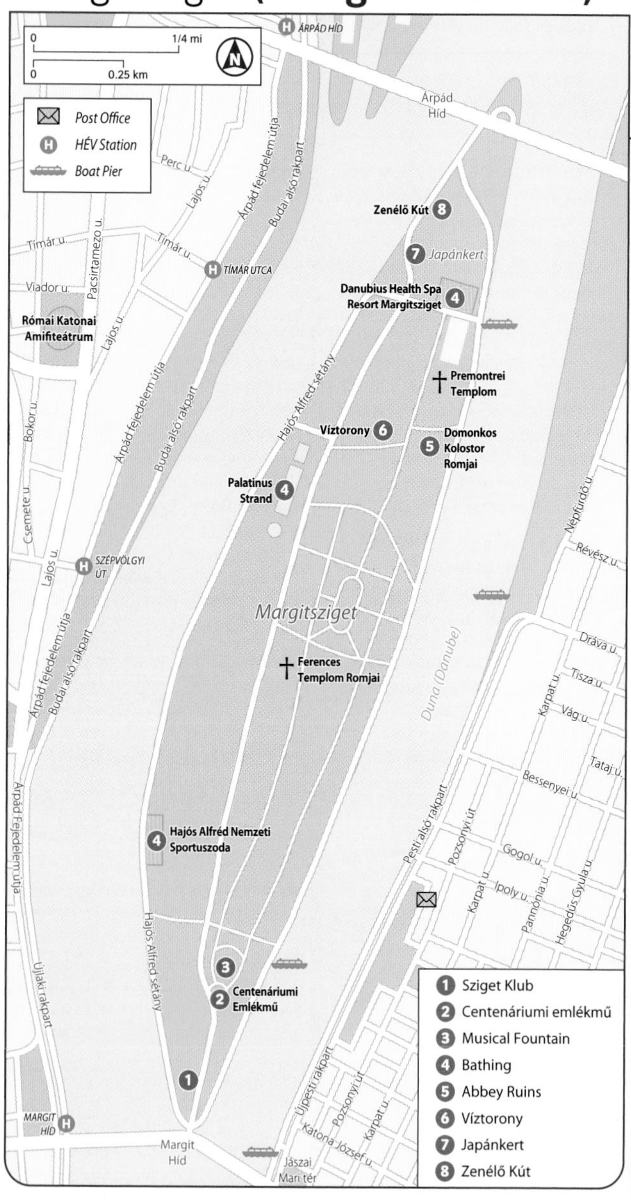

Leafy Margaret Island (Margitsziget) is a haven for morning runners and midnight lovers. Located minutes from the downtown in the middle of the mighty Danube between Buda and Pest, locals come to escape the bustle of the city, as well as to party al fresco in summer (see Nightlife p 109). START: **Tram 4/6 to Margit Sziget or take bus 26, which stops at several points on the island.**

1 ★★ **Sziget Klub.** Entering from the central Margit híd, after about 100m (320 ft) on the left you come to my favorite tennis club. It may say "Only for Members," but if they have a court free you'll get a game; sadly it's the only remaining tennis club on the island. The riverside setting is a lovely place to play tennis and the club also has a summer terrace bar. ☎ *20/203-7488 (English-speaking). www.szigetklub.hu. 4 Courts in summer; 2 in winter. Bring your own rackets.3,800 Ft court hire for 1hr (non-members).*

2 **Centenáriumi emlékmű (Centenary Monument).** Carry on straight and you'll be greeted by the twisty Centenary Monument whose intertwining symbolism represents the fusion of Buda and Pest. It has stood on this spot since 1972 when it marked 100 years since Budapest became one entity. 🕘 *5 min.*

3 kids **Musical Fountain.** A bit further on you'll come to the curious spectacle of the musical fountain, which really requires no explanation other than it spurts out classical music intermittently. The spray carried by the breeze on to your boiling frame is a godsend for cooling off in the heat of summer. 🕘 *5 min.*

Locals lazing around the Musical Fountain.

4 ★★★ kids **Bathing.** Walk to the Buda side from the fountain and you'll find the **Hajós Alfréd Nemzeti Sportuszoda** swimming complex (p 29, 7), which hosts major swimming competitions. Further upstream, also facing the Buda side, is the altogether more relaxed holiday camp-like **Palatinus Strand** (p 29, 6). For

Boatyard Island (Hajógyári sziget)

"Boatyard Island" is the next island upriver from Margaret Island and has big green open spaces that are given over to the **Sziget Festival** for one week each year (p 165). It's also home to some of the capital's glitziest nightclubs (Nightlife, p 109). For golf enthusiasts, there's also a driving range.

A River Runs Through It—the River Danube

The banks of the mighty but murky Danube tend to be dominated by roads, but the stretch on the Pest side just north of the Chain Bridge to Margaret Bridge makes for a pleasant stroll, as does the whole of Margaret Island. Boat trips are a good way of viewing the city from another perspective, and there are a number of boat operators offering tours from Vigadó tér on the Pest bank.

After a conventional ride around the city's key sights, the **River Ride** bus then plunges into the Danube itself to make this a sightseeing tour with a difference. The 2-hour tours depart from Roosevelt tér 7–8 several times daily (www.riverride.com).

more pampered but indoor thermal bathing, head to the Danubius Health Spa Resort Margitsziget close to Árpád híd (www.danubius hotels.com/en). *2–3 hr.*

5 ★ kids **Abbey Ruins.** The foundations of the 13th-century St. Margaret's Abbey are located roughly on the middle of the island, Pest side. Although there's been some obvious mortaring going on and some modern additions, it's still a pleasant place to contemplate the past. About another 100m (320 ft) further on, in an upstream direction, there's a replica functioning church. What would saintly Princess Margit (Margaret)—given to God by her father, Béla IV, for sparing his country from the Mongols—make of all the hedonism on her hallowed island? *15 min.*

The watertower dating back to 1911.

6 ★★ **Víztorony (Watertower).** The watertower stood as a beacon of Hungary's industrial prowess at its time of construction in 1911. Designer and Budapest Engineering University Professor Szilárd Zielinski managed to add a few Art Nouveau touches to the striking 57m high (187-ft.) structure. The watertower is not currently open but a drink at the theater bar directly underneath is a good way to appreciate it. The bar is the most laidback theater bar I know and one for which flip flops are highly appropriate. *10 min.*

7 kids **Japánkert (Japanese Garden).** This delightful spot provides a diversion for children who can seek out varied species of fish, turtles, and frogs to the trickling sound of the waterfall. *15–30 min.*

8 kids **Zenélő Kút (Musical Well).** The last time I visited this well, it was actually talking about the Island's history, but hang around until music starts pumping out. *15 min.* ●

6 The Best Dining

Dining Best Bets

Best **Asian**
★★★ Nobu, *Kempinski Hotel Corvinus, Erzsébet tér 7–8 (p 106)*

Best **Balkan**
★ Montenengrin Gurman, *Rákóczi út 54 (p 106)*

Best **Bargain Gourmet**
★★★ Csalagány 26, *Csalagány utca 26 (p 99)*

Best **Bistro**
★★ Café Kör, *Sas utca 17 (p 99)*

Best **Burger**
★★★ Gresham Kávéház, *Four Seasons Gresham Palace Hotel, Széchenyi tér 5–6 (p 104)*

Best **Burrito**
★ Arriba Taqueria, *Teréz körút 25 (p 103)*

Best **Bargain Gourmet**
★★★ Csalagány 26, *Csalagány utca 26 (p 99)*

Best **Celebrity (Chinese) Chef Meal**
★★★ Wangmester, *Gizella út 46A (p 108)*

Mexican fare at Arriba Taqueria. Previous page: Arcade Bistro.

Best **Cheap 'n' Cheerful Goulash**
★ Pozsonyi kisvendéglő, *Radnóti Miklós utca 38 (p 102)*

Best **Courtyard Dining**
★ Fészek, *Kertész utca 36 (p 99)*

Best **Curry**
★ Taj Mahal, *Szondi utca 40 (p 108)*

Best **Danube Dining**
★★ Spoon, *Moored opposite Hotel Intercontinental (p 108)*

Best **Fin de Siècle Hungarian Gourmet**
★★ Múzeum, *Múzeum Körút 12 (p 101)*

Best **Fusion**
★★ Baraka, *Andrássy Hotel MaMaison, Andrássy út 111 (p 103)*

Best **Italian**
★★★ Fausto's Étterem, *Székely Mihály utca 2 (p 104)*

Best **Nouveau Hungarian**
★★★ Onyx, *Vörösmarty tér 7–8 (p 102)*

Best **Pizza**
★ New York Pizza, *Szondi utca 37 (p 106)*

Best **Retro**
★★★ Kádár Étkezde, *Klauzál tér 10 (p 100)*

Best **Solet (Jewish Bean Stew)**
★★ Fülemüle, *Kőfaragó utca 5 (p 100)*

Best **Sushi**
★★ Okuyama no Sushi, *Kolosy tér 5–6 (p 107)*

Best **Wine Restaurant**
★★★ Klassz, *Andrássy út 41 (p 101)*

Outer Pest Dining

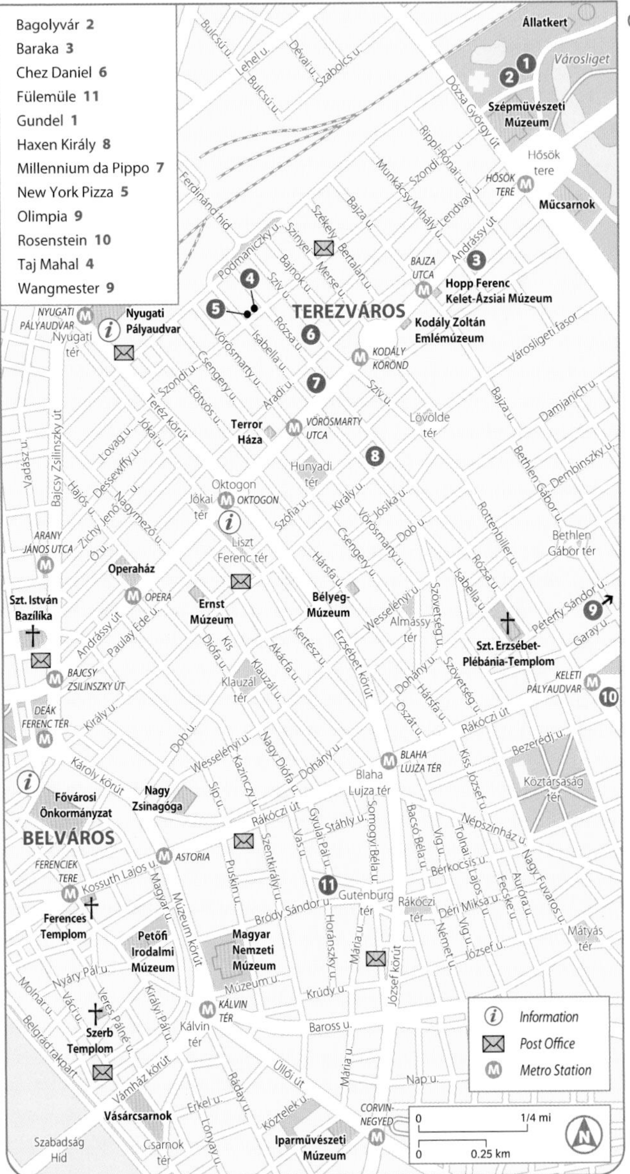

Central Pest Dining

Arriba Taqueria 17
Balletcipő 22
Biarritz 5
Bock Bistro 24
Borkonyha 30
Café Bouchon 18
Café Kör 10
Costes 42
Cyrano 14
Fausto's Étterem 29
Fausto's Osteria 36
Fészek 26
Firkász 3
Govinda Vegetáriánus Étterem 8
Gresham Kávéház 11
Hummus Bar 9
Iguana Bar & Grill 6
Il Terzo Cerchio 35
Indigo 16
Kádár Étkezde 28
Károlyi Étterem-Kávéház 38
Két Szerecsen Kávéház 23
Kiskakukk 2
Kispipa 27
Klassz 21
Kőleves 33
Le Bourbon 32
M! 25
Menza 20
Momotaro Ramen 7
Montenengrin Gurman 34
Mosselen 4
Múzeum 37
Nobu 31
Onyx 13
Pampas Argentine Steak House 40
Pata Negra 41
Peppers! Mediterranean Grill 15
Pozsonyi kisvendéglő 1
Rézkakas 39
Ristorante Krizia 19
Spoon 12

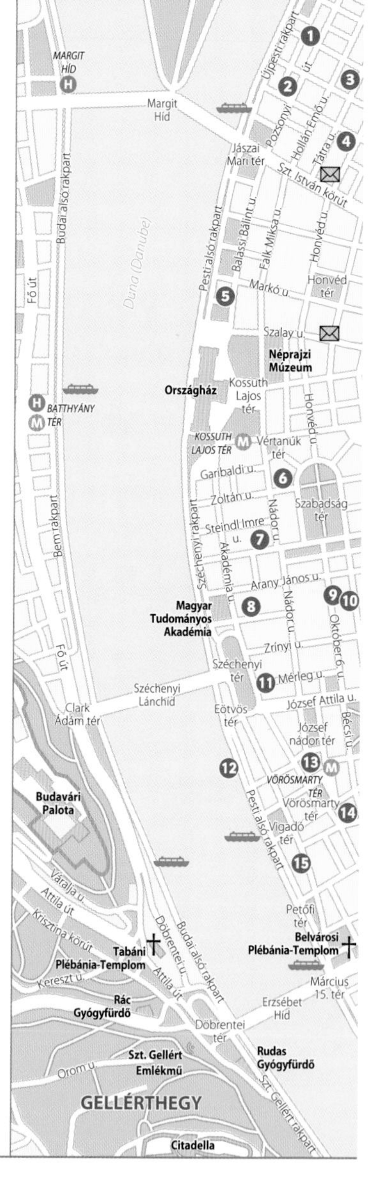

Information
Post Office
Metro Station
HÉV Station
Boat Pier
TEREZVÁROS
BELVÁROS
Westend City Center
Nyugati Pályaudvar
NYUGATI PÁLYAUDVAR
Nyugati tér
LEHEL TÉR
Lehel tér
Hopp Ferenc Kelet-Ázsiai Múzeum
BAJZA UTCA
Kodály körönd
KODÁLY KÖRÖND
Kodály Zoltán Emlémúzeum
VÖRÖSMARTY UTCA
Terror Háza
Liszt Ferenc Emlémúzeum
Lövölde tér
Hunyadi tér
Oktogon
OKTOGON
Jókai tér
Liszt Ferenc tér
Operaház
OPERA
Ernst Múzeum
Bélyeg-Múzeum
Almássy tér
Rózsák tére
ARANY JÁNOS U.
Szt. István Bazílika
BAJCSY ZSILINSZKY ÚT
Erzsébet tér
DEÁK FERENC TÉR
Deák Ferenc tér
Klauzál tér
BLAHA LUJZA TÉR
Blaha Lujza tér
Nagy Zsinagóga
Fővárosi Önkormányzat
ASTORIA
FERENCIEK TERE
Ferences Templom
Petőfi Irodalmi Múzeum
Magyar Nemzeti Múzeum
Gutenburg tér
Rákóczi tér
Józsefvárosi Plébánia-Templom
Horváth Mihály tér
KÁLVIN TÉR
Kálvin tér
Szabó Ervin Könyvtar
Andrássy út
Teréz körút
Erzsébet körút
József körút
Múzeum körút
Károly körút
Vámház körút
Rákóczi út
Üllői út
Váci út
Kossuth Lajos u.
Ferdinánd híd
Bajcsy Zsilinszky út
Városligeti fasor
Baross u.
0 1/4 mi
0 0.25 km
16 17 18 19 20 21 22 23 24 25 26 27 28 29 30 31 32 33 34 35 36 37 38 39 40 41 42

Buda Dining

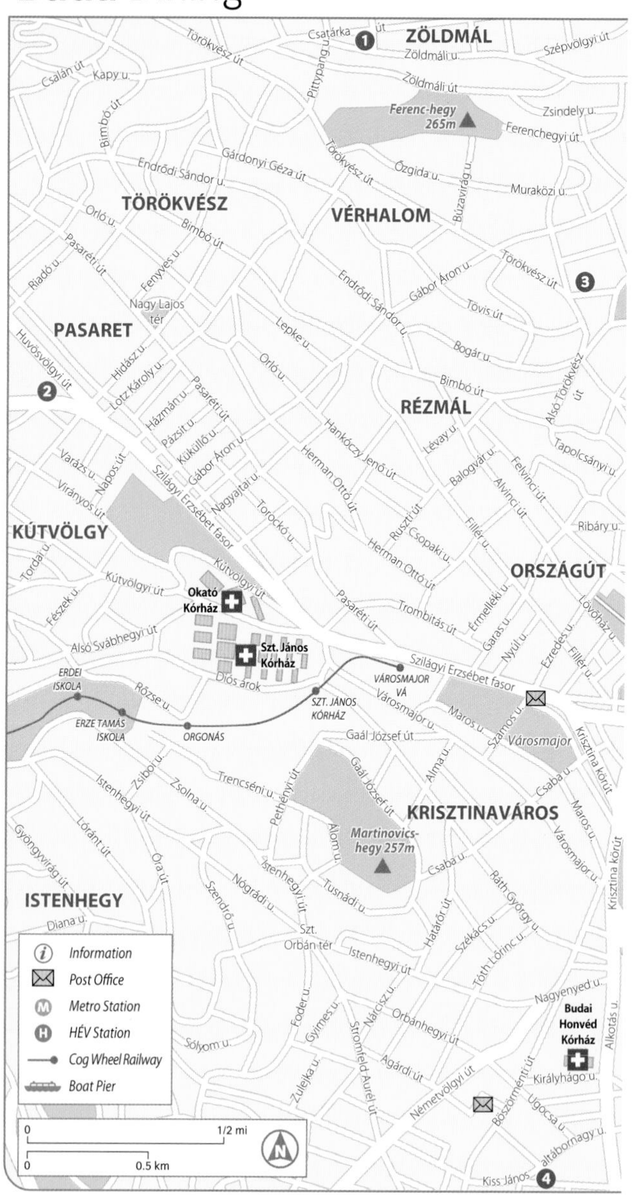
ZÖLDMÁL
TÖRÖKVÉSZ
VÉRHALOM
PASARET
RÉZMÁL
KÚTVÖLGY
ORSZÁGÚT
KRISZTINAVÁROS
ISTENHEGY
Ferenc-hegy 265m
Martinovics-hegy 257m
Okató Kórház
Szt. János Kórház
Budai Honvéd Kórház
Városmajor
VÁROSMAJOR VÁ
SZT. JÁNOS KÓRHÁZ
ERDEI ISKOLA
ERZE TAMÁS ISKOLA
ORGONÁS
Nagy Lajos tér
Szt. Orbán tér
Information
Post Office
Metro Station
HÉV Station
Cog Wheel Railway
Boat Pier
0
1/2 mi
0
0.5 km
N

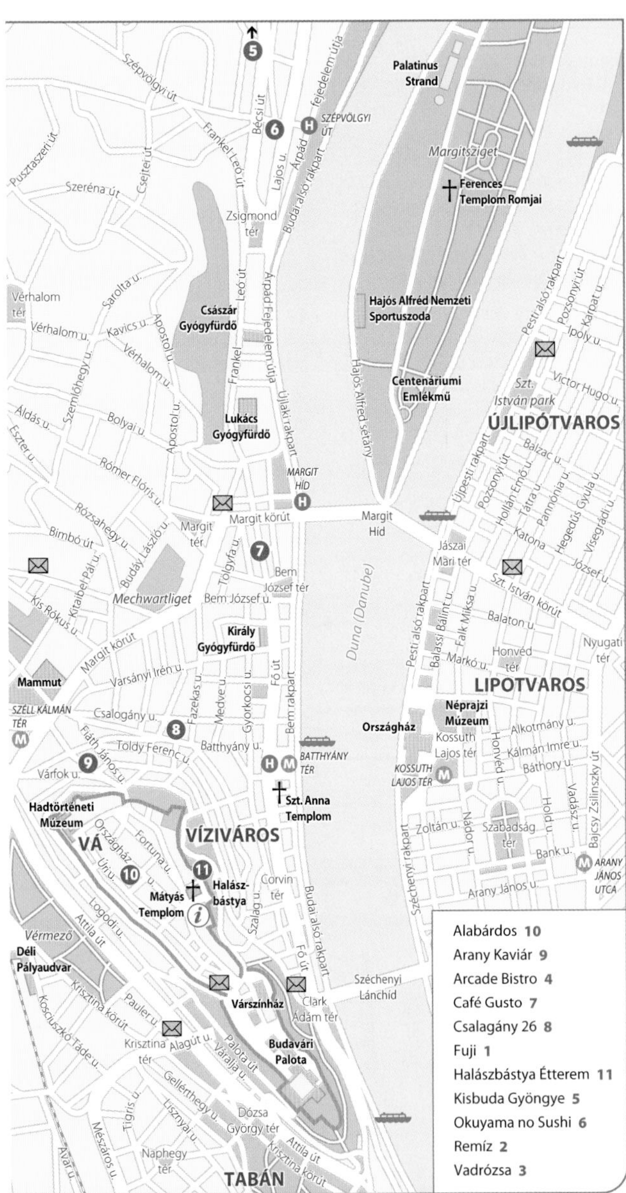
Palatinus Strand
Margitsziget
Ferences Templom Romjai
Hajós Alfréd Nemzeti Sportuszoda
Centenáriumi Emlékmű
Szt. István park
ÚJLIPÓTVAROS
LIPOTVAROS
Császár Gyógyfürdő
Lukács Gyógyfürdő
Király Gyógyfürdő
Mammut
SZÉLL KÁLMÁN TÉR
Mechwartliget
Margit tér
Margit híd
MARGIT HÍD
Duna (Danube)
Országház
Néprajzi Múzeum
Kossuth Lajos tér
KOSSUTH LAJOS TÉR
Szabadság tér
ARANY JÁNOS UTCA
BATTHYÁNY TÉR
Szt. Anna Templom
VÍZIVÁROS
Hadtörténeti Múzeum
Mátyás Templom
Halászbástya
Corvin tér
Vérmező
Déli Pályaudvar
Várszínház
Clark Ádám tér
Széchenyi Lánchíd
Budavári Palota
Krisztina tér
Dózsa György tér
Naphegy tér
TABÁN
SZÉPVÖLGYI ÚT
Zsigmond tér
Vérhalom tér
Jászai Mari tér
Bem József tér
Honvéd tér
Nyugati tér
Szépvölgyi út
Frankel Leó út
Bécsi út
Árpád fejedelem útja
Budai alsó rakpart
Pusztaszeri út
Szeréna út
Sarolta u.
Kavics u.
Vérhalom u.
Apostol u.
Szemlőhegy u.
Áldás u.
Bolyai u.
Eszter u.
Rómer Flóris u.
Rózsahegy u.
Bimbó út
Kitaibel Pál u.
Kis Rókus u.
Margit körút
Varsányi Irén u.
Csalogány u.
Fiáth János u.
Toldy Ferenc u.
Várfok u.
Batthyány u.
Fő út
Bem rakpart
Újlaki rakpart
Hajós Alfréd sétány
Pesti alsó rakpart
Pozsonyi út
Katona
Szt. István körút
Balaton u.
Markó u.
Alkotmány u.
Kálmán Imre u.
Báthory u.
Zoltán u.
Nádor u.
Bank u.
Arany János u.
Széchenyi rakpart
Bajcsy Zsilinszky út
Országház u.
Fortuna u.
Úri u.
Logodi u.
Attila út
Krisztina körút
Pauler u.
Alagút u.
Palota út
Váralja u.
Gellérthegy u.
Lisznyai u.
Mészáros u.
Avar u.
Kosciuszkó Tádé u.
Tigris u.
Szalag u.
Alabárdos 10
Arany Kaviár 9
Arcade Bistro 4
Café Gusto 7
Csalagány 26 8
Fuji 1
Halászbástya Étterem 11
Kisbuda Gyöngye 5
Okuyama no Sushi 6
Remíz 2
Vadrózsa 3

Budapest **Dining A to Z**

Hungarian

★★ **Alabárdos** BUDA *HUNGARIAN* Gourmet heaven in a Gothic setting with unique takes on Hungarian cuisine from only the best in local fresh ingredients. ***Országház utca 2. ☎ 1/356-0851. Main course 3,400 Ft–5,700 Ft. AE, MC, V. Lunch only Sat, dinner daily. Bus: 16/16A/116 to Szentháromság tér. Map p 96.***

★★ **Arcade Bistro** BUDA *HUNGARIAN/CONTINENTAL* This stylishly modern sister of Pest's Café Kör (p 99) ups the gourmet stakes with delicacies such as Guinea hen with green asparagus and goose liver. ***Kiss János Altábornagy utca 38. ☎ 1/225-1696. Main course 3,580 Ft–5,250 Ft. MC, V. Lunch & dinner Mon–Sat. Lunch only Sun. Tram: 59/59A to János Altábornagy utca or 61 to Csörsz utca. Map p 96.***

★ **Babel** CENTRAL PEST *HUNGARIAN/INTERNATIONAL* Dine beside an open kitchen that crafts its own inspired and imaginative versions of Hungarian and international dishes. ***Szarku utca 1. ☎ 1/338-2143. Main course 3,500 Ft–6,500 Ft. AE, DC, MC, V. Dinner Tues–Sat. Metro: M2 to Ferenciek tere/M3 to Kálvin tér. Map p 94.***

Classic Hungarian served up at Biarritz.

Bagolyvár OUTER PEST *HUNGARIAN* This women-run restaurant (the "Owl's Castle") does Magyar cuisine, in an early 20th-century setting, as a Hungarian mother makes it. This sister of gourmet Gundel (p 100) is housed in a mock Transylvanian castle. ***Állatkerti út 2. ☎ 1/468-3110. 1,750 Ft–4,490 Ft. AE, DC, MC, V. Lunch & dinner daily. Metro: M1 to Hősök tere. Map p 93.***

Biarritz CENTRAL PEST *HUNGARIAN/INTERNATIONAL* A few steps away from Parliament, this stylish eatery does classic Hungarian and continental dishes well, but excels in merging the two. Take advantage of the terrace on warm days. ***Kossuth tér 18. ☎ 1/311-4413. Main course 2,650 Ft–4,950 Ft. AE, MC, V. Lunch & dinner daily. Tram: 2 to Szalay utca. Map p 94.***

★ **Bock Bistro** CENTRAL PEST *HUNGARIAN/MEDITERRANEAN* Luxury Latin look with tasty tapas and succulent meat dishes, with a comprehensive wine list led by Villány heavyweight József Bock. Chef Lajos Bíró brilliantly lifts heavy Hungarian with southern subtlety. ***Corinthia Grand Hotel Royal, Erzsébet körút 43–49. ☎ 1/321-0340. Main course 3,400 Ft–6,700 Ft. MC, V. Lunch & dinner Mon–Sat. Metro: M1 to Oktogon. Tram: 4/6 to Oktogon. Map p 94.***

★★ **Borkonyha** CENTRAL PEST *HUNGARIAN/CONTINENTAL* This vinous bistro uses modern kitchen technology to whip up divine nouveau Magyar, but also Transylvanian and various European dishes, from classic fresh ingredients. Top drawer wines are served by über-knowledgeable staff. *Sas utca 3. ☎ 1/266-0835. Main course 2,400 Ft–5,700 Ft. MC, V. Lunch & dinner Mon–Sat. Metro: M1 to Bajcsy-Zsilinsky út. Map p 94.*

★ **Café Bouchon** CENTRAL PEST *HUNGARIAN/FRENCH* Welcoming bistro with Art Nouveau influences in the decor and new takes on Hungarian cuisine and continental favorites. *Zichy Jenő utca 33. ☎ 1/353-4094. Main course 2,390 Ft–2,980 Ft. No credit cards. Lunch & dinner Mon–Sat. Metro: M1 to Oktogon, M3 to Nyugati pályaudvar. Map p 94.*

★★ **Café Kör** CENTRAL PEST *HUNGARIAN/CONTINENTAL* A buzzing bistro and although it's a bit cramped, plenty of customers ensure ever-consistent Hungarian and continental fare. *Sas utca 17. ☎ 1/311-0053. Main course 1,900 Ft–4,200 Ft. No credit cards. Lunch & dinner Mon–Sat. Metro: M3 to Arany János utca. Map p 94.*

★★★ **Csalagány 26** BUDA *HUNGARIAN/CONTINENTAL* A remarkable value lunch menu makes this plain-looking bistro a good bet, although it's more expensive in the evening. Dishes are prepared using only fresh seasonal ingredients. *Csalagány utca 26. ☎ 1/201-7892.*

Try Villány producer József Bock's wine at the Bock Bistro.

Main course 1,400 Ft–4,000 Ft. MC, V. Lunch & dinner Tues–Fri, dinner only Sat; closed Jul 20–Aug 5. Metro: M2 to Batthyány tér. Map p 96.

★ kids **Fészek** CENTRAL PEST *HUNGARIAN* This artists' club, with its cloistered courtyard, is steeped in atmosphere: Excellent *sztrapacska*—flour and potato dumplings with bacon and ewe cheese. *Kertész utca 36. ☎ 1/322-6043. Main course 1,600 Ft–2,500 Ft. No credit cards. Lunch & dinner daily. Tram: 4/6 to Király utca. Map p 94.*

★ **Firkász** CENTRAL PEST *HUNGARIAN* Fine cuts are prepared from

Old world charm at Firkász.

Seasonal Hungarian dishes at Gundel.

refined recipes at Firkász. Old newspaper articles cover the walls and a piano player enhances the old-world atmosphere in the evening. *Tátra utca 18. ☎ 1/450-1119. Main course 1,490 Ft–4,900 Ft. MC, V. Lunch & dinner daily. Tram: 2/4/6 to Jászai Mari tér. Map p 94.*

★★ **Fülemüle** OUTER PEST *HUNGARIAN/JEWISH* "The Nightingale" serves a non-kosher blend of Hungarian and Jewish cuisine, which predates modern fusion trends, in a warm family setting. *Kőfaragó utca 5. ☎ 1/266-7947. Main course 2,300 Ft–4,900 Ft. MC, V. Lunch & dinner daily. Metro: M2 to Blaha Lujza tér. Tram: 4/6 to Blaha Lujza tér. Map p 93.*

★★ **Gundel** OUTER PEST *HUNGARIAN* A feast of the finest china, tablecloths, artworks, and splendor entices you before you even get to sample the seasonally inspired food. Although they will give you a jacket to put on to smarten you up, Gundel's 1894 Wine Cellar downstairs offers a less formal but still memorable experience. *Állatkerti út 2. ☎ 1/468-4040. Main course 3,900 Ft–10,620 Ft. AE, DC, MC, V. Lunch & dinner daily. Metro: M1 to Hősök tere. Map p 93.*

★ **Halászbástya Étterem** BUDA *HUNGARIAN* A remarkable setting in the belly of the fairytale Fisherman's Bastion (see p 62) with quality gourmet Magyar and the service to back up the view and luxury. A Gypsy band plays every afternoon. *Halászbástya – Északi Híradástorony (Fisherman's Bastion – northern tower). ☎ 1/201-6935. Main course 4,400 Ft–8,700 Ft. AE, MC, V. Lunch & dinner daily. Bus: 16/16A/116 to Szentháromság tér. Map p 96.*

★★ **Haxen Király** OUTER PEST *HUNGARIAN/BAVARIAN* Pine-paneling and wooden furnishings galore welcome carnivores with generous portions of quality goose liver, goose leg, wild boar, and pork knuckle. *Király utca 100 (corner of Rózsa utca). ☎ 1/351-6793. Main course 2,860 Ft–4,860 Ft. AE, MC, V. Lunch & dinner daily. Metro: M1/M2/M3 to Deák tér. Map p 93.*

★★★ **Kádár Étkezde** CENTRAL PEST *HUNGARIAN/JEWISH* Non-kosher, Jewish-like crispy goose leg with red cabbage served in a real retro setting where guests often share tables. The *solet* bean stew and *matzo* ball soup are on the Saturday menu. *Klauzál tér 10. ☎ 1/321-3622. Main course 800 Ft–1,900 Ft. No credit cards. Lunch Tues–Sat. Tram: 4/6 to Király utca. Map p 94.*

★ **Károlyi Étterem-Káveház** CENTRAL PEST *HUNGARIAN/MEDITERRANEAN* A restaurant-cum-coffeehouse in the grand Károlyi Palace featuring a restored Biedermeier interior and a sublime courtyard. *Károlyi Mihály utca 16. ☎ 1/328-0240. Main course 2,800 Ft–4,700 Ft. AE, MC, V. Lunch & dinner daily. Metro: M3 to Ferenciektere or Kálvin tér. Map p 94.*

★★★ **Kisbuda Gyöngye** BUDA *HUNGARIAN* The high-end menu features continental and Mediterranean twists such as goose liver

Vegetarian options available at the hip Köleves.

risotto, served in a charming early 20th-century setting that's well worth the trek out to Óbuda. ***Kenyeres utca. 34.*** ☎ ***1/368-9227. Main course 1,900 Ft–4,200 Ft. AE, MC, V. Lunch & dinner Mon–Sat. Tram: 17 to Nagyszombat utca. Map p 96.***

★★ **Kiskakukk** CENTRAL PEST *HUNGARIAN/CONTINENTAL* Arches and heavy wood depict the original "Little Cuckoo" restaurant, which dates back to 1913. Delicacies include goose liver cream soup. ***Pozsonyi út 12.*** ☎ ***1/450-0829. Main course 2,000 Ft–3,000 Ft. AE, MC, V. Lunch & dinner daily. Tram: 2/4/6 to Jászai Mari tér. Map p 94.***

★ **Kispipa** CENTRAL PEST *HUNGARIAN* Indulge in traditional gastronomy with a refined pre-war vibe and old-world continental dishes with plenty of game on the menu. ***Akácfa utca 38.*** ☎ ***1/342-2587 or 1/342-3969. Main course 1,000 Ft–5,560 Ft. AE, DC, MC, V. Lunch & dinner daily. Metro: M1 to Oktogon. Tram: 4/6 to Wesselényi utca. Map p 94.***

★★★ **Klassz** CENTRAL PEST *HUNGARIAN/CONTINENTAL* Foie gras risottos, lamb knuckle, and Mangalica pig steak feature at this creative and hip minimalist-designed wine restaurant. No bookings so turn up early. ***Andrássy út 41. No phone. Main course 1,500 Ft–2,890 Ft. AE, MC, V. Lunch & dinner Mon–Sat; lunch only Sun. Metro: M1 to Opera. Map p 94.***

★★ **Kőleves** CENTRAL PEST *HUNGARIAN* Expect hearty meaty fare alongside Jewish, international, and veggie options at the cool and slightly alternative "Stone soup." ***Kazinczy utca 35/Dob utca 26 corner.*** ☎ ***1/322-1011. Main course 1,280 Ft–3,680 Ft. AE, MC, V. Lunch & dinner daily. Metro: M1/M2/M3 to Deák tér. Map p 94.***

★ **Menza** CENTRAL PEST *HUNGARIAN* A popular spot for unpretentious fare on fashionable Liszt Ferenc tér. The fun retro kitsch decor is based on the ubiquitous Socialist-era canteen. ***Liszt Ferenc tér 2.*** ☎ ***1/413-1482. Main course 1,490 Ft–3,490 Ft. AE, MC, V. Lunch & dinner daily. Metro: M1 to Oktogon. Tram: 4/6 to Oktogon. Map p 94.***

★★ **Múzeum** CENTRAL PEST *HUNGARIAN* Bastion of old Budapest and gourmet Magyar charm, plus good sea fish, under a striking Zsolnay tiled roof. A very pleasant trip back in time. ***Múzeum Körút 12.*** ☎ ***1/267-0375. Main course 2,800 Ft–5,900 Ft. AE, MC, V. Dinner***

Retro styling at Menza.

Mon–Sat. Metro: M3 to Kálvin tér. Map p 94.

★★ **Olimpia** OUTER PEST *HUNGARIAN/CONTINENTAL* Look forward to deep flavors, and contemporary creativity at very reasonable prices, at this buzzing Pest bistro. Go for all three courses of the lunch menu for 2,050 Ft to avoid leaving hungry because portions can be small. ***Alpár utca 5.*** ☎ ***1/321-2805. Main course 1,500 Ft. Lunch & dinner Mon–Fri, dinner only Sat. No credit cards. Metro: M2 to Keleti pályaudvar. Map p 93.***

★★★ **Onyx** CENTRAL PEST *HUNGARIAN* This classy modern eatery with a Michelin star brings great local cuisine into the modern culinary age. Try the "Hungarian Evolution" tasting menu for 19,900 Ft. ***Vörösmarty tér 7–8.*** ☎ ***06/30-508-0622. Main course 6,500 Ft–19,500 Ft. AE, V, MC. Lunch & dinner Tues–Sat. Metro: M1 to Vörösmarty tér. Map p 94.***

★ **Pozsonyi kisvendéglő** CENTRAL PEST *HUNGARIAN* People line up patiently for reassuringly old-fashioned, cheap and cheerful classics. You can even grab a beer as you wait. ***Radnóti Miklós utca 38 (corner of Pozsonyi út).*** ☎ ***1/329-2911. Main course 800 Ft–1,900 Ft. No credit cards. Breakfast, lunch & dinner daily. Tram: 2/4/6 to Jászai Mari tér. Map p 94.***

★★ **Remíz** BUDA *HUNGARIAN/CONTINENTAL* Remíz has a classy casual atmosphere. The front room features a raised alcove that resembles the front of a tram. In summer, tasty spare ribs are grilled up in the garden. ***Budakeszi út 5.*** ☎ ***1/275-1396. Main course 1,500 Ft–3,000 Ft. AE, MC, V. Lunch & dinner daily. Tram: 17. Bus: 22 to Szépilona. Map p 96.***

★ **Rézkakas** CENTRAL PEST HUNGARIAN A top-notch Gypsy ensemble accompanies high-end classic Magyar dishes in a classy, traditional setting. The "Copper Cockerel" specializes in smoked versions of the finest delicacies, such as goose liver. ***V. Kerület, Veres Pálné.*** ☎ ***1/318-0038. Main course 3900 Ft–5900 Ft. AE, V, MC. Lunch & dinner daily. Metro: M2 to Ferenciek tere/M3 to Kálvin tér. Map p 94.***

★★ **Rosenstein** OUTER PEST *JEWISH/HUNGARIAN/INTERNATIONAL* "Everything is kosher, that tastes good" says owner/chef Tibor Rosenstein on his kitchen philosophy. Tibor's son Robi helps bring dad's traditional fusion fare into the present and the results are stunning.

Classy Hungarian fare Onyx.

The decor also bridges past and present nicely. *Mosonyi utca 3.* ☎ *1/333-3492. Main course 1,800 Ft–6,200 Ft. MC, V. Lunch & dinner Mon–Sat. Metro: M2 to Keleti pályaudvar. Map p 93.*

★★★ **Vadrózsa** BUDA *HUNGARIAN* Fine dining turn-of-the-century style, in a baroque villa circled by a plush garden. Gorgeous-looking cuts of meat, game, and fish will be paraded enticingly before you. *Pentelei Molnár utca 15.* ☎ *1/326-5817. Main course 5,240 Ft–7,880 Ft. AE, DC, MC, V. Lunch & dinner daily. Bus: 11/91 to Vend utca. Map p 96.*

International Cuisines

★ **Arany Kaviár** BUDA *RUSSIAN* The best in Beluga, Sevruga, and Iranian caviar, blinis and pickled fish, plus posh stroganoff in a retro Romanov setting. *Ostrom utca 19.* ☎ *1/201-6737 or 1/225-7370. Main course 3,500 Ft–7,900 Ft. AE, DC, MC, V. Lunch & dinner daily. Metro: M2 to Széll Kálmán tér. Tram: 4/6 to Széll Kálmán tér. Map p 96.*

★ **Arriba Taqueria** CENTRAL PEST *MEXICAN* Head to this colorful Mexican for freshly steamed tacos, quesadillas, and burritos with juicy steak, chorizo, and fresh condiments galore. Wash it all down with a *Tecate* beer. *Teréz körút 25.* ☎ *1/374-0057. Main course 1,200 Ft–1,600 Ft. AE, DC, MC, V. Lunch & dinner Mon–Sat. Metro: M1 to Oktogon. Tram: 4/6 to Oktogon. Map p 94.*

★ **Balletcipő** CENTRAL PEST *INTERNATIONAL* This gastro pub's eclectic menu somehow works, especially the Philly Cheese Steak sandwich. The tables spill out onto a shabby chic pedestrian street in the summer. *Hajós utca 14 (corner of Ó utca).* ☎ *1/269-3114. Main course 1,950 Ft–2,990 Ft. No credit cards. Lunch & dinner daily. Metro: M1 to Opera or M3 to Arany János utca. Map p 94.*

★★★ **Baraka** OUTER PEST *FUSION* Dark, sleek, and minimalist, Baraka fits well into the Bauhaus Andrássy Hotel (p 140) and sets the fusion standards with ambitious-sounding but delicious concoctions. *MaMaison Andrássy Hotel. Andrássy út 111.* ☎ *1/483-1355. Main course 3,900 Ft–6,700 Ft. AE, DC, MC, V. Lunch & dinner daily. Metro: M1 to Bajza utca. Map p 93.*

Café Gusto BUDA *ITALIAN* Exquisite Italianate salads and starters, cold pastas, and sumptuous tiramisu served in an intimate, antique-laden, bijou setting. *Frankel Leó utca. 12.* ☎ *1/316-3970. Main course 1,000 Ft–2,000 Ft. Breakfast, lunch & dinner daily. Metro: M2 to Battyhány tér. Tram: 4/6 to Margit híd Budai hídfő. Map p 96.*

★ **Chez Daniel** OUTER PEST *FRENCH* Maverick French chef Daniel Labrosse conjures up nouveau French cuisine par-excellence. There's also a lovely courtyard for dining in the summer. *Szív utca 32.* ☎ *1/302-4039. Main course 2,200 Ft–5,000 Ft. AE, DC, MC, V. Lunch & dinner daily. Metro: M1 to Kodály körönd. Map p 93.*

★★★ **Costes** CENTRAL PEST. *CONTINENTAL* A sleek Michelin star restaurant serving-up creative dishes from prime ingredients. Try the "Corrèze" veal sweetbreads with licorice, and roasted baby carrots with gingerbread. *Raday utca 4* ☎ *1/219-0696. Main course 6,500 Ft–8,500 Ft. Lunch & dinner Wed–Sun. Metro: M3 to Kálvin Tram: 4/6. Map p 94.*

★ **Cyrano** CENTRAL PEST *INTERNATIONAL* Pricey but consistently creative restaurant offering fresh-ingredient fueled takes on

Try Fuji for great sushi lunch boxes.

old favorites. *Kristóf tér 7–8. ☎ 1/226-3096. Main course 3,490 Ft–4,790 Ft. AE, MC, V. Breakfast, lunch & dinner daily. Metro: M1/M2/ M3 to Deák tér. Map p 94.*

★★★ **Fausto's Étterem** CENTRAL PEST *ITALIAN* Dine at this classy, minimalist-decorated restaurant on exquisite, traditional Italian food enhanced by subtle wider-world touches and flawless ingredients. *Székely Mihály utca 2. ☎ 1/877-6210. Main course 3,500 Ft–6,000 Ft. AE, MC, V. Lunch & dinner Mon–Fri; dinner only Sat. Metro: M1 to Opera. Map p 94.*

★★★ **Fausto's Osteria** CENTRAL PEST *ITALIAN* Fausto's take on classic Italian cuisine is informal but gets the ingredients just right. Like its sibling Fausto's Etterem (above), it also received a recommendation from Michelin in 2007. *Dohány utca 5. ☎ 1/269-6806. Main course 2,900 Ft–5,900 Ft. AE, MC, V. Lunch & dinner Mon–Sat. Metro: M2 to Astoria. Map p 94.*

★★ kids **Fuji** BUDA *JAPANESE* Sushi is rolled before watchful customers in a highly authentic setting. Great lunch boxes include sashimi, tempura, and grilled fish. *Csatárka utca 54 (corner of Zöldlomb utca and Zödkert utca). ☎ 1/325-7111. Main course 3,500 Ft–9,800 Ft. AE, DC, MC, V. Lunch & dinner daily. Bus: 29 to Zöldkert út. Map p 96.*

Govinda Vegetáriánus Étterem CENTRAL PEST INDIAN Great value vegetarian Indian food from the Krishnas in this funky cellar. Wash it all down with the spicy homemade soft drinks. *Vigyázó Ferenc utca 4. ☎ 1/269-1625. Main course 1,550 Ft–1,850 Ft (menus). No credit cards. Lunch & dinner Mon–Sat. Metro: M3 to Arany János utca. Map p 94.*

★★★ **Gresham Kávéház** CENTRAL PEST *CONTINENTAL* A suave coffeehouse/bistro inside an Art Nouveau landmark where you can enjoy continental cuisine with sublime international touches—topped off with a view of the Chain Bridge. *Four Seasons Gresham Palace Hotel, Széchenyi tér 5–6. ☎ 1/268-5100. Main course 3,600 Ft–5,800 Ft. AE, DC, MC, V. Lunch & dinner daily. Metro: M1 to Vörösmarty tér. Tram: 2 to Roosevelt tér. Map p 94.*

★ **Hummus Bar** CENTRAL PEST *ISRAELI* Locals flock here for the flavorsome hummus and falafel served with delectable *lafa* and pita bread, alongside authentic Israeli meat dishes like Jerusalem Mix: chicken breast, liver and heart, grilled with onions. *Október 6 utca 19. ☎ 1/354-0108. Main course 990 Ft–1,800 Ft. Lunch & dinner daily. MC, V. Metro: M3 to Arany János utca. Map p 94.*

Iguana Bar & Grill CENTRAL PEST *TEX-MEX* The American expat crowd pile in for Tex-Mex that approaches the quality from back home. Enjoy the potent margaritas and a guaranteed lively Cantina atmosphere. *Zoltán utca 16. ☎ 1/301-0215. Main course 1,790 Ft–3,690 Ft. AE, DC, MC, V. Lunch & dinner daily. Metro: M2 to Kossuth tér. Map p 94.*

★★ Il Terzo Cerchio CENTRAL PEST *ITALIAN* A strong Italian contingent frequents this upmarket trattoria whose house pizza is a tasty assortment of tomato, buffalo mozzarella, and Parma ham. *Dohány utca 40. ☎ 1/354-0788. Main course 1,850 Ft–6,400 Ft. MC, V. Lunch & dinner daily. Metro: M2 to Blaha Lujza tér. Map p 94.*

★ Indigo CENTRAL PEST *INDIAN* A fine Indian all-rounder with an impressive variety of classic Indian dishes, but particularly excelling in lamb curries. The comfy chic decor makes this a place to linger as well. *Jókai utca 13. ☎ 1/428-2187. Main course 1,900 Ft–3,000 Ft. Lunch & dinner daily. Metro: M1 to Oktogon. Tram: 4/6. Map p 94.*

★★ Két Szerecsen Kávéház CENTRAL PEST *MEDITERRANEAN* Med-influenced cuisine and decor, with subtle Magyar and international touches. The "Two Saracens" is also good for tapas or just a drink on the terrace. *Nagymező utca 14. ☎ 1/343-1984. Main course 2,390 Ft–3,990 Ft. DC, MC, V. Lunch & dinner daily. Metro: M1 to Opera. Map p 94.*

★★ Le Bourbon CENTRAL PEST *FRENCH* Chef Laurent Vandenameele draws on his wide Michelin-starred French restaurant experience, with dishes such as semi-cooked goose foie gras and smoked duck breast. *Le Méridien Budapest, Erzsebet tér 9–10. Main course 4,100 Ft–6,800 Ft. AE, DC, MC, V. Lunch & dinner Mon–Fri, Sun; dinner only Sat. Metro: M1/M2/M3 to Deák tér. Map p 94.*

★ M! CENTRAL PEST *FRENCH/HUNGARIAN* No-nonsense bijou bistro that lets the creative and daily changing menu do the talking. Well worth visiting now that Francophile founder Miklós Sulyok is back. *Kertész utca 48. ☎ 1/342-8991. Main course 1,500 Ft–2,900 Ft. No credit cards. Dinner daily. Metro: M1 to Oktogon. Tram: 4/6 to Király utca. Map p 94.*

Millennium da Pippo OUTER PEST *ITALIAN* Resembling a station of the Millennium Underground

Iguana Bar & Grill.

Okuyama no Sushi.

that zips under the same street, the food is reassuringly rustic and of good quality. ***Andrássy út 76 (corner of Rózsa utca). ☎ 1/374-0880. Main course 2,300 Ft–4,050 Ft. MC, V. Lunch & dinner daily. Metro: M1 to Vörösmárty utca. Map p 93.***

★★ **Momotaro Ramen** CENTRAL PEST *ASIAN* An excellent ramen noodle soup washed down by the free green tea may suffice, but the tasty Szechuan is a delight. ***Széchenyi utca 16. ☎ 1/269-3802. Main course under 800 Ft. No credit cards. Lunch & dinner daily. Metro: M2 to Kossuth tér. Tram: 2 to Kossuth tér. Map p 94.***

★ **Montenengrin Gurman** CENTRAL PEST BALKAN Dine on authentic *Pljeskavica* (similar to a minced veal patty) and *Csevapcsicsi* (grilled sausage), freshly prepared by Serbian and Montenegrin chefs, with red Vranac wine and a funky Balkan soundtrack. ***Rákóczi út 54 ☎ 1/782-0806. Main course 830 Ft–1,740 Ft. No credit cards. Lunch & dinner daily. Metro: M3 to Blaha Lujza tér. Map p 94.***

Mosselen CENTRAL PEST *BELGIAN/CONTINENTAL* Fans of Belgian beer can choose from several varieties on draft while sampling eccentrically named dishes such as "The Favorite of the Leuven Professors" (duck steak). ***Pannónia utca 14 (corner of Katona József utca). ☎ 1/452-0535. Main course 2,390 Ft–4,690 Ft. AE, V, MC. Lunch & dinner daily. Tram: 2/4/6 to Jászai Mari tér. Map p 94.***

★ **New York Pizza** OUTER PEST *AMERICAN* This is the place I head when I need my fix of ultra-thin fold-over New York-style pizza, but it's also a perfect place just to hang out. The burgers, baked *ziti* pasta, and breakfasts are also first class. ***Szondi utca 37. ☎ 1/219-0696. Main course 950 Ft–2,690 Ft. MC, V. Breakfast, lunch & dinner daily. Metro: M3 to Nuygati pályaudvar/M1 to Oktogon. Map p 93.***

★★★ **Nobu** *Nouveau Japanese* CENTRAL PEST *JAPANESE* This internationally acclaimed nouveau gourmet nirvana exquisitely enhances traditional Japanese with subtle South American twists. Classics include Yellowtail Sashimi with Jalapeno and Broiled Black Cod in Miso. *Kempinski Hotel Corvinus.* ***Erzsébet tér 7–8. ☎ 1/429-4242. Main course 4,000 Ft–11,000 Ft. Dinner Mon–Sat. Lunch & dinner Sun. AE, DC, MC, V. M1/M2/M3 to Deák tér. Map p 94.***

★★ Okuyama no Sushi BUDA *JAPANESE* Stellar sushi is rolled from ocean delights by the intricate Japanese hand of Tokyo-trained chef Sachi Okuyama in this no-nonsense cellar joint. Hot options include noodle soups. ***Kolosy tér 5–6. ☎ 1/250-8256. Main course 1,200 Ft–5,000 Ft. No credit cards. Lunch & dinner Tues–Sun. Bus: 6/60/86 to Kolosy tér. Map p 96.***

★ Pampas Argentine Steak House CENTRAL PEST *STEAK* Enjoy stylish blood-red decor and juicy steaks from quality imported Argentine Angus cuts, T-bone from the UK, plus Japanese Kobe steak. ***Vámház körút 6. ☎ 1/411-1750. Main course 2,600 Ft–14,900 Ft. MC, V. Lunch & dinner daily. Metro: M3 to Kálvin tér. Tram: 47/49 to Kálvin tér. Map p 94.***

Pata Negra CENTRAL PEST *SPANISH* Traditional, tasty tapas with many of the ingredients, such as *jamon* (ham) and Manchego sheep's cheese. imported from Spain. Almost authentic tiled interior plus seats outside next to a church. ***Kálvin tér 8. ☎ 1/215-5616. Main course 850 Ft–2,200 Ft. No credit cards. Lunch & dinner daily. Metro: M3 to Kálvin tér. Map p 94.***

★★ kids Peppers! Mediterranean Grill CENTRAL PEST *MEDITERRANEAN* Delicious Mediterranean-style dishes from local ingredients such as *Mangalica* pork and *Racka* lamb, plus imported

The Budapest Bistro

The Budapest dining scene has been transformed by competition and a growth in discerning Hungarian foodies in the last few years. The financial crisis has also led to many of those restaurants that do remain prospering by using the classic bistro formula of putting good value dishes together from seasonal ingredients and getting plenty of people in. Accordingly, Budapest currently abounds with bargain lunch menus starting a bit below 1,000 Ft.

Aside from munching on *kolbász* (sausage) at a butchers (*hús-hentesáru*), an *étkezde* is a basic lunch joint and serves no-nonsense Hungarian classics such as *paprikás csirke* (chicken paprika), *Rántott hús* (deep fried pork in breadcrumb), and *Bableves* (bean soup). In such establishments salads can still be straight from the pickle jar and vegetables even deep fried.

Etterem is the word for restaurant, although many places have dispensed with the word, choosing to go solely by their name. A *Vendéglő* is a more traditional inn.

Although *libamaj* (fois gras) is usually outstanding, with much of it exported to France, Budapest is also a good place for game dishes.

Spoon.

salumi to be enjoyed in a stylish setting. This is a great option for Sunday brunch. ***Budapest Marriott Hotel, Apáczai Csere János utca 4.*** *☎ 1/737-7377. Main course 3,100 Ft–5,600 Ft. AC, DC, MC, V. Breakfast, lunch & dinner daily. Metro: M1 to Vörösmarty tér. Map p 94.*

★★ **Ristorante Krizia** CENTRAL PEST *ITALIAN* A charming and hardly discovered slice of Italy where a savvy touch is applied to traditional Italian cuisine, making poor man's food a rich experience. ***Mozsár utca 12.*** *☎ 1/331-8711. Main course 2,680 Ft–8,800 Ft. AE, MC, V. Lunch & dinner Mon–Sat. Metro: M1 to Oktogon. Tram: 4/6 to Oktogon. Map p 94.*

★★ **Spoon** DANUBE PEST SIDE *INTERNATIONAL* Spoon is the top pick of the boat restaurants, although the classy cuisine itself warrants a visit regardless of the inspiring Buda views and cool decor. Ocean-fresh fish and seafood and quality meat feature strongly. ***Opposite Hotel Intercontinental.*** *☎ 1/411-0933. Main course 2,900 Ft–10,900 Ft. AE, DC, MC, V. Lunch & dinner. Metro: M1 to Vörösmarty tér. Map p 94.*

★ **Taj Mahal** OUTER PEST *INDIAN* Highly consistent, traditional and authentic curry house specializing in Karahi, Balti, Handi, and Tandoori dishes. Cricket games are often screened here too. ***Szondi utca 40.*** *☎ 1/301-0447. Main course 1,210 Ft–3,250 Ft. AE, MC, V. Lunch & dinner Tues–Sun. Metro: M1 to Nyugati pályaudvar. Tram: 4/6 to Nyugati pu. Map p 93.*

★★★ **Wangmester** OUTER PEST *CHINESE* Szechuan is served here, much more flavorsome than you usually find in Budapest, with bargain lunch menus on weekdays for under 1,000 Ft, although you'll feel the difference in quality when ordering a la carte. ***Gizella út 46A.*** *☎ 1/251-2959. Main course 1,500 Ft–2,990 Ft. AE, V, MC. Lunch & dinner. Metro: M2 to Stadionok. Map p 93.*

7 The Best **Nightlife**

Nightlife Best Bets

Best **Al Fresco Bar**
★★★ Holdudvar, *Margaret Island (p 122)*

Best **Boho Bar**
★★ Kiadó Kocsma, *Jókai tér 3 (p 118)*

Best **Cocktail**
★★★ Boutiq'Bar, *Paulay Ede utca 5 (p 116)*

Best **Comic Strip Decor**
★★ Szóda, *Wesselényi utca 18 (p 120)*

Best **Courtyard Bar**
★★★ Kőleves kert, *Kazinczy utca 37 (p 123)*

Best place to **Drink with the Locals**
★ Wichmann, *Kazinczy utca 55 (p 120)*

Szóda.

Best **Garage Bar**
★★ Kuplung, *Király utca 46 (p 118)*

Best **Gay Club**
★★★ CoXx Men's Club, *Dohány utca 38 (p 121)*

Best **Glitzy Dance Club**
★★★ Dokk, *Hajógyárisziget 122 (p 121)*

Best **Intimate Night Club**
★★★ Fészek Club, *Kertész utca 36 (p 121)*

Best **Lesbian Hospitality**
★★ Café Eklektika, *Nagymező utca 30 (p 121)*

Best **Martini**
★★★ Gresham Bar, *Four Seasons Gresham Palace Hotel, Roosevelt tér 5–6 (p 117)*

Best place to **Pose Under the Stars**
★★★ Bed Beach, *Hajógyárisziget (p 121)*

Best **Retro Bar**
★★ Bambi Presszó, *Frankel Leó utca 2–4 (p 116)*

Best **Rooftop Terrace**
★★★ Corvintető, *Corvin Áruház, Blaha Lujza tér 1–2 (p 122)*

Best **30-something Boho Hangout**
★★ Ellátó, *Klauzál tér 2 (p 122)*

Best place to **Watch Live Soccer**
★★ Caledonian Scottish Pub, *Mozsár utca 9 (p 116)*

Best **Wine Bar**
★★★ DiVino, *Szent István tér 3 (p 123)*

Previous page: Alfresco drinking at Holdudvar.

Buda Nightlife

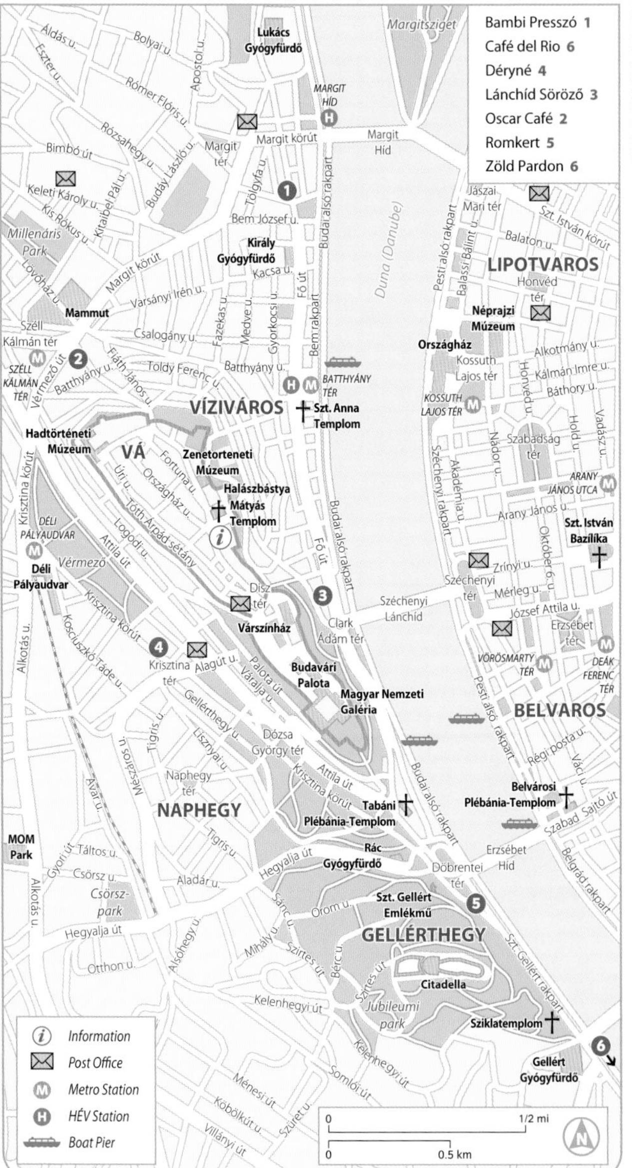

Pest Nightlife

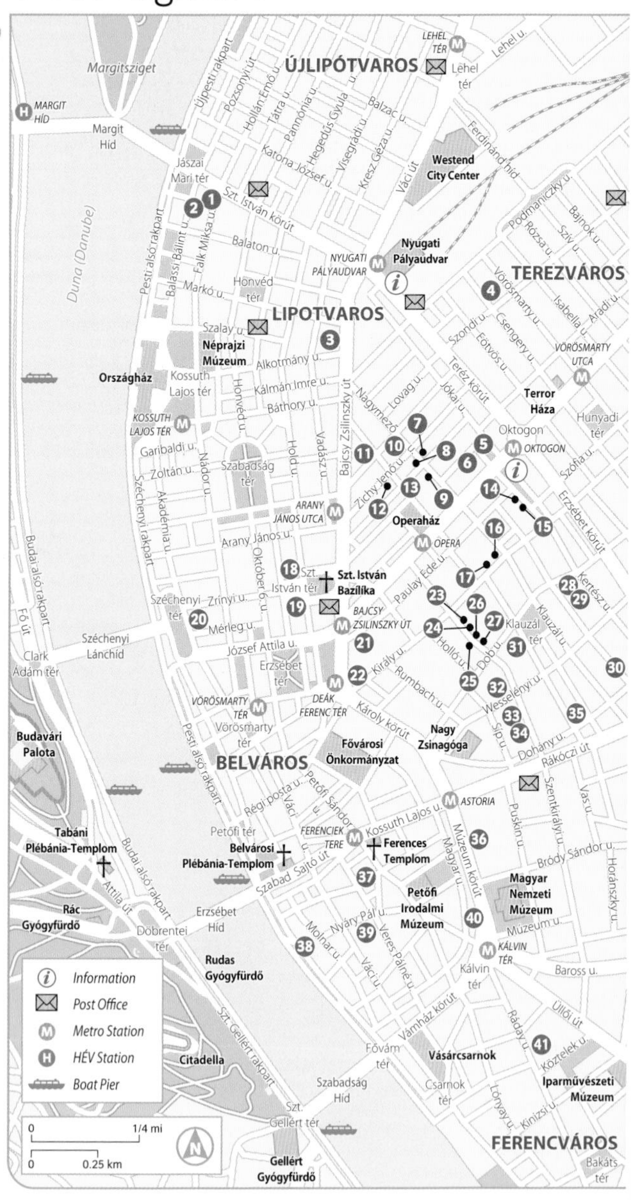

SZÉCHENYI FÜRDŐ
Szépművészeti Múzeum
Kós Károly sétány
Hermina út
Mexikói út
Francia út
Hungária körút
Hősök tere
HŐSÖK TERE
Magyar Mezőgazdasági Múzeum
Petőfi Csarnok
Műcsarnok
Közlekedési Múzeum
Városliget
Ripl-Rónai u.
Munkácsy Mihály u.
Szondi u.
Kmety György u.
Andrássy út
Délibáb u.
BAJZA UTCA
Aradi u.
Hopp Ferenc Kelet-Ázsiai Múzeum
Felvonulási tér
Ilka u.
Jávor u.
Ajtósi Dürer sor
Stefánia út
Zichy Géza u.
Kodály körönd
Kodály Zoltán Emlékmúzeum
KODÁLY KÖRÖND
Városligeti fasor
Dózsa György út
Bajza u.
Damjanich u.
Abonyi u.
Szabó
Thököly út
Lövölde tér
Peterdy u.
Cházár András u.
Országos Földtani Múzeum
ERZSÉBETVÁROS
Király u.
Bethlen Gábor u.
Dembinszky u.
Marek József u.
Cserhát u.
József u.
Jósika u.
Vörösmarty u.
Dob u.
Rottenbiller u.
István út
Murányi u.
Hernád u.
Alpár u.
Kisstadion
Rózsa u.
Isabella u.
Bethlen Gábor tér
Nefelejcs u.
Puskás Ferenc Stadion
Wesselényi u.
Rózsák tere
Garay u.
Verseny u.
Almássy tér
Szt. Erzsébet Plébánia-Templom
Keleti Pályaudvar
Erzsébet körút
Dohány u.
Szövetség u.
Munkás u.
Hársfa u.
Rákóczi út
BLAHA LUJZA TÉR
Blaha Lujza tér
Bezerédj u.
János Pál Pápa tér
Népszínház u.
Bacsó Béla u.
Víg u.
Berkocsis u.
Rákóczi tér
Déri Miksa u.
Fecske u.
Auróra u.
József körút
Német u.
József u.
Horváth Mihály tér
JÓZSEFVÁROS
Kisfaludy u.
Nap u.
Vajdahunyad u.
Nagy Templom u.
Leonardo da Vinci u.
CORVIN-NEGYED
Futó u.
Üllői út
Tűzoltó u.
Anker Klub 22
Bar Ladino 28
Boutiq'Bar 21
B7 10
Buena Vista 15
Café Eklektika 9
Caledonian Scottish Pub 6
Capella 38
Corvintető 43
CoXx Men's Club 35
DiVino 19
Drop Shop Wine Bar & Store 2
Dürer kert 46
Egri Borozó 3
El Rapido 34
Ellátó 31
Ellátó kert 25
Fat Mo's 39
Fészek Club 29
400 24
Gresham Bar 20
Grinzingi 37
Incognito 14
Instant 8
Irish Cat 40
Jelen 42
Kertem 45
Kiadó Kocsma 5
Kőleves kert 27
Kuplung 17
Mika Tivadar Mulató 26
Most 12
Museum Cukrászda 36
Negro 18
Noiret 11
Old Man's Music Pub 30
Paris Texas 41
Piaf 7
Pótkulcs 4
Sandokan Lisboa 13
Sirály 16
Szimpla Kert 33
Szóda 32
Tokaji Borozó 1
Vittula 44
Wichmann 23

Islands Nightlife

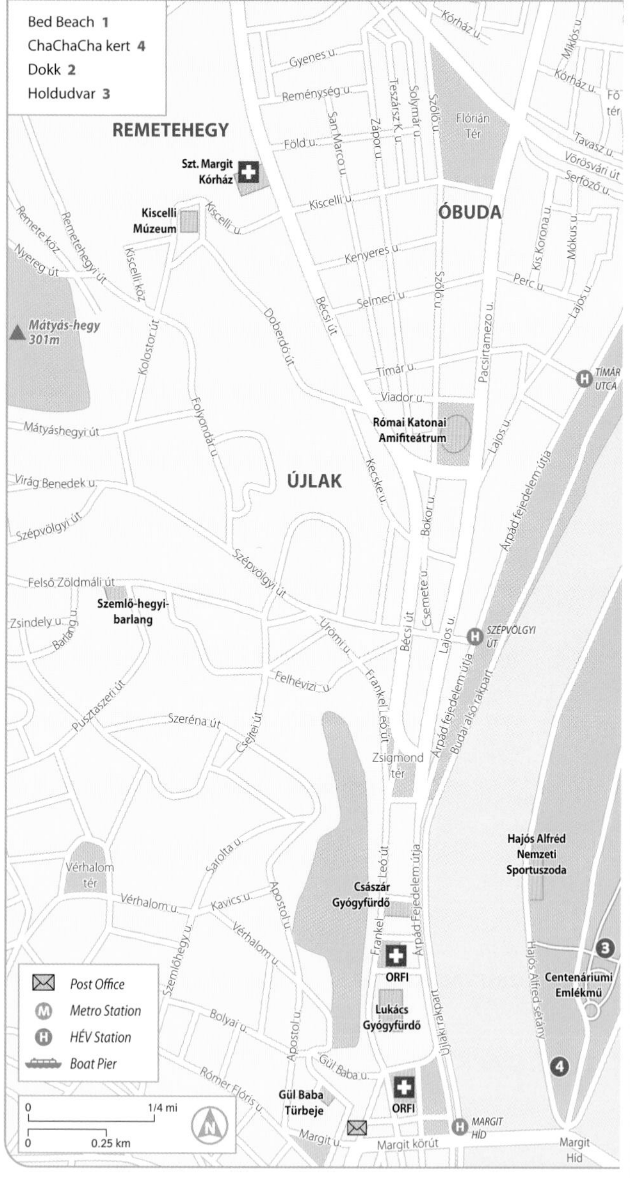

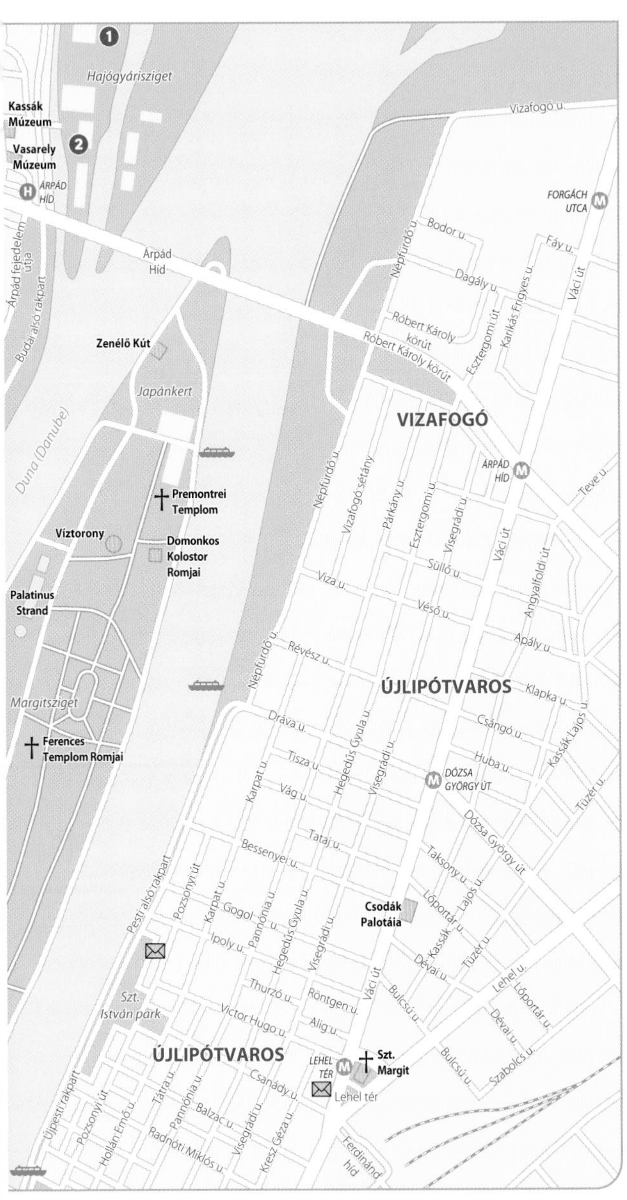
Hajógyárisziget
Kassák Múzeum
Vasarely Múzeum
ÁRPÁD HÍD
Árpád fejedelem útja
Budai alsó rakpart
Árpád Híd
Zenélő Kút
Japánkert
Duna (Danube)
Premontrei Templom
Víztorony
Domonkos Kolostor Romjai
Palatinus Strand
Margitsziget
Ferences Templom Romjai
Vizafogó u.
FORGÁCH UTCA
Bodor u.
Fáy u.
Népfürdő u.
Dagály u.
Karikás Frigyes u.
Váci út
Róbert Károly körút
Esztergomi út
VIZAFOGÓ
ÁRPÁD HÍD
Teve u.
Vizafogó sétány
Párkány u.
Esztergomi u.
Visegrádi u.
Süllő u.
Viza u.
Véső u.
Angyalföldi út
Apály u.
Révész u.
ÚJLIPÓTVAROS
Klapka u.
Csángó u.
Dráva u.
Hegedűs Gyula u.
Huba u.
Kassák Lajos u.
Tisza u.
DÓZSA GYÖRGY ÚT
Kárpát u.
Vág u.
Tüzér u.
Dózsa György út
Tataj u.
Bessenyei u.
Taksony u.
Pesti alsó rakpart
Pozsonyi út
Gogol u.
Pannónia u.
Csodák Palotáia
Lőportár u.
Ipoly u.
Dévai u.
Thurzó u.
Röntgen u.
Bulcsú u.
Lehel u.
Szt. István park
Victor Hugo u.
Alig u.
ÚJLIPÓTVAROS
LEHEL TÉR
Szt. Margit
Szabolcs u.
Csanády u.
Lehel tér
Újpesti rakpart
Tátra u.
Balzac u.
Hollán Ernő u.
Radnóti Miklós u.
Kresz Géza u.
Ferdinánd híd

Budapest Nightlife A to Z

Bars & Pubs

★★ **Anker Klub** PEST With an industrial/warehouse look, laid back atmosphere, and cheap drinks, Anker Klub is usually heaving, although it's more of a big bar than a club. For a classier, and pricier, cocktail head a few doors down the street to Bar Domby at no. 4. *Anker Köz 1–3. No phone. Metro: M1/M2/ M3 to Deák tér. Map p 112.*

★ **Bambi Presszó** BUDA Named after a Socialist-period drink, Bambi Presszó has original swinging Socialist 1960s' decor with red PVC, old guys playing dominos, plus a great terrace. Go early as it closes around 9pm. *Frankel Leó utca 2–4 (corner of Bem József utca). ☎ 1/212-3171. Tram: 4/6 to Budai hídfő. Map p 111.*

★ **Bar Ladino** PEST Shabby cool bar/eatery with funky brown wallpaper where old dudes playing cards in the afternoon give way to a 30-something crowd in the evening. A good place to meet up before taking on the bars of Jewish District VII. *Dob utca 53. No phone. www.ladino.hu. Tram: 4/6 to Király utca. Map p 112.*

Nordic minimalism at Buena Vista.

★★★ **Boutiq'Bar** PEST Classy nouveau speak-easy cocktail joint with a striking red interior. Expert mixers breathe new life into classic cocktails, such as spicing up the Caipirinha and adding mango to the Daiquiri. The menu is a history book of great cocktails brought into the present. Open Tuesday–Saturday from 6pm 'till late. *Paulay Ede utca 5. ☎ 06/30-229-1821. www.boutiqbar.hu. Metro: M1/M2/M3 to Deák tér. Map p 112.*

Buena Vista PEST Trendy but classy with slick Nordic minimalist design, linseed-oiled floors, mahogany tables, and a wide selection of drinks. There's a terrace on fashionable Liszt Ferenc tér and a restaurant upstairs. *Liszt Ferenc tér 4–5. ☎ 1/344-6303. www.buena-vista.hu. Metro: M1 to Oktogon. Tram: 4/6 to Oktogon. Map p 112.*

★★ **Caledonian Scottish Pub** PEST Draft Scottish bitter (or "heavy" as it's known in Scotland) Belhaven Best flows freely in this cozy soccer-oriented gastropub that's noted for its all-day Scottish breakfast. *Mozsár utca 9. ☎ 1/311-7611. www.caledonia.hu. Metro: M1 to Oktogon. Tram: 4/6 to Oktogon. Map p 112.*

★★ **Déryné** BUDA This converted coffeehouse close to the Castle District, is a tasteful mix of trendy lounge, cocktail, and wine bar, with a bistro, high-end restaurant and breakfast joint all under one roof. *Krisztina tér 3.* ☎ *1/255-1407. www.cafederyne.hu. Tram: 18/56. Bus: 105 to Krisztina tér. Map p 111.*

★★ **Ellátó** PEST Attracting a slightly older arty crowd, "the bringer" delivers a lively and sometimes tangibly flirty atmosphere. Sip draft Staropramen, or decent wines by the glass in the bar or seating area in the backroom. Also serves up internationally influenced bar food. *Klauzál tér 2. No phone. Metro: M1 to Opera. Tram: 4/6 to Király utca. Map p 112.*

El Rapido PEST A colorful, Mexican-looking storefront beckons you in. It's a deli-cum-kitchen upstairs, but descend the stairs and find yourself in a fully-fledged junk shop replete with wall-to-wall retro bric-a-brac that's for sale and makes a great backdrop for drinking. The tasty grub is cheap and attracts a young, alternative crowd. *Kazinczy utca 10.* ☎ *06/30-279-2861. www.elrapido.hu. Metro: M2 to Astoria. Map p 112.*

Fat Mo's PEST A fun speak-easy style joint with a long bar and intimate dance floor. Fat Mo's is for those who want to avoid the big club experience but still want to get down and boogie. *Nyáry Pál utca 11.* ☎ *1/267-3199. www.fatmo.hu. Metro: M3 to Ferenciek tere or Kálvin tér. Map p 112.*

★★★ **400** PEST This Serbian-run, arty 400-sq. m (4,306-sq. ft.) space has a converted warehouse look, crowned by a large bar in the middle, and is one of the Jewish District's most popular draws. It does decent food (including Serbian), has a fine terrace, appeals to mixed age groups, and is good at any time of the day. *Kazinczy utca 52/b.* ☎ *06/20-776-0764. www.400bar.hu. Metro: M1/M2/M3 to Deák tér. Map p 112.*

Fat Mo's speak-easy style.

★★★ **Gresham Bar** PEST Try the magical martinis in this pricey but classy cocktail bar, which adds grasshopper motifs and an alabaster ceiling to Art Nouveau surroundings. *Four Seasons Gresham Palace Hotel, Roosevelt tér 5–6.* ☎ *1/268-5100. Metro: M1 to Vörösmarty tér. Tram: 2 to Roosevelt tér. Map p 112.*

Incognito PEST Long-established favorite in über-trendy Liszt Ferenc Square with more character than most. A fitting jazz soundtrack goes with the more discerning crowd but there's still a flirty edge. *Liszt Ferenc tér 3.* ☎ *1/342-1471. Metro: M1 to Oktogon. Tram: 4/6 to Oktogon. Map p 112.*

★★★ **Instant** PEST This new kid on the alternative block is already drawing in hordes. Join the crowd in the covered courtyard or explore the nooks and crannies upstairs where you'll find several bars each with their own vibe. Look out for the dentist's chair. *Nagymező utca 38. www.instant.co.hu/en. Metro: M1 to*

Opera. Tram: 4/6 to Oktogon. Map p 112.

Irish Cat PEST A steamy weekend atmosphere warms up winter nights as dancing breaks out around the bar, fueled by an enthusiastic mixed age and nationality crowd. Guinness and food also served. *Múzeum körút 41. ☎ 1/266-4085. www.irishcat.hu. Metro: M3 to Kálvin tér. Map p 112.*

★ **Jelen** PEST The "Boys Don't Cry" poster by The Cure at the entrance of Jelen welcomes those looking to relive their student days. Serbian and Hungarian food is served. *Blaha Lujza tér 1–2 (corner of Márkus Emilia utca and Stáhly utca). ☎ 06/26-344-3155. Metro: M2 to Blaha Lujza tér. Tram: 4/6. Map p 112.*

★★ **Kiadó Kocsma** PEST Cool hangout with a bright street-level cafe and an arty intellectual library booth-like setting downstairs. The Magyar-style pub grub is pretty decent too. *Jókai tér 3. ☎ 1/331-1955. Metro: M1 to Oktogon. Tram: 4/6 to Oktogon. Map p 112.*

★★ **Kuplung** PEST The "Clutch" is a cool underground Boho hangout with graffiti covered walls that was once a garage. A ping-pong table is on hand for those up to the challenge. *Király utca 46. ☎ 06/30-986-8856. www.kuplung.net. Metro: M1 to Opera. Map p 112.*

Lánchíd Söröző BUDA A great place for a beer after a hard day's Buda sightseeing. Simple and unpretentious, and decked out in old memorabilia, the welcome is a warm one. This was my favorite watering hole when I worked close by. *Fő utca 4. ☎ 1/214-3144. www.lanchidsorozo.hu. Tram: 19 to Clark Ádám tér. Bus: 86/105 to Clark Ádám tér. Map p 111.*

★★★ **Mika Tivadar Mulató** PEST This converted one-time copper and steel works is a very happening spot in the cooler months. The contemporary design embraces elements of the building's past as chandeliers hang from the stucco ceiling. It has a lively garden bar in the summer, which completes a trio of top outdoor spots on the same street with Kőleves kert and Ellátó kert. *Kazinczy utca 47. ☎ 06/20-965-3007. www.mikativadarmulato.hu. Metro: M1/M2/M3 to Deák tér. Map p 112.*

★★ **Most** PEST Meaning "now" in Hungarian, this venue was the

Old memorabilia adorns the walls at Lánchid Söröző.

Museum Cukrászda.

"in place" when it opened in 2009 and continues to attract a lively mixed crowd. The book wallpaper is a nice token gesture to intellectual aspirations, but who needs books when you have indoor and outdoor nooks and crannies to explore? *Zichy Jenő utca 17.* ☎ *06/30-248-3322. Metro: M3 to Arany János utca. Map p 112.*

★ **Museum Cukrászda** PEST A busy cake and coffee shop by day, and by night a favorite of assorted revelers who come to sober up on solids—but often keep on drinking until the sun comes up. Attractive terrace that's nice for seeing in the new day. *Múzeum körút 10.* ☎ *1/452-0888. Metro: M2 to Astoria. Map p 112.*

★ **Negro** PEST Dark and sultry chi-chi lounge room/cocktail bar with a terrace leading onto the stunning basilica-dominated Szent István tér. The bar is actually located in the square's only ugly building, meaning you see the square at its best. *Szent István tér 11.* ☎ *1/302-0136. Metro: M1 to Bajcsy-Zsilinszky út. Map p 112.*

Noiret PEST Pool and darts cellar with a party vibe and a jukebox pumping out greatest hits soundtracks. *Dessewffy utca 8–10 (corner of Hajós utca).* ☎ *1/331-6103. www.noiret.hu. Metro: M3 to Arany János utca. Map p 112.*

Old Man's Music Pub PEST A good venue to head to for a last drink and a free dance to old classics, or for local rock gigs. The mature female clientele make this music pub just as much the "Old Girl's" as the "Old Man's." *Akácfa utca 13.* ☎ *1/322-7645. www.oldmansmusicpub.com. Metro: M2 to Blaha Lujza tér. Tram: 4/6. Map p 112.*

Oscar Café BUDA A city slickers-oriented Buda bar that's known for top cocktails, good wine, and draft beer, which pardons the now-dated Hollywood theme that, fortunately, is hidden with the dim lighting. *Ostrom utca 14.* ☎ *1/212-8017. Metro: M2 to Széll Kálmán tér. Tram: 4/6. Map p 111.*

★ **Paris Texas** PEST An old favorite on the trendy Ráday utca

Admire the Manga wallpaper at Szóda.

party strip, whose venues often lack substance over style. Here, however, enjoy a real pub atmosphere, a decent cocktail list, and a pleasant outside seating area. ***Ráday utca 22. ☎ 1/218-0570. Metro: M3 to Kálvin tér. Tram: 47/49. Map p 112.***

★ **Pótkulcs** PEST Set behind a nondescript gate, the "Spare Key" is easy to miss but difficult to leave. Tavern-like on one side by the bar, Pótkulcs becomes a grungy cellar on the other. Popular with the student and young alternative crowd, it also serves plenty of veggie pub grub. ***Csengery utca 65/B. ☎ 1/269-1050. www.potkulcs.hu. Metro: M3 to Nyugati. Tram: 4/6. Map p 112.***

★★ **Sandokan Lisboa** PEST The colorfully tiled interior and decaying townhouses on this pedestrian street, onto which the action spills in summer, conjure up the city of Lisbon. There may be no Portuguese beer but the thirst-quenching draft Spanish San Miguel is close enough. ***Hajós utca 23 (corner of Ó utca). ☎ 1/302-7002. Metro: M1 to Opera. Map p 112.***

★ **Sirály** PEST A twisty staircase connects this multi-level arty venue that's everything from a buzzing bar/coffeehouse, to a concert and theater venue, Internet hotspot, exhibition space, and occasional cinema. ***Király utca 50. ☎ 06/20-957-2291. www.siraly.co.hu. Tram: 4/6 to Király utca. Map p 112.***

★★★ **Szimpla Kert** PEST The great survivor of temporary nightspots that sprung up in derelict buildings has made this, its second location, its permanent home. The free Wi-Fi makes this many people's unofficial office too. ***Kazinczy utca 14. No phone. www.szimpla.hu. Metro: M2 to Astoria. Bus: 7 to Astoria. Map p 112.***

★ **Szóda** PEST The alternative ambience here is provided by a backdrop of Japanese Manga comic strip wallpaper and retro red plastic seats attracting a young arty crowd. There's a fun dance floor downstairs in fall and winter. ***Wesselényi utca 18. ☎ 06/70-389-6463. www.szoda.com. Metro: M2 to Astoria. Tram: 4/6 to Wesselényi utca. Map p 112.***

★ **Vittula** PEST Grungy hip cellar bar frequented by a friendly and up-for-it mixed nationality clientele. The alternative rock soundtrack is supplemented by occasional DJs and live music. ***Kertész utca 4. No phone. www.vittula.hu. Metro: M2 to Blaha Lujza tér. Map p 112.***

★ **Wichmann** PEST Classic smoky drinking den in a lovely old house that, with the long wooden tables and bar, give it an old-world tavern feel. Come for cheap wine, beer, and spirits shared by an eclectic crowd. ***Kazinczy utca 55. ☎ 1/322-6174. Tram: 4/6 to Király utca. Map p 112.***

Clubs

★★ **B7** PEST Big booming "rhythm and bling" dance club in the heart of central Pest, providing glitzy nightlife action without having to trek out to the big clubs of Hajógyárisziget. Open Wednesday to Saturday 10pm to 5am only. *Nagymező utca 48–48. ☎ 06/30-670-1404. www.b7.hu. Admission varies. Metro: M1 to Oktogon or Opera. Map p 112.*

★★★ **Dokk** HAJÓGYÁRISZIGET Über-trendy club with top dance DJs in a spacious converted warehouse on Hajógyárisziget (Boatyard Island). The sight of so many beautiful girls under one roof gets the men's pulses racing. The action moves outdoors to Dokk Beach in summer. *Hajógyárisziget 122. ☎ 06/30-535-2747. www.dokkdisco.hu. Cover varies. Suburban train: HÉV to Filatorigát. Map p 114.*

★★★ **Fészek Club** PEST Amazing bijou artists cellar club with a risqué atmosphere and borderline bordello decoration. You never know what you're going to get here—it ranges from seriously arty one night to gangster bling the next. *Kertész utca 36. ☎ 1/342-6549. www.feszek-muveszklub.hu. Free–300 Ft. Tram: 4/6 to Király utca. Map p 112.*

★★★ **Piaf** PEST This Budapest classic rocks through 'till dawn with Parisian-style sleaze upstairs and a greatest hits soundtrack downstairs. The slightly mature crowd should know better but can't resist coming back. Ring the bell to get in. *Nagymező utca 25. ☎ 1/312-3823. www.piafklub.hu. 800 Ft cover, including one drink. Metro: M1 to Oktogon or Opera. Tram: 4/6 to Oktogon. Map p 112.*

Gay & Lesbian

★★ **Café Eklektika** PEST Displays the same lovely lesbian hospitality as its like-named predecessor but now in a more mature location and under a stucco ceiling. A great hangout any time of day and admission is free. *Nagymező utca 30. ☎ 1/266-1266. www.eklektika.hu. Metro: M1 to Oktogon or Opera. Map p 112.*

★★ **Capella** PEST This Pest waterfront hotspot attracts a mixed bunch, mostly piling in for the midnight drag show. A lively crowd twists the night away to dance and disco in camped-up surroundings. *Belgrád rakpart 23. ☎ 06/70-597-7755. wwww.capella.hu. Admission varies. Wed–Sat. Map p 112.*

★★★ **CoXx Men's Club** PEST Hidden gents' club with themed nights including macho, military cruising, and a "bear club." Tastefully done but quite hardcore. *Dohány utca 38. ☎ 1/344-4884. www.coxx.hu. 1,000 Ft cover. Metro: M2 to Blaha Luiza tér. Map p 112.*

Summer Bars/Venues

★★★ **Bed Beach** HAJÓGYÁRISZIGET Whiter than white decor, the ideal backdrop for hot hedonistic nights with hardcore dance music on Budapest's glitzy nightlife island. The place to be seen but not for a quiet drink. *Hajógyárisziget. ☎ 06/30-436-4400. www.bedbeach.hu. Suburban train: HÉV to Filatorigát. Map p 114.*

Garden Party

The hot summer bars and venues are usually open May to September but sometimes open later due to bad weather. Many come and go but the ones listed here are expected to be open in 2011 and beyond.

★★ Café del Rio BUDA Dress-up in chic attire and sip expensive cocktails at this fancy outdoor venue that pumps out dance music to a backdrop of palm trees and undeniably beautiful girls. *Goldmann György tér 1. ☎ 06/30-297-2158. www.rio.hu. Free entry with exception of major concerts. Tram: 4/6 to Petőfi híd budai hídfő. Map p 111.*

★★ ChaChaCha kert MARGARET ISLAND Sandwiched between tennis courts and a sports stadium, this outdoor venue goes from a relaxed place to take an early evening drink to groove central as everyone takes to the al fresco dance floor (on hot summer nights Wed–Sat). After summer the action moves indoors and underground to a cool cellar labyrinth at Bajcsy Zsilinszky út 63, close to Nuygati station. *Tram: 4/6 to Margit Sziget. www.chachacha.hu. Bus: 26 to Szigeti bejáró. Map p 114.*

★★★ Corvintető PEST Set atop a Socialist-era shopping complex, Corvin is a cool spot on steamy summer nights. The rooftop is open summers only but the Bohemian warehouse-type hangout is worth checking out any time of year. (You'll need to climb several flights of stairs.) *Corvin Áruház, Blaha Lujza tér 1–2 (entrance from Somogyi Béla utca). ☎ 06/20-772-2984. www.corvinteto.hu. Metro: M2 to Blaha Lujza tér. Tram: 4/6 to Blaha Lujza tér. Map 112.*

★ Dürer kert PEST Drink and think in this cool, less-frequented courtyard of the Arts University. Tree stumps, colorful lights plus DJs and gigs at weekends, with a fun interior maze of extreme retro rooms that are also open in winter. *Ajtósi Dürer sor 19–21. ☎ 1/789-4444. www.durerkert.com. Trolley bus: 74 to Ajtósi Dürer sor. Map p 112.*

★★ Ellátó kert PEST Yet another outdoor "ruin" pub on Kazinczy utca (opened in 2010), though the "Supplier Garden" has its own boho vibe and cool clientele. Funky murals, multi-colored chairs, and ping pong, darts, and pool to burn off the beer. Magyarized Mexican food provides solid nourishment. *Kazinczy utca 48. www.ellatokert.blogspot.com. Metro: M1/M2/M3 to Deák tér. Map p 112.*

★★★ Holdudvar MARGARET ISLAND Converted from a famous casino, this trendy nightspot

Trendy nightspot Holdudvar.

Egri Borozó.

successfully marries old-world charm with modern touches. The garden bars are surrounded by trees and lit up by funky orange lanterns, plus there's a gallery, dance floor and a restaurant. *Margaret Island.* ☎ *1/236-0155. www.holdudvar.net. Tram: 4/6 to Margaret Island. Bus: 26 to Hajós Alfréd Uszoda. Map p 114.*

★★ **Kertem** PEST The extremely laidback "My Garden" feels like everyone's garden. Old vinyl discs decorate the bar, while the sleeves of incredibly schmaltzy looking singers line the route to the toilets. Christmas lights add funky color after dark. *Olof Palme sétány 3. No phone. Metro: M1 to Hősök tere. Map p 112.*

★★★ **Kőleves kert** PEST There's a beach bar atmosphere here, with pebbles underfoot, in the heart of the Jewish district. Cheap drinks and an alternative and friendly vibe prove to be a joy on hot summer nights. Who needs the sea? *Kazinczy utca 37.* ☎ *1/322-1011. Metro: M1/ M2/M3 to Deák tér. Map p 112.*

★★ **Romkert** BUDA This venue is dramatically situated between the river and the foot of Gellért Hill, in a garden under the beautiful Turkish dome of the Rudás Baths. There's always a steady flow of cocktails and the music scene is set for a serious al fresco party. *Döbrentei tér 9 (Garden of the Rudas Baths). www. romkert.eu. Tram: 18/19 to Döbrentei tér. Map p 111.*

Zöld Pardon BUDA Festival-like atmosphere attracting an up-for-it student crowd. Varied attractions include a fruit brandy house, a games and dance area, plus loads of live music. *Southern side of Goldmann György tér. www.zp.hu. Tram: 4/6 to Petőfi híd, Budai hídfő. Map p 111.*

Wine Bars

★★★ **DiVino** PEST Cool and contemporary new wine joint opposite the Basilica offering a fine vinous tour around Hungary via 100 wines available by the glass and at very competitive prices. One of the 27 young winemakers featured is usually on hand. *Szent István tér 3.* ☎ *06/30-231-1132. Metro: M1 to*

Bajcsy-Zsilinsky út/M3 to Arany János utca. Map p 112.

★★★ **Drop Shop Wine Bar & Store** PEST Modern design with classic wine bar atmosphere, Drop Shop fills up in the evening, when booking is recommended. Although the selection is two-thirds foreign, including iconic names, it successfully showcases upcoming local winemakers with 60 wines by the glass and 200 bottles on the shelves. *Balassi Bálint utca 27. www.dropshop.hu.* ☎ *06/30-345-3739. Tram: 2/4/6 to Jászai Mari tér. Map p 112.*

Egri Borozó PEST Unpretentious wine cellar with Flintstone-like furniture selling barrels of cheap and cheerful wine in green ceramic jugs and mugs. Not sure if it's the quantity or quality that gives the next-day headache—but that's a small price to pay. *Bajcsy-Zsilinszky út 72.* ☎ *1/302-1724. Metro: M3 to Nyugati pályaudvar, or Arany János utca. Map p 112.*

Grinzingi PEST Rough-and-ready wine bar with a great atmosphere where five different types of wine from the Mátra region flow in a scary quantity. The chairs are chunky and fixed to the floor so nobody falls off. *Veres Pálné utca 10.* ☎ *1/317-4624. www.grinzingi.hu. Metro: M3 to Ferenciek tere. Map p 112.*

★ **Tokaji Borozó** PEST Descend the steps into this crypt-like setting that swallows up people from all walks of life heading home from work. You certainly won't find the finest examples of the sweet *Tokaji Aszú* here but you will find a great wine cellar atmosphere and some hearty bites. *Falk Miksa utca 32.* ☎ *1/269-3143. Tram: 4/6 to Jászai Mari tér. Map p 112.*

8 The Best Arts & Entertainment

Arts & Entertainment Best Bets

Best **Art Nouveau Auditorium**
★★★ Ferenc Liszt Music Academy (Liszt Ferenc Zeneakadémia), *Liszt Ferenc tér 8 (p 131)*

Best place to **Catch International Jazz Acts**
★★ Budapest Jazz Club, *Múzeum utca 7 (p 133)*

Best **Contemporary Performance Art**
★★★ Trafó House of Contemporary Arts, *Liliom utca 41 (p 130)*

Best **Converted Industrial Arts Complex**
★★★ Millenáris, *Kis Rókus utca 16–20 (p 130)*

Best **English Language Comedy**
★★ Smiley's, *Szent István körút 13 (p 132)*

Best **Floating Rock Concerts**
★★★ A38 Ship, *Moored on the River Danube next to Petőfi híd (p 132)*

Best **Folk Concerts**
★★★ Fonó Budai Zeneház, *Sztregova utca 3 (p 133)*

Best **Free Underground Concerts**
★★★ Gödör, *Erszebet tér (p 133)*

Best **Heavenly Acoustics**
★★★ Mátyás Templom (Matthias Church), *Szentháromság tér 2 (p 131)*

Best **High Brow Arts Complex**
★★ Művészetek Palotája (Palace of Arts), Komor *Marcell utca 1 (p 130)*

Best **Independent & Gay Movies**
Cirko-geyzir, *Balassi Bálint utca 15–17 (p 130)*

Best **Night at the Opera**
★★★ Opera House, *Andrássy út 22 (p 132)*

Best **Preserved Fin-de-Siècle Cinema**
★★★ Uránia, *Rákóczi út 21 (p 131)*

Best place to **See Internationally Acclaimed Local Dance Troupe**
★★ Ram Colosseum, *Kárpát utca 23–25 (p 132)*

Best **State-of-the-Art Classic Music Venue**
★★ Béla Bartók National Concert Hall, *Palace of Arts, Komor Marcell utca 1 (p 131)*

Best place to **Tap into the Local Jazz Scene**
★ Columbus Jazz Club, *Permanently moored on the River Danube at Vigadó tér (p 133)*

Matthias Church for heavenly acoustics. Previous page: Ram Colosseum.

Buda Arts & Entertainment

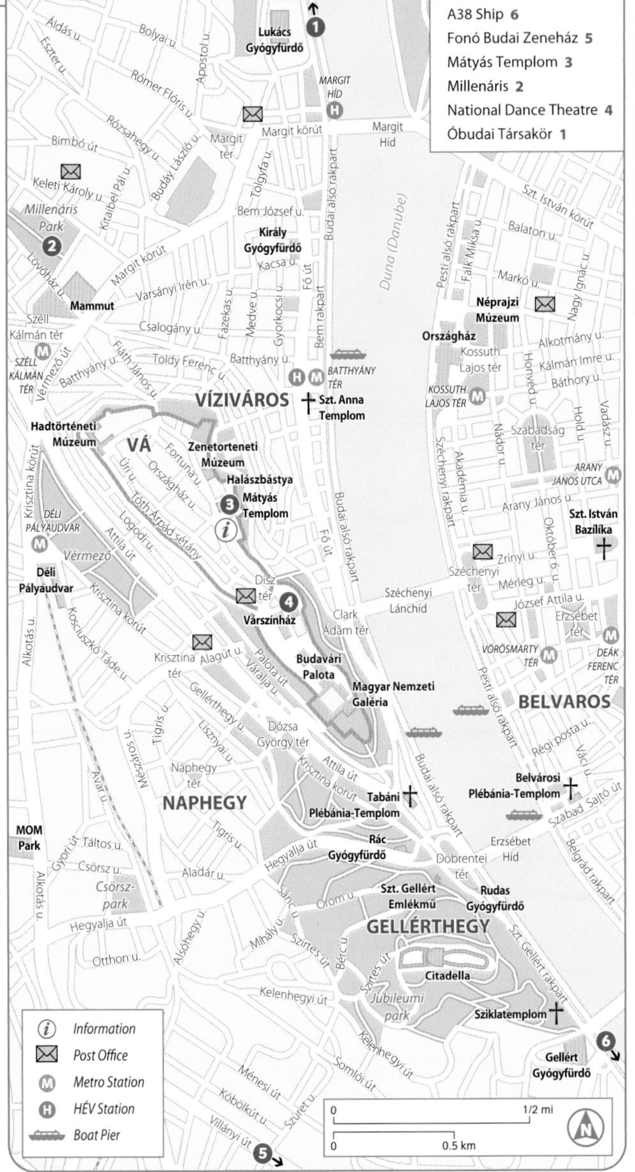

Pest Arts & Entertainment

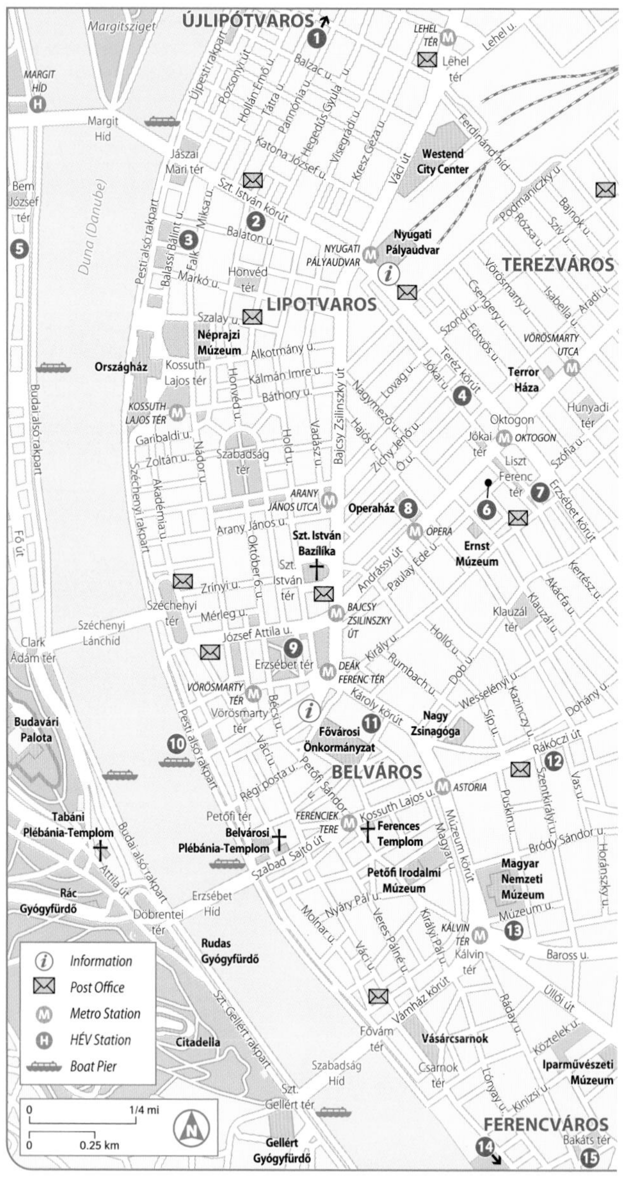

Széchenyi Fürdő
Szépművészeti Múzeum
Hősök tere
Hősök tere
Műcsarnok
Magyar Mezőgazdasági Múzeum
Petőfi Csarnok
Közlekedési Múzeum
Városliget
Bajza utca
Hopp Ferenc Kelet-Ázsiai Múzeum
Felvonulási tér
Kodály körönd
Kodály Zoltán Emlémúzeum
Kodály körönd
Lövölde tér
ERZSÉBETVÁROS
Országos Földtani Múzeum
Kisstadion
Bethlen Gábor tér
Puskás Ferenc Stadion
Rózsák tere
Szt. Erzsébet-Plébánia-Templom
Almássy tér
Keleti Pályaudvar
Baross tér
Keleti pályaudvar
Blaha Lujza tér
Blaha Lujza tér
Köztársaság tér
Teleki László tér
Rákóczi tér
Mátyás tér
Horváth Mihály tér
Kálvária tér
JÓZSEFVÁROS
Corvin-negyed
Botanikus kert
Klinikák
Béla Bartók National Concert Hall 14
Budapest Arena 23
Budapest Jazz Club 13
Cirko-geyzir 3
Columbus Jazz Club 10
Erkel Színház 18
Filter Klub 19
Giero 6
Gödör 9
Jedermann 15
Liszt Ferenc Zeneakadémia 7
Mappa 16
Merlin 11
Művész 4
Művészetek Palotája 14
Nádor Terem 22
Opera House 8
Örökmozgó 20
PECSA 21
Ram Colosseum 1
Smiley's 2
Trafó House of Contemporary Arts 17
Uránia 12
Vízraktér 5

Arts & Entertainment A to Z

Arts Centers

★★★ kids **Millenáris** BUDA Über-cool converted industrial complex packed with urban art and installations, which holds film festivals, concerts, and DJ nights. There's also a nice outdoor area for children. *Kis Rókus utca 16–20.* ☎ *1/336-4000. www.millenaris.hu. Tickets vary. Metro: M2 to Moszkva tér. Tram: 4/6 to Széna tér. Map p 127.*

★★ **Művészetek Palotája (Palace of Arts)** PEST This high-tech and chic art house is the centerpiece of the new "Millennium City Center" with the Ludwig Gallery, Béla Bartók National Concert Hall, and Festival Theater among its attractions. *Komor Marcell utca 1.* ☎ *1/555-3001. Tickets vary. Tram: 2 to Millenniumi Kulturális Központ. Map p 128.*

★★★ **Trafó House of Contemporary Arts** PEST This hotbed of cutting-edge expression plays host to a variety of local and international performance arts, many of which are accessible for non-Hungarian speakers. *Liliom utca 41.* ☎ *1/215-1600. www.trafo.hu. Tickets vary. Metro: M2 to Ferenc Körút. Map p 128.*

★★ **Vízraktér** BUDA Turfed out by the local council from its previous Pest location in fall 2011, the arty crew from Tűzraktér is back in a striking new location at the Turkish era Király Baths. This offbeat cultural complex hosts eclectic concerts, a human circus and exhibitions to a remarkable colorful Turkish backdrop. The bars are seriously atmospheric. *Fö utca 84.* ☎ *0620/434-1020. www.vizrakter.hu. Tickets vary. Metro: M2 to Batthyány tér. Map p 128.*

Cinema

★★ **Cirko-geyzir** PEST A little gem of an intimate independent cinema that screens lots of obscure international films, and is also the place to find gay cinema. *Balassi*

Millenáris.

Bálint utca 15–17. ☎ 1/269-1915. www.cirkofilm.hu. Metro: M3 to Nyugati. Tram: 2/4/6 to Jászai Mari tér. Map p 128.

★★ **Művész** PEST Popular central cinema that screens a wide range of mainly less-commercial films, new and not so new. It leans toward the arty, but not too esoteric to repel a fair crowd. Many films are shown in English, with Hungarian subtitles. The website provided is in Hungarian but can still tell non-Hungarian speakers what's on. *Teréz körút 30. ☎ 1/459-5050. http://www.artmozi.hu/muvesz/Muvesz_net/muvesz.html. Metro: M1 to Oktogon. Tram: 4/6 to Oktogon. Map p 128.*

★★ **Örökmozgó** PEST Art house cinema that specializes in screening international and Hungarian classics from the Hungarian National Film Archive. Look out for themed film weeks. *Erzsébet körút 39. ☎ 1/342-2167. www.filmarchive.hu/orokmozgo/program/index.php (Hungarian only). Tram: 4/6 to Király utca. Map p 128.*

★★★ **Uránia** PEST The Moorish-influenced Uránia has been restored to its fin-de-siècle splendor and has viewing boxes that make for a special experience, quite different to watching a Hollywood blockbuster in an ordinary commercial cinema. Drop into the coffeehouse, even if you can't make one of its Hungarian or international films. *Rákóczi út 21. ☎ 1/486-3413. www.urania-nf.hu. Metro: M2 to Astoria or Blaha Lujza tér. Map p 128.*

Classical & Opera

★★★ **Béla Bartók National Concert Hall** PEST Home to the Hungarian Philharmonic Orchestra led by the world-famous pianist Zoltán Kocsis, this state-of-the-art venue has the same dimensions as a Gothic cathedral and the acoustics to match. *Palace of Arts, Komor Marcell utca 1. ☎ 1/555-3300. Tickets vary. Tram: 2 to Millenniumi Kulturális Központ. Map p 128.*

Erkel Színház PEST Socialist-realist from the outside, but with pleasing acoustics inside. Although I once saw Nick Cave and the Bad Seeds here, it's used mainly to share Budapest's opera and ballet burden with the Opera House and Thalia Theater. *Köztársaság tér 30. ☎ 1/333-0540. www.opera.hu. Tickets vary. Metro: M2 to Blaha Lujza tér. Map p 128.*

★★★ **Liszt Ferenc Zeneakadémia (Ferenc Liszt Music Academy)** PEST Facing funding cuts, this 130-year-old education institution is paying for itself by putting on more of its own concerts, featuring the cream of Hungarian talent. Regular performances are held in the awesome Art Nouveau auditorium. This is an experience not to be missed. See p 24, ❽. *Liszt Ferenc tér 8. ☎ 1/342-0179. Tickets vary. Metro: M1 to Oktogon. Map p 128.*

★★★ **Mátyás Templom (Matthias Church)** BUDA Heavenly surroundings and acoustics make for an outstanding classical music experience. The kind of place that's built to handle all that Handel's *Messiah* can throw at it. *Szentháromság tér 2. ☎ 1/355-5657. www.matyastemplom.hu. Tickets vary. Bus: 16/16A/116 to Szentháromság tér. Map p 127.*

★★ **Nádor Terem** PEST The intimate bijou Art Nouveau Nádor Hall, hidden away in the Institute of the Blind, is a prime venue for strings, chamber music, and virtuoso performances. *Ajtósi Dürer sor 39. ☎ 1/344-7072. www.hangverseny.hu. Closed Jul and Aug. Tickets on sale before*

The state-of-the-art Ram Colosseum.

performance, prices vary. Metro: M1 to Mexikói út. Map p 128.

★★ **Óbudai Társakör** ÓBUDA The Franz Liszt Chamber Orchestra, Budapest Strings, and Auer String Quartet are regulars at this wonderfully restored enclave of "Old Buda," sadly a gatecrasher these days in the realm of high rises. ***Kiskorona utca 7.*** *☎ 1/250-0288. www.obudaitarsaskor.hu. Tickets vary. Suburban train: HÉV to Árpád híd. Map p 127.*

★★★ **Opera House** PEST At the cutting edge when it was opened by Franz Joseph I in 1884, both in terms of design and functionality, the Opera House is desperate to replace the creaking East German stage and concrete pit to restore the once-outstanding acoustics. She still looks beautiful though, and the great-value opera and ballet is a must. *See p 10, ❽. Andrássy út 22. ☎ 1/353-0170 for tickets. www.opera.hu. Tickets vary. Metro: M1 to Hősök tere. Map p 128.*

Comedy

★★ **Smiley's** PEST Critically acclaimed stand up comedians from the English-speaking world, magicians, and Hungarian and expat bands can often be seen here. Check out the adjoining Fun Palace Pub for live English Premiership soccer games and other sports. ***Szent István körút 13.*** *☎ 06/30-695-2866. www.smileysklub.weebly.com. Tickets vary. Metro: M3 to Nyugati. Tram: 2/4/6 to Jászai Mari tér. Map p 128.*

Dance

★ **National Dance Theatre** BUDA Ballet, folk, modern, and contemporary dance are on tap in this handsome theater. ***Színház utca 1–3.*** *☎ 1/201-4407. www.dancetheatre.hu. Tickets vary. Bus: 16/16A/116 to Dísz tér. Map p 127.*

★★ kids **Ram Colosseum** PEST This state-of-the-art venue opened in 2011 and serves as a showcase for the versatile, creative, and internationally renowned Hungarian dance troupe *Experidance*. Ram offers many other concerts and performances from gypsy orchestras to puppet theater. ***Kárpát utca 23–25.*** *☎ 1/222-5254. www.ramcolosseum.com. Tickets vary. Trolley bus: 75 to Vág utca. Map p 128.*

Live Folk, Rock, Pop & Jazz

★★★ **A38 Ship** RIVER DANUBE Local and international acts, including names as big as John Cale, perform on this very hip Ukrainian ship. Alongside the music, there's a cool industrial bar in the engine room and swanky restaurant on the top deck. ***Moored next to Petőfi híd (Petőfi Bridge).*** *☎ 1/464-3940. www.a38.hu. Tickets vary. Closed Sun. Tram: 4/6 to Petőfi híd, budai hídfő. Map p 127.*

Budapest Arena PEST The multipurpose Papp László Budapest Sport Arena, to give this huge spaceship-like building its full name, hosts world-famous names. ☎ *1/422-2600. www.budapestarena.hu. Tickets vary. Metro: M2 to Stadionok. Map p 128.*

★★ **Budapest Jazz Club** PEST Local and international acts, with many well-known American artists, drop off here on their European tours. Expect top acoustics, many styles of jazz, and regular jam sessions on Fridays and Saturdays. *Múzeum utca 7.* ☎ *06/70-413-9837. www.bjc.hu. Tickets vary. Metro: M2 to Kálvin tér. Map p 128.*

★ **Columbus Jazz Club** DANUBE This is the best place to tap into the local jazz scene. Prices for drinks, however, are high on this slightly cheap-looking floating jazz venue, but the music makes up for it. *Permanently moored at Vigadó tér.* ☎ *1/266-9013. Tickets vary. Tram: 2 to Vigadó tér. Map p 128.*

Filter Klub PEST Absolutely no filtering of the end product goes on in this raw hard rock hangout. Plenty of young punk bands strut their stuff for free, especially on school nights. *Almássy utca 1.* ☎ *06/30-921-4212. www.filterclub.hu. Free entry. Metro: M2 to Blaha Lujza tér. Tram: 4/6 to Wesselényii utca or Blaha Lujza tér. Map p 128.*

★★★ **Fonó Budai Zeneház** BUDA Top Hungarian and Transylvanian folk acts on Wednesdays, with powerful and unrestrained Csángó, a folk style from a Hungarian minority hailing from deepest Romania and Moldavia. Gypsy dance classes, too. *Sztregova utca 3.* ☎ *1/206-5300. www.fono.hu. Tickets vary. Tram: 47 to Kalotaszeg utca. Map p 127.*

★ **Giero** PEST Tiny cellar place where Gypsy Jazz musicians meet up to jam and hang out. Electric atmosphere and decent rustic cooking. Free, but a few tips get them to really go for it. *Paulay Ede utca 56. Free entry. Metro: M1 to Oktogon. Map p 128.*

★★★ **Gödör** PEST Weird, wonderful, and varied program of concerts sees all the beats from across the globe sounding in this stylish subterranean setting under Erszebet tér. Local gypsy greats Romano Drom are a feature. *Erszebet tér.*

The multi-purpose Budapest Arena.

Where to Buy Tickets

www.jegymester.hu is a comprehensive online booking system that also works in English. It sells tickets for opera, music concerts, theater, dance, exhibitions, festivals across Hungary, and children's entertainment—and you can pick your seats online. It also has an office at Bajcsy-Zsilinszky út 31 (☎ 1/302-3333).

Broadway Jegyiroda (Hollán Ernő utca 10, ☎ 1/340-4040. jegy @broadwayjegyiroda.hu) sells tickets to many concerts, theater performances, and festivals in the capital and beyond, featuring both Hungarian and international artists.

Tickets can also be bought directly from most of the places featured. As anywhere, always try to book ahead to avoid disappointment.

☎ 06/20-201-3868. www.godorklub.hu. Tickets vary, often no cover charge. Metro: M1/M2/M3 to Deák tér. Map p 128.

★★ **Jedermann** PEST Given a Midas touch makeover by Dutch bar guru extraordinaire Hans van Vliet, himself a trombone player, this hip and arty jazz bar attracts an intellectual crowd. There's live jazz on Wednesdays and Saturdays, plus often on Thursdays, and it has good food plus a cool outdoor terrace. A breathe of fresh air after passing many soulless establishments on trendy Raday utca. *Ráday utca 58. Part of the Goethe Institute. ☎ 06/30-406-3617. www.jedermannkavezo.blogspot.com. Tram: 4/6 to Mester utca. Map p 128.*

★★★ **Mappa** PEST The cellar club of the truly progressive Trafó unsurprisingly pulls in many budding alternative bands. *Liliom utca 41. ☎ 1/456-2053. www.trafo.hu. Tickets vary. Metro: M3 to Ferenc körút. Tram: 4/6 to Ferenc körút. Map p 128.*

PECSA PEST This retro kitsch venue attracts the likes of big less-commercial stars such as Morrissey and Nick Cave. *See p 48, 8.*

Theater

★ **Merlin** PEST Regular performances in English from the Madhouse and Scallabouche theater companies, lots of contemporary dance from local and touring troupes, and DJ nights. For more on the two English language theater groups, who also perform elsewhere, check out www.scallabouche.com. *Gerlóczy utca 4. ☎ 1/317-9338. www.merlinszinhaz.hu. Tickets vary. Metro: M1/M2/M3 to Deák tér or M3 to Astoria. Map p 128.* ●

9 The Best Lodging

Lodging Best Bets

Continental Hotel Zara. Previous page: Four Seasons Hotel Gresham Palace Budapest.

Best Art Deco Hotel
★★ Andrássy Hotel MaMaison, *Andrassy út 111 (p 140)*

Best Art Nouveau Hotel
★★★ Four Seasons Hotel Gresham Palace Budapest, *Széchenyi tér 5–6 (p 142)*

Best Arty Accommodations
★★ Brody House, *Bródy Sándor utca 10 (p 141)*

Best Bargain View
Citadella Hotel, *Citadella sétány (p 141)*

Best Boutique Hotel
★★ Zara Boutique Hotel, *Só utca 6 (p 146)*

Best Cheap 'n' Cheerful Socialist-era Lodgings
Medosz, *Jókai tér 9 (p 145)*

Best Designer Hotel
★★★ Lánchid 19, *Lánchíd utca 19–21 (p 144)*

Best Hostel For Fun Seekers
Carpe Noctem, *Szobi utca 5 (p 141)*

Best Hotel for Vampire Lovers
★ Soho Hotel, *Dohány utca 64 (p 146)*

Best Newcomer
★★★ Continental Hotel Zara, *Dohány utca 42–44 (p 141)*

Best Old World Ambience
★★ Danubius Hotel Gellért, *Szent Gellért tér 1 (p 142)*

Best Restored Old Favorite
★★★ Corinthia Grand Royal Hotel, *Erzsébet körút 43–49 (p 141)*

Best Spa Hotel
★★ Ramada Resort Budapest, *Íves út 16 (p 145).*

Best Views
★★ Marriott, *Apaczai Csere Janos utca 4 (p 145)*

Best Villa
★★★ Uhu Villa, *Keselyű utca 1/a (p 146)*

Best When Money is No Object
★★★ Four Seasons Hotel Gresham Palace Budapest, *Széchenyi tér 5–6 (p 142)*

Buda Lodging

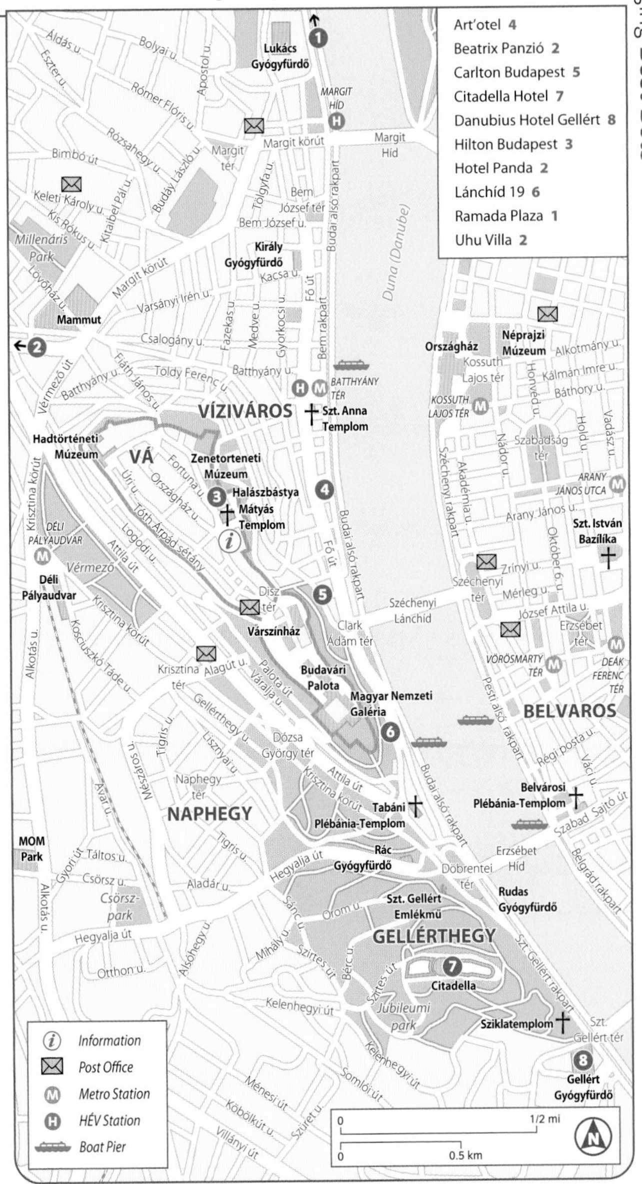

Pest Lodging

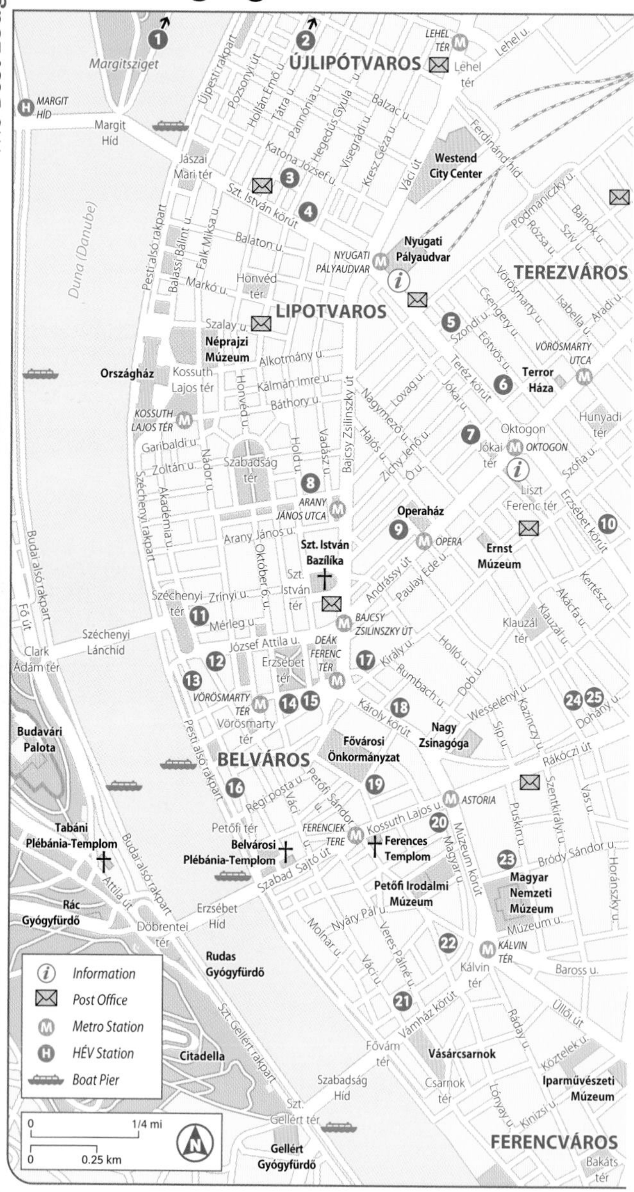

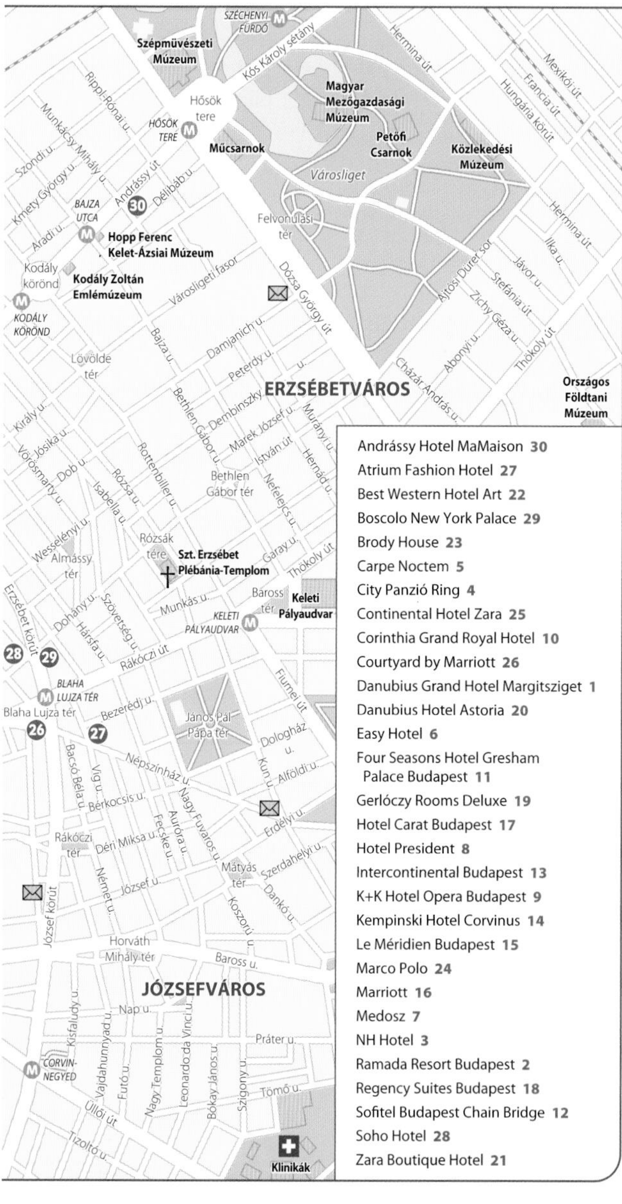
Széchenyi Fürdő
Szépművészeti Múzeum
Hősök tere
Hősök tere
Műcsarnok
Magyar Mezőgazdasági Múzeum
Petőfi Csarnok
Közlekedési Múzeum
Városliget
Kós Károly sétány
Hermina út
Mexikói út
Francia út
Hungária körút
Rippl-Rónai u.
Munkácsy Mihály u.
Szondi u.
Kmety György u.
Andrássy út
Délibáb u.
Bajza utca
Aradi u.
Hopp Ferenc Kelet-Ázsiai Múzeum
Kodály körönd
Kodály Zoltán Emlékmúzeum
Kodály körönd
Felvonulási tér
Városligeti fasor
Dózsa György út
Ajtósi Dürer sor
Stefánia út
Jávor u.
Ilka u.
Zichy Géza u.
Abonyi u.
Thököly út
Cházár András u.
Országos Földtani Múzeum
Damjanich u.
Bajza u.
Lövölde tér
Peterdy u.
ERZSÉBETVÁROS
Bethlen Gábor u.
Dembinszky u.
Marek József u.
Murányi u.
István út
Hernád u.
Király u.
Jósika u.
Vörösmarty u.
Dob u.
Rottenbiller u.
Bethlen Gábor tér
Nefelejcs u.
Isabella u.
Rózsa u.
Wesselényi u.
Almássy tér
Rózsák tere
Szt. Erzsébet Plébánia-Templom
Garay u.
Thököly út
Baross tér
Keleti Pályaudvar
Keleti Pályaudvar
Munkás u.
Erzsébet körút
Dohány u.
Szövetség u.
Hársfa u.
Rákóczi út
Fiumei út
Blaha Lujza tér
Blaha Lujza tér
Bezerédj u.
János Pál Pápa tér
Dologház u.
Népszínház u.
Bacsó Béla u.
Vig u.
Berkocsis u.
Kun u.
Alföldi u.
Nagy Fuvaros u.
Aurora u.
Fecske u.
Erdélyi u.
Rákóczi tér
Déri Miksa u.
Mátyás tér
Szerdahelyi u.
Német u.
József u.
Dankó u.
József körút
Koszorú u.
Horváth Mihály tér
Baross u.
JÓZSEFVÁROS
Nap u.
Kisfaludy u.
Vajdahunyad u.
Futó u.
Nagy Templom u.
Leonardo da Vinci u.
Bókay János u.
Szigony u.
Práter u.
Tömő u.
Corvin-negyed
Üllői út
Tűzoltó u.
Klinikák
Andrássy Hotel MaMaison 30
Atrium Fashion Hotel 27
Best Western Hotel Art 22
Boscolo New York Palace 29
Brody House 23
Carpe Noctem 5
City Panzió Ring 4
Continental Hotel Zara 25
Corinthia Grand Royal Hotel 10
Courtyard by Marriott 26
Danubius Grand Hotel Margitsziget 1
Danubius Hotel Astoria 20
Easy Hotel 6
Four Seasons Hotel Gresham Palace Budapest 11
Gerlóczy Rooms Deluxe 19
Hotel Carat Budapest 17
Hotel President 8
Intercontinental Budapest 13
K+K Hotel Opera Budapest 9
Kempinski Hotel Corvinus 14
Le Méridien Budapest 15
Marco Polo 24
Marriott 16
Medosz 7
NH Hotel 3
Ramada Resort Budapest 2
Regency Suites Budapest 18
Sofitel Budapest Chain Bridge 12
Soho Hotel 28
Zara Boutique Hotel 21

Budapest **Lodging A to Z**

★★ Andrássy Hotel MaMaison PEST Stylish Art Deco hotel with all the mod cons and designer furniture to match. It's conveniently close to Heroes' Square and houses fusion cuisine benchmark Baraka (p 103). *Andrássy út 111. ☎ 1/462-2100. www.mamaison.com. 68 units. Doubles 84€–156€. AE, DC, MC, V. Metro: M1 to Bajza utca or Hősök tere. Map p 138.*

★ Art'otel BUDA Chic hotel with a lovely Buda riverside setting, plus easy access to the Castle District and Pest, and great views to the Chain Bridge and Parliament. *Bem rakpart 16–19. ☎ 1/487-9487. www.artotel.com. 165 units. Doubles 85€–248€, without breakfast (14€). AE, MC, V. Metro: M3 to Batthány tér. Map p 137.*

★ Atrium Fashion Hotel PEST "Fashion hotel" with a striking central atrium and minimalist bijou rooms. The neighborhood is not the most salubrious but it's lively and central. *Csokonai utca 14. ☎ 1/299-0777. www.atriumhotelbudapest.com. 57 units. Doubles 54€–186€ w/breakfast. AE, MC, V. Metro: M3 to Blaha Lujza tér. Map p 138.*

kids Beatrix Panzió BUDA Clean and simple with a sense of 1970s' retro hangover, Beatrix has a relaxing homely atmosphere. Self-catering "Mediterranean" apartments for 55 to 65€ per person are also available. *Széher út 3. ☎ 1/275-0550. www.beatrixhotel.hu. 22 units. Doubles 50€–60€ w/breakfast. No credit cards. Tram: 56 to Kelemen László utca. Map p 137.*

★ Best Western Hotel Art PEST Tucked away in a charming and laidback narrow street just a step away from the action, the Art Deco columns recall this building's arty past while the modern rooms are spotless. *Király Pál utca 12. ☎ 1/266-2166. www.bwhotelart.hu. 32 units. Doubles 72€–123€ w/breakfast. AE, DC, MC, V. Metro: M3 to Kálvin tér. Map p 138.*

★★★ Boscolo New York Palace CENTRAL PEST Seriously sumptuous from the moment you walk in to the modern but classically

Andrássy Hotel MaMaison's terrace.

influenced Italianate lobby, this hotel also houses the legendary New York Kávéház (coffeehouse) (p 35). *Erzsébet körút 9–11. ☎ 1/886-6111. www.boscolohotels.com. 112 units. Doubles 145€–250€ w/breakfast. AE, DC, MC, V. Metro: M3 Blaha Lujza tér. Map p 138.*

★★ **Brody House** PEST Individually designed bedrooms with en suite facilities named after the cutting-edge Brody House artists whose works feature in the rooms. This hip arts center, fits in beautifully with the renewal of Pest's Palace Quarter, and gives off a creative vibe. *Bródy Sándor utca 10. ☎ 1/266-1211. www.brodyhouse.com. 8 units. Doubles 55€–95€ w/breakfast. MC, V. Metro: M2 to Kálvin tér/M3 to Astoria. Map p 138.*

★ **Carlton Budapest** CASTLE DISTRICT Great location on a steep quiet street at the foot of the Castle District close to the Danube and Chain Bridge. Rooms are immaculate but can be on the small side. *Apor Péter utca 3. ☎ 1/224-0999. www.carltonhotel.hu. 95 units. Doubles 65€–115€ w/breakfast. AE, DC, MC, V. Metro: M2 to Batthány tér. Map p 137.*

Carpe Noctem PEST This scooped the World's Most Fun Hostel and overall number 5 at Hostelworld's 2009 Hoscars ceremony. This clean, super sociable hostel, with orthopedic mattresses, is run by helpful culture vultures. Over 40s not admitted, though they are welcome at the team's more tranquil Carpe Noctem Vitae (www.carpenoctempenthouse.hostel.com). *Szobi utca 5, III/8a. ☎ 06/20-365-8749. www.carpenoctemhostel.com. 24 mixed dorm beds. 3,300 Ft–6,000 Ft. No credit cards. Forints only. Metro: M3 to Nyugati pályaudvar. Map p 138.*

Citadella Hotel BUDA Basic hotel with superb views over the river to most of Pest and much of Buda, from where the Austrian occupiers used to keep watch over the Magyars below. *Citadella sétány. ☎ 1/466-5794. www.citadella.hu. 12 units. Doubles 30€–49€. No credit cards. Bus: 27. Map p 137.*

City Panzió Ring PEST Tidy, comfortable, no-thrills, reasonably priced, and on a major Pest thoroughfare close to Margaret Island. Can be noisy in rooms overlooking the street but these are brighter than facing the courtyard. *Szent István Körút 22. ☎ 1/340-5450 or 1/340-4884. www.taverna.hu. 39 units. Doubles 47€–72€ w/breakfast. AE, MC, V. Metro: M2 to Nyugati pályaudvar. Map p 138.*

★★★ **Continental Hotel Zara** PEST Award-winning new four-star superior hotel in a building that once housed a public bathing house. The remarkable Art Nouveau exterior has been strikingly restored while Art Deco dominates the interior. It has modern design rooms, conference facilities, and a roof garden, and houses the popular Azaz restaurant. *Dohány utca 42–44. ☎ 1/815-1000. www.continentalhotelbudapest.com. 272 units. Doubles 70€–110€ w/breakfast. AE, MC, V. Metro: M2 to Blaha Lujza tér. Map p 138.*

★★★ **Corinthia Grand Royal Hotel** PEST Behind the beautifully restored Habsburg-period facade lies a seriously swish interior that brilliantly combines the best of old and new. The swanky rooms, awesome atrium, grand ballroom, and spa facilities are a treat. *Erzsébet körút 43–49. ☎ 1/479-4000. www.corinthiahotels.com. 414 units. Doubles 130€–350€, without breakfast (28€). AE, DC, MC, V. Metro: M1 to Oktogon. Map p 138.*

The Tepper Room, Brody House.

★ Courtyard by Marriott PEST This four-star version of the Marriott provides contemporary comfort in a traditional setting. It's sufficiently slick and practical, located in a lively part of Pest, if not the most salubrious. Popular with business travelers. *Blaha Lujza tér 3–5. ☎ 1/235-4888. www.courtyardbudapestcitycenter.com. 235 units. Doubles 89€–160€ w/breakfast. AE, DC, MC, V. Metro: M2 to Blaha Lujza tér. Map p 138.*

★★ Danubius Grand Hotel Margitsziget MARGARET ISLAND This handsome old-world riverside building is handily connected to the outstanding spa and sporting facilities of its sportier-looking Margaret Island twin by tunnel. *Margitsziget. ☎ 1/889-4752. www.danubiusgroup.com/grandhotel. 164 units. Doubles 137€–180€ w/breakfast. AE, DC, MC, V. Bus: 26 to Szállodák (Hotels). Map p 138.*

★★ Danubius Hotel Astoria PEST Bastion of old-world charm in a very central location, this hotel is clean and comfortable with plenty of marble, elaborate carpets, crystal chandeliers, myriad mirrors, and stained-glass windows. *Kossuth Lajos utca 19–21. ☎ 1/889-6000. www.danubiusgroup.com/astoria. 135 units. Doubles 69€–120€. AE, MC, V. Metro: M3 to Astoria.*

★★ Danubius Hotel Gellért BUDA You experience a unique lived-in atmosphere here, seemingly unchanged since the last days of the Austro-Hungarian Empire. This hotel features an Art Nouveau exterior with seriously eclectic rooms. Now has free Wi-Fi and guests also have free access to the deliciously Art Nouveau Gellért Baths via a private elevator. *Szent Gellért tér 1. ☎ 1/889-5501. www.danubiusgroup.com/gellert. 234 units. Doubles 70€–240€. AE, DC, MC, V. Tram: 18/19/47/49 to Szent Gellért tér. Map p 137.*

Easy Hotel PEST Bargain prices for clean, albeit orange, rooms in downtown Pest. Book online in the same way as budget air tickets, whereby the cheaper rooms sell out first. *Eötvös utca 25/a. www.easyhotel.com. 59 units. Doubles from 35€. Pay over the Internet. with all major credit cards. Tram: 4/6 to Oktogon.* *Map p 138.*

★★★ Four Seasons Hotel Gresham Palace Budapest
PEST Looking right onto the splendor of the Chain Bridge and with stunningly restored Art Nouveau interior and rooms, outstanding service, breakfasts, and spa, this is the place to splash out. The rooms maintain an elegant but not over-stated Art Nouveau style. *Széchenyi tér 5–6. ☎ 1/268 6000. www.fourseasons.com/budapest. Doubles 290€–410€ w/breakfast. AE, DC, MC, V. Tram: 2. Bus: 16/105 to Széchenyi István tér.* *Map p 138.*

★★ Gerlóczy Rooms Deluxe
PEST Immaculate rooms elegantly furnished and true to the style of this charming 1892 building, which also houses the excellent Gerlóczy coffeehouse (p 36). It overlooks a charming and less discovered square. *Gerlóczy utca 1. ☎ 1/501-4000. www.gerloczy.hu/roomsdelux/. 15 units. Doubles 114€ w/breakfast. AE, MC, V. Metro: M1/M2/M3 to Deák tér.* *Map p 138.*

★★ Hilton Budapest BUDA
This Hilton is built around the remnants of a 13th-century Dominican church, which are still visible, and in the heart of Castle Hill, with splendid views to Pest. Popular for business conferences. *Hess András tér 1–3. ☎ 1/889-6600. www.budapest.hilton.com. 322 units. Doubles 128€–208€, without breakfast (28€). AE, DC, MC, V. Bus 16/16A/116 to Szentháromság tér.* *Map p 137.*

★ Hotel Carat Budapest PEST
A modern design hotel featuring contrasting shades of color, seamlessly integrated into a pristinely refurbished Belle Epoque townhouse. This four-star superior hotel has a great location on trendy Király utca. *Király utca 6. ☎ 1/235-4600. www.hotelcarat.hu. 50 units. Doubles 59€–99€ w/breakfast. AE, MC, V. Metro: M1/M2/M3 to Deák tér.* *Map p 138.*

Hotel Panda BUDA Fresh, spacious, and colorful, this Socialist-era hotel overlooks Bauhaus Pasaréti tér. Spa facilities include massage and sauna. *Pasaréti út 133. ☎ 1/394-1932. www.budapesthotelpanda.hu. 29 units. Doubles 70€–80€ w/breakfast. AE, MC, V. Bus: 5 to Pasaréti tér.* *Map p 137.*

Elegant décor at Gerlóczy Rooms Deluxe.

Kempinski Hotel Corvinus.

★★★ Hotel President PEST Luxurious five-star hotel that strikingly fuses old world style with modern touches, located directly opposite Odon Lechner's Art Nouveau masterpiece of the National Savings Treasury. *Hold utca 3–5. ☎ 1/373-8200. www.hotelpresident.hu. 110 units. Doubles from 109€. AE, DC, MC, V. Metro: M3 to Arany János utca. Map p 138.*

★★ Intercontinental Budapest PEST Although the building is looking a bit dated, the Pest riverside location next to the Chain Bridge and opposite Buda Castle is still hard to beat. Pleasant decor with very good conference facilities. *Apaczai Csere János utca. 12–14. ☎ 1/327-6333. www.budapest.intercontinental.com. 402 units. Doubles 100€–250€ w/breakfast. AE, DC, MC, V. Metro: M1 to Vörösmarty tér. Map p 138.*

K+K Hotel Opera Budapest PEST A superior offering in a prime central location, next to the Opera House but down a quiet side street. Modern, elegant, warm colors, and comfortable furnishings. *Révay utca 24. ☎ 1/269-0222. www.hu.kkhotels.com. 200 units. Doubles 70€–150€ w/breakfast. AE, MC, V. Metro: M1/M2/M3 to Deák tér. Map p 138.*

★★ Kempinski Hotel Corvinus PEST The king of Budapest's luxury hotels, until a wave of others came along to challenge its crown. Although starting to look a bit dated you can find some competitive prices by booking ahead. Home to Budapest's nouveau Japanese Nobu restaurant. *Erzsébet tér 7–8. ☎ 1/429 3777. www.kempinski-budapest.com. 366 units. Doubles 120€–439€, without breakfast (25€). AE, DC, MC, V. Metro: M1/M2/M3 to Deák tér. Map p 138.*

★★★ Lánchíd 19 BUDA Seriously chic designer hotel with each room decorated with its own unique arty touches. Splash out on a suite for 292€, laze in the bath, and watch the Danube flow by. *Lánchíd utca 19–21. ☎ 1/419-1900. www.lanchid19hotel.hu. 48 units. Doubles 65€–110€, without breakfast (12€). MC, V. Tram 19 or buses 16/105 to Clark Ádám tér. Map p 137.*

★★ Le Méridien Budapest PEST This classy and central hotel is big boutique rather than large chain and has a top French restaurant, Le Bourbon (p 105). *Erzsébet tér 9–10. ☎ 1/429-5500. www.lemeridien-budapest.com. 218 units. Doubles from 239€.. AE, DC, MC, V. Metro: M1/M2/M3 to Deák tér. Map p 138.*

Marco Polo PEST A bargain option offering everything from private rooms to dorms in the heart of the Jewish district's bar scene. Prices start from as little as 12€ per night in the dorm, with curtains dividing each bunk. *Nyár utca 6. ☎ 1/413-2555. www.marcopolo*

hostel.com. 56 units. Doubles 48€–84€. Metro: M2 to Blaha Lujza tér. Tram: 4/6 to Blaha Lujza tér. Map p 138.

★★ **Marriott** PEST Renovated from top to bottom a couple of years back, with rooms kitted out with the mega-comfy Marriott Revive Bedding and fantastic views over the river to the Buda Palace. Drink Bling deluxe water in the AQVA Lounge Bar. *Apaczai Csere Janos utca 4. ☎ 1/486 5000. www.marriott.com. 364 units. 119€–225€, excluding taxes and breakfast. AE, DC, MC, V. Metro: M1 to Vörösmarty tér. Map p 138.*

Medosz Pest The building could be considered a Socialist-period monstrosity but it's ideally located in downtown Pest, well priced, clean, and comfortable, and just the place for someone looking to sleep behind the original "iron curtain." *Jókai tér 9. ☎ 1/374-3000. www.medosz hotel.hu. 69 units. Doubles 59€–69€ w/breakfast. AE, MC, V. Metro: M1 to Oktogon. Tram: 4/6 to Oktogon. Map p 138.*

★★ **NH Hotel** PEST Stylish and exceedingly modern hotel tucked away behind the Vígszínház, the oldest theater in Budapest. It's close to Margaret Island, and blends in tastefully with the old buildings in neighborhood. *Vígszínház utca 3. ☎ 1/814-0000. www.nh-hotels.com. Doubles 113€–164€ w/breakfast. AE, DC, V, MC. Metro: M2 Nuygati. Map p 138.*

★ **Ramada Plaza** ÓBUDA Luxury choice for business or pleasure on the banks of the Danube in Óbuda over the water from Margaret Island. Excellent thermal and wellness facilities on the site where Romans once bathed. *Árpád fejedelem útja 94. ☎ 1/436-4100. 182 units. 100€–240€ w/breakfast. AE, DC, MC, V. Suburban railway: HÉV to Árpád híd. Map p 137.*

★★ **Ramada Resort Budapest** OUTER PEST Swish wellness and conference hotel on the edge of Budapest with direct access to Aquaworld water theme park, which entails a separate charge. *Íves út 16. ☎ 1/231-3600. www.ramadaresort budapest.hu. 309 units. Doubles 100€–180€ w/breakfast. AE, MC, V. Bus: Free shuttle bus departs from outside the Museum of Fine Arts next to Heroes' Square every hour on the hour, except noon, 1pm, and 3pm. Map p 138.*

★ **Regency Suites Budapest** PEST Opened in 2010, this centrally located hotel boasts the biggest room sizes in the category in the city. Terrific view of Budapest from its rooftop bar, plus a pleasant bijou conference room that looks out onto the Basilica. A direct bus

Uhu Villa offers a quiet retreat within the city limits.

from the airport stops here. *Madách Imre tér 2.* ☎ *1/801-6300. www.regencysuites.hu. 42 units. Doubles 80€–100€ w/breakfast. AE, DC, MC, V. Metro: M1/M2/M3 to Deák tér. Map p 138.*

★★ **Sofitel Budapest Chain Bridge** PEST Socialist-era exterior but delightful interior with expertly applied modern touches including a funky airplane in the striking lobby. *Széchenyi tér 2.* ☎ *1/266-1234. www.sofitel.com. 350 units. 193€–350€ double, 2,500€ suite, excluding taxes and breakfast (27€). AE, DC, MC, V. Metro: M1 to Vörösmarty tér. Map p 138.*

★ **Soho Hotel** PEST Designer hotel that extends into the townhouse next door. The smallish rooms feature Swedish wooden floors and sound proofing while the two vampire suites will thrill gothic lovers. *Dohány utca 64.* ☎ *1/872-8292. www.sohoboutiquehotel.com. 74 units. Doubles 59€–139€ w/breakfast. AE, DC, MC, V. Metro: M2 to Blaha Lujza tér. Map p 138.*

★★★ **Uhu Villa** BUDA Cozy, friendly, and tastefully decorated with its own swimming pool, Uhu offers peace and quiet within the city limits. Most love it but a few gripe about its hilltop location, 10 minutes on foot from the nearest tram stop. *Keselyű utca 1/a.* ☎ *1/275-1002. www.uhuvilla.hu. 12 units. Rooms from 65€–100€, without breakfast (10€). MC, V. Tram: 56 to Akadémia. Map p 137.*

★★ **Zara Boutique Hotel** PEST Minimalism nicely executed with no expense spared on furnishings, Zara is a cool option in this enjoyable part of downtown Pest. No wellness facilities but guests can use sister hotel Continental Hotel Zara's (see p 141) plush facilities for free. *Só utca 6.* ☎ *1/357-6170. www.zarahotels.com. 74 units. Doubles 90€–129€ w/breakfast. AE, MC, V. Metro: M3 to Kálvin tér. Map p 138.* ●

Rooftop garden, Continental Hotel Zara.

10 The Best Day Trips & Excursions

The Danube Bend

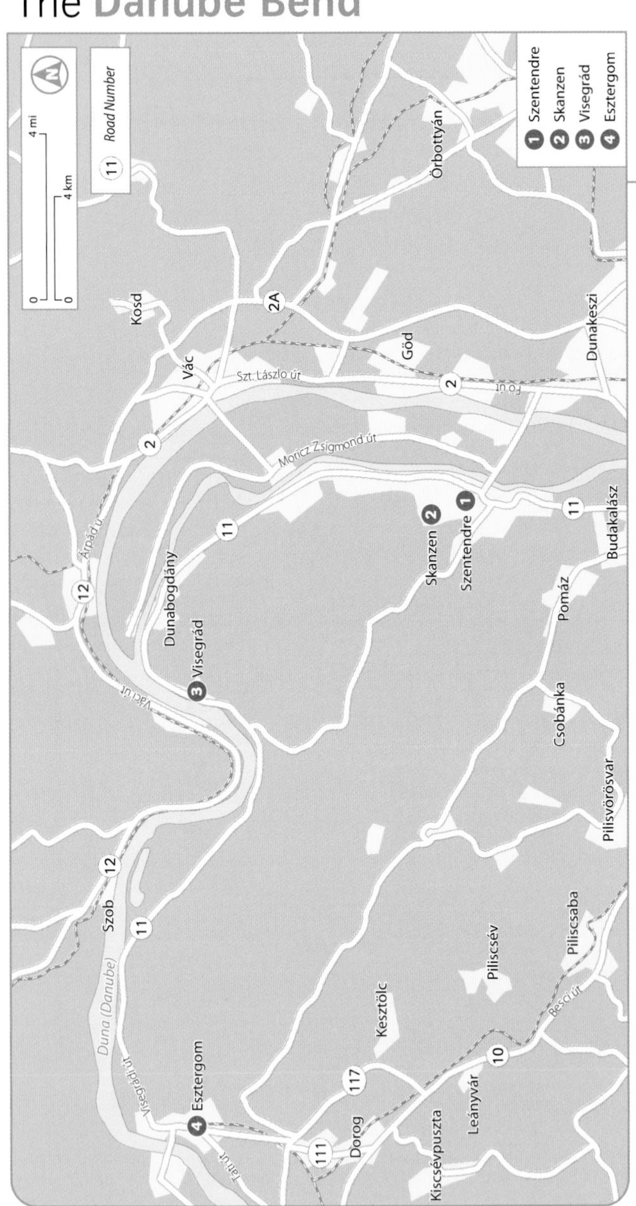

Previous page: Lake Balaton.

One of the prettiest stretches of the entire length of the Danube is blessed with three towns steeped in history, each of which I describe here. At a push, you could see them all in a day, but a more manageable approach might involve Szentendre on one day, and Visegrád and Esztergom together on another. START: **Batthány tér to take HÉV suburban train to Szentendre; or Árpád híd bus station in Pest for Visegrád; or Pest's Nuygati station for Esztergom.**

Travel Tip

Road 11 connects all the towns in this tour and follows the twisting Danube.

★★★ ❶ **Szentendre.** Of all the easy short hops from Budapest, Szentendre packs in the most history and color. The town is certainly on the tourist radar and attracts large numbers of visitors. See Minitour, p 150.

❷ ★★ kids **Skanzen.** A sprawling open-air ethnographical museum that offers far more than a mere walk around the exhibits. Skanzen brings the past to life with buildings and scenes from various parts of the country recreated, and youngsters are encouraged to join in and make traditional wares. *2–3 hr. Sztaravodai út. ☎ 26/502-500. www.skanzen.hu. 1,400 Ft adults, 700 Ft children 6–26 and seniors 62–70. Apr–Oct Tues–Sun 9am–5pm. Bus: 7 from Szentendre's Hév station. Follow the signs to Szabadtéri Néprajzi Múzeum. Also direct bus from Budapest—check website for details.*

From Szentendre it's 22km (13.5 miles) by road to Visegrád.

❸ ★★★ **Visegrád.** The smallest town in Hungary is towered over by an imposing medieval citadel, which along with the lower castle was originally built by Béla IV in the 13th century to keep out the Mongols. The Royal Palace dates from the 14th century when Charles Robert of Anjou (1307–42) moved the Royal Court here. You can visit it at the **Mátyás Király Múzeum** (King Mathias Museum) at Fő utca 27 (☎ 26/398-026; www.visegradmuzeum.hu). The **Visegrád International Royal Palace Fair** (www.palotajatekok.hu) takes place annually in July with a medieval parade, jousting tournaments with dueling knights, and traditional medieval music. *3–4 hr. www.visegrad.hu. Bus: from Szentendre or Árpád híd bus station in Pest.*

From Visegrád it's 24km (15 miles) to Esztergom.

❹ ★★★ **Esztergom.** Although the center of the Hungarian Catholic

The colorful town of Szentendre.

1A Požarevačka Church, the first Serbian Orthodox church you'll encounter on your way from the station, sets the scene: it seems like just another Hungarian baroque Catholic church from the outside, but notice how it points east as Serbian Orthodox churches do and is somewhat out of sync with its neighboring buildings. Inside, the intricate iconostasis that dates back to 1742 is actually older than the church itself by around 20 years. The chocolate box beauty of the cobblestoned main square **1B Fő tér** was bankrolled for the most part by wealthy Serbian immigrants, and has the Orthodox **1C Blagoveštenska Church** as its centerpiece. Take some time to explore the beautiful cobbled main streets that run off the main square, going where the mood takes you, and then lose the tourist hordes by exploring the steep, narrow streets. This is one of the joys of being in Szentendre and reveals the town's real beauty.

Next, walk up to the Catholic church of **1D Szent János.** Although the church itself is nothing to write home about, the views of the town, the river, and the surrounding hills make the short uphill walk from the main square so worthwhile.

The burgundy-colored **1E Belgrade Orthodox Church** is situated behind high protective walls and served as the seat of the Serbian Orthodox Church during the occupation by the Turks. The adjoining museum is full of religious articles related to church life, colorful in the way that only Orthodox ecclesiastical items can be.

Finally, take a walk along the banks of the Danube, where the river is wide and majestic. *3 hr. Szentendre Tourist Information Office, Dumtsa J. utca 22. ☎ 26/317-965. www.szentendre.extra.hu. Last stop on HÉV suburban train that starts at Batthány tér (approx. 40 min).*

Szentendre Shopping

Although there are heaps of tacky souvenirs to find here, you can still seek out some unique things too in the town's boutiques and galleries. Shops such as the **Blue Land Folklor** (Alkotmány utca) has proper non-schmaltzy folk art, whilst **Palmetta** (Bogdányi út 14) stocks cutting-edge designer textiles from Anna Regős and **Salon de Bohéme** at (Péter Pál utca 2b) houses the owner Szidónia Szép's contemporary fashions among collections by many other like-minded unconventional designers.

Church, Esztergom has a remarkable number of bars, and in this easy-going riverside border town, like most frontier posts, there's no shortage of opportunities to enjoy yourself. The biggest church in Hungary, **Esztergom Basilica** (☎ 33/402-354; www.bazilika-esztergom.hu), is situated on St. Thomas Hill, opposite what must be one of Hungary's smallest. Climb the hill (it's a 3.5km/2-mile walk or take bus no. 1 or 6) to see the neoclassical cathedral and step inside to admire the world's largest painted altarpiece. From the hill you can stare over to Slovakia (in the summer you can walk up to the cupola of the cathedral, though it's not for the claustrophobic with its narrow walkways and staircase) or walk over the bridge and enjoy some fine Slovakian draft beer. 🕘 *3–4 hr. Bus: from Visegrád. Train: direct from Pest's Nyugati station.*

Learn about traditional household crafts at Skanzen.

A Wine Country Detour

Hungary's wines are one of its best-kept secrets and its wine regions are an engaging blend of rustic charm and state-of-the-art new wineries. It's best to call wineries ahead of visiting and worth staying over at most of Hungary's wine regions. START: **All regions can also be reached by train or bus (check www.elvira.hu and www.volanbusz.hu respectively for timetables).**

1 ★★★ **Eger.** The region famous for the generally lowly reputed, mass-market Bull's Blood wine now has Bikavér Superior, a more refined, limited-yield version of the classic red blend as its flagship. The increasingly sophisticated Central European indigenous grape Kékfrankos forms the backbone of most Bikavér. Eger is also a serious region for white wines. Two notable wineries are: **Nimród Kóvács winery** at Verőszala utca 66 (☎ 36/537-232; www.kovacsnimrodwinery.com) and **St. Andrea,** the latter being a few kilometers out of town close to a thermal resort in Egerszalók at Ady Endre utca 88 (☎: 36/474-018; www.standrea.hu). *140km (87 miles) east of Budapest on E71/M3, taking E71/M3 then exit 114 and road 33.*

2 **Etyek.** Etyek makes for a nice excursion in itself but its crispy white wines are even more reason to make the 30km (19-mile) trip from Budapest. Up on Öreg hegy, **Etyeki Kúria** (☎ 0630-922-5261) has mastered reductive fruity style Pinot Gris, but also look out for its floral and elegant Királyleányka and delicious Sauvignon Blanc. Its Pinot Noir is much decorated. *30km (19 miles) west of Budapest on E60/M1, exiting at Biatorbágy.*

Travel Tip

In Badacsony a dedicated bus runs between some excellent wineries from June to September.

3 **Lake Balaton.** The many soils and micro-climates around the "Hungarian Sea" present the Hungarian wine world in microcosm. The black volcanic basalt "organ pipes" that rise up at **Badacsony** set the tone for the area's predominantly white mineral-infused wines. **Szeremley** wines put Badacsony on

Grapes growing around Lake Balaton.

the path to renown and the winery has an excellent restaurant with sweeping views of the lake where you can taste. *On the other side of the lake out on Kishegy in Balatonlelle in the Balaton Boglár region, the Konyári Winery (☎ 85/700-096; www.konyari.hu), makes big, spicy Bordeaux-style blends, exciting Kékfrankos, as well as sophisticated whites. Saint Orbán Wine House Restaurant at Kisfaludy S. utca 5 in Badacsony. ☎ 87/431-382. www.szeremley.com. M7 to Balaton.*

❹ **Pannonhalma.** Near the town of Győr, the **Benedictine Monastery of Pannonhalma** at Pannonhalma, Vár 1 (☎ 96/570-171; www.apatsagipinceszet.hu) is situated strikingly above a quaint village. The UNESCO-listed monastery is well worth visiting in its own right and has its own state-of-the-art gravity-fed winery making excellent Tramini, Riesling, and Pinot Noir, among others. It also has the stunning **Viator** restaurant (☎ 96/570-200), which impresses in terms of its contemporary design and its quality kitchen that's run by the same people behind Budapest favorite Klassz (p 101). *133km (82.5 miles) west of Budapest on E60/M1–82.*

❺ ★★ **Szekszárd.** Rapidly emerging from the big red shadow cast by Villány, Szekszárd is also doing well in international competitions with Bordeaux blends. The red Kadarka grape is a local specialty and can make delicious light but spicy reds. One of its finest proponents is the **Bodri cellar,** which has won international awards for many different wines. It unveiled a brand new winery and visitor center in summer 2010 at Vitéz utca 1 (☎ 06/20-440-6666; www.bodribor.hu). Eight kilometers (5 miles) south of Szekszárd in the direction of Mohács, **Takler** makes big, award-winning tannic reds and offers accommodation at Decsi-Szőlőhegy PL. 57 (☎ 74/311-961; www. www.takler.com). Unlike in Villány, wineries are far apart. *180km (112 miles) south of Budapest. Take E73.*

❻ ★★★ **Somló.** Hungary's smallest wine region is known for its fiery, savory white wine. Britain's Queen Victoria loved it, especially when she heard about the propensity for women who imbibed wines made from Somló grape Juhfark (Sheep Tail) to mother male offspring. The **Kreinbacher winery** (☎ 88/506-212) is one that has succeeded in making polished, well-balanced, and fruity wines that have plenty of Somló's minerality in them. *164km/102 miles west of Budapest. Take E71/M7 until exit 64 and connect with the E66/8 and head past Veszprém*

Nimród Kóvács winery, Eger.

Villany, Hungary's leading red wine region.

to Somlóvásárhely where you'll see Somló Hill.

7 ★★★ **Tokaj.** Tokaj has the world's oldest wine classification system and its sumptuous elixirs were once the favorites of European royalty. Hungary's one undeniably world-class region is blessed with its position at the confluence of the Bodrog and Tisza rivers. The mist that rises here enables "noble rot" that concentrates the sweetness of wine. The region is also privileged with unique volcanic soils and a distinct portfolio of grapes led by Furmint and Hárslevelű. The only problem for Tokaj now is that sweet wine isn't the flavor of modern times. Yet the taste of one of these sublime elixirs, when made in the modern style, emphasizes freshness and sumptuous acidity, rather than overt sweetness. Also, less intense late-harvest styles and bone-dry Furmints are gaining ground. **Disznókő** at Mezőzombor, the Mád-Tarcal junction of the 37 road (☎ 47/569-410; www.disznoko.hu), is one of the easiest to visit, and one of the best, as well as the first you'll encounter coming in from Budapest. *Tokaj town is 233km (145 miles) north-east of Budapest. Take E71/M3—E71—E71/M30—E71/3 and take junction 37 to enter the region.*

8 ★★★ **Villány.** Although Cabernet Sauvignon and Merlot are good here in Hungary's leading red wine region, it's the lesser-known Bordeaux varietal Cabernet Franc that seems most at home and capable of unique expression. Local grape Portugieser makes enjoyable easy-drinking reds. Most of Villány's wineries can be accessed on foot, on and around the high street. **Attila Gere,** whose blockbusting Bordeaux-style reds helped put Villány in the spotlight, has a large modern winery and visitor center at Erkel Ferenc utca 2/A (☎ 72/492-839; www.gere.hu), plus the four-star superior **Crocus Wellness Hotel** and top restaurant in the village center at Diófás tér 4–12 (☎ 72/492-195). The **Sauska** winery has shot straight to the top with reds of outstanding fruit and power. It's located between the Attila Gere and Wunderlich wineries. ☎ *72/592-120. 234km (145.5 miles) south of Budapest. Take the same direction as Szekszárd, passing it and later taking road 57.*

Lake Balaton

The oft dubbed "Hungarian Sea" is circled by a range of varied attractions and is much more than a place to go sailing with the in-crowd or for basking on the banks of the water. These contrasting towns will give you an essence of Balaton and are best enjoyed over a few days. START: **Trains depart regularly from Budapest's Déli station (for an interactive timetable go to www.elvira.hu) and take between 1¾ and 3 hours.**

1 ★★ **Balatonfüred.** The biggest resort town on the northern shore has an elegant old world feel, at least in parts, which is surviving well alongside the modern hotel developments. Take a stroll around the waterfront, stopping for some deep-fried fish and maybe a swim on the deeper northern side. *Balatonfüred Tourist Information Office, Kisfaludy utca 1. ☎ 87/580-480. www.balatonfured.hu.*

2 ★★★ **Tihány.** This pretty peninsula town is just 4km (2.5 miles) from Balatonfüred. The narrowest point of the lake is topped off by the epic twin-towered **Tihanyi Bencés Apátság** (Benedictine Abbey), which hangs dramatically over the water. It features an eerie crypt housing the engraved tomb of András, Hungary's very first king of that name, buried here in 1060. He also founded the still-functioning Abbey. *Tihany Tourist Information Office, Kossuth utca 20. ☎ 87/448-804. www.tihany.hu.*

3 ★★★ **Keszthely.** A rare pearl of baroque beauty after countless repetitive resorts, Keszthely is home to the **Festetics Palace** at Szabadság utca 1 (☎ 83/314-194; www.helikonkastely.hu). The abode of charitable counts, they built a hospital and the world's first agricultural university, the latter now being part of the University of Pannonia. *Keszthely Tourist Information Office, Kossuth utca 28. ☎ 83/314-144. www.keszthely.hu.*

Lake Balaton.

4 **Hévíz.** A uniquely curative thermal lake close to Keszthely, rich in minerals, with the contents of the lake changed every 3 days. Now that's fresh! *www.spaheviz.hu. 2,400 Ft for 3 hr.*

5 **Siófok.** This is the undisputed party capital of Balaton, but it also has some pleasant beaches away from the action. The southern side has a very shallow shelf around waist height, which makes the water warm. *Siófok Tourist Information Office, Víztorony (Water Tower). ☎ 84/315-355. www.siofoktourism.com.*

Pécs

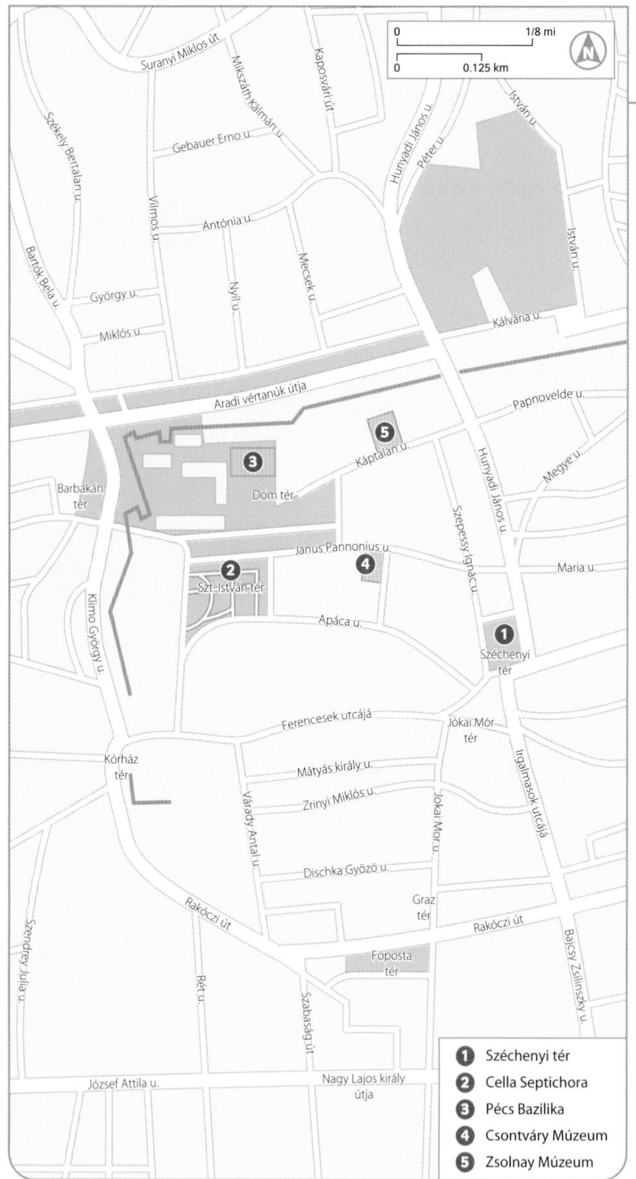
0
1/8 mi
0
0.125 km
N
Suranyi Miklos út
Mikszáth Kálmán u.
Kaposvári út
Székely Bertalan u.
Gebauer Erno u.
Hunyadi János u.
Péter u.
István u.
Vilmos u.
Antónia u.
Bartók Bela u.
Nyíl u.
Mecsek u.
István u.
György u.
Miklós u.
Kálvária u.
Aradi vértanúk útja
Papnovelde u.
Káptalan u.
Megye u.
Barbakán tér
Dóm tér
Hunyadi János u.
Szepessy Ignác u.
Janus Pannonius u.
Maria u.
Szt. István tér
Klimo György u.
Apáca u.
Széchenyi tér
Ferencesek utcájá
Jókai Mór tér
Kórház tér
Mátyás király u.
Irgalmasok utcájá
Zrinyi Miklós u.
Várady Antal u.
Jokai Mor u.
Dischka Győző u.
Graz tér
Rakóczi út
Rakóczi út
Bajcsy Zsilinszky u.
Szendrey Julia u.
Főposta tér
Rét u.
Szabaság út
József Attila u.
Nagy Lajos király útja
1 Széchenyi tér
2 Cella Septichora
3 Pécs Bazilika
4 Csontváry Múzeum
5 Zsolnay Múzeum

Pécs is often touted as the Hungarian town with a mellow Mediterranean vibe, but you can also feel an influence from the Eastern Mediterranean Muslim world. This European City of Culture can be enjoyed on foot with all the attractions close to each other. START: **Train from Déli pályaudvar (Southern train station).**

1 ★★★ kids **Széchenyi tér.** This sloping and striking old town central square displays in its architecture some of the most significant periods in the city's history. The **Church of St. Mary** in Turkish times was the Mosque of Pasha Gazi Kasim and still has a praying niche toward Mecca. Below it there's a baroque holy statue, and a remarkable Art Nouveau Zsolnay fountain. The classy bar- and restaurant-lined Király utca runs off the square. The Mediterranean-style bistro **Corso Restaurant** at Király utca 14 (☎ 72/525-198; www.susogo.hu) is best of an ever-improving bunch. ⌚ *45 min. Széchenyi tér.*

2 ★★★ **Cella Septichora (Early Christian Cemetery).** A short walk away, this UNESCO-listed series of 4th-century underground burial chambers features lavish murals depicting Christian themes and memorial chapels above ground. ⌚ *45 min. Séta tér, just above Szent István tér. www.septichora.hu. 1,200 Ft adults, 600 Ft children. Apr–Oct Tues–Sun 10am–6pm; Nov–Mar Tues–Sun 10am–4pm.*

3 ★★ **Pécs Bazilika (Cathedral).** An impressive neo-Romanesque cathedral with elaborate frescoes painted by local and international artists including Bertelan Székely, Károly Lotz, Moritz von Beckerath, and Karl Andrea. ⌚ *45 min. Dóm tér.* ☎ *72/513-030. Apr–Oct Mon–Sat 9am–5pm, Sun 1–5pm; Nov–Mar Mon–Sat 10am–4pm, Sun 1–4pm.*

4 ★★★ **Csontváry Múzeum.** Csontváry is my favorite Hungarian artist, mainly for his originality and ability to breathe new life into tired themes. This superb museum houses a comprehensive collection of his works. ⌚ *1 hr. Janus Pannonius utca 11.* ☎ *72/310-554. 1,200 Ft adults, 600 Ft children, 3,400 Ft family, free for under-6s. Apr–Oct Tues–Sun 10am–6pm; Nov–Mar Tues–Sun 10am–4pm.*

The town Hall on Széchenyi tér.

5 ★★ **Zsolnay Múzeum.** The tiles that adorn many of Budapest's finest buildings like St. Matthias Church (p 61, **2**) and the Applied Arts Museum (p 15, **8**) hail from Pécs' Zsolnay. See the rise and fall of its irrepressible iridescent eosin technology. ⌚ *45 min. Káptalan utca 2.* ☎ *72/514-040. 1,200 Ft adults, 600 Ft children, 3,400 Ft family, free for under-6s. Apr–Oct Tues–Sun 10am–6pm; Nov–Mar Tues–Sun 10am–4pm.*

Eger

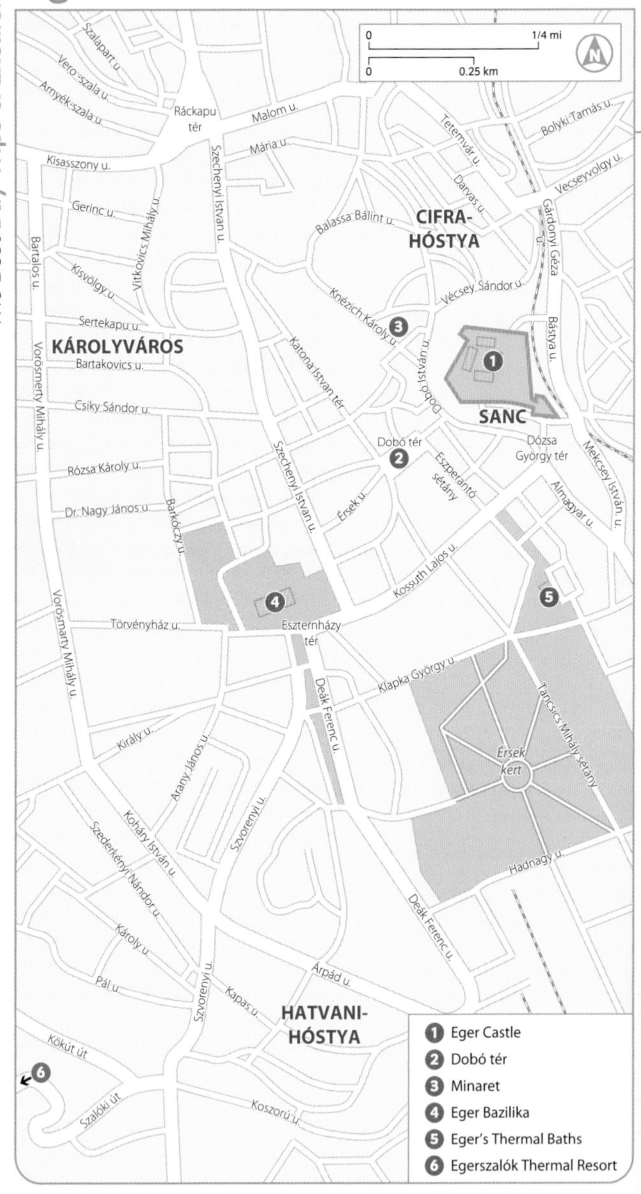
0
1/4 mi
0
0.25 km
N
Szalapart u.
Vero-szala u.
Árnyék-szala u.
Ráckapu tér
Malom u.
Mária u.
Kisasszony u.
Tetemvár u.
Bolyki Tamás u.
Darvas u.
Vecseyvölgy u.
Gerinc u.
Vitkovics Mihály u.
Szechenyi István u.
Balassa Bálint u.
CIFRA-HÓSTYA
Gárdonyi Géza u.
Bartalos u.
Kisvölgy u.
Vécsey Sándor u.
Knézich Károly u.
Sertekapu u.
Bástya u.
KÁROLYVÁROS
Bartakovics u.
Katona István tér
Dobó István u.
Csiky Sándor u.
SANC
Vorösmerty Mihály u.
Dobó tér
Dózsa György tér
Rózsa Károly u.
Eszperantó sétány
Mekcsey István u.
Almagyar u.
Dr. Nagy János u.
Érsek u.
Barkóczy u.
Kossuth Lajos u.
Törvényház u.
Eszterházy tér
Klapka György u.
Deák Ferenc u.
Tancsics Mihály sétány
Király u.
Arany János u.
Érsek kert
Szvorenyi u.
Koháry István u.
Szederkényi Nándor u.
Hadnagy u.
Károly u.
Árpád u.
Pál u.
Szvorenyi u.
Kapas u.
HATVANI-HÓSTYA
Kökút út
Szalóki út
Koszorú u.
1 Eger Castle
2 Dobó tér
3 Minaret
4 Eger Bazilika
5 Eger's Thermal Baths
6 Egerszalók Thermal Resort

Eger, together with its castle, is an iconic symbol of Hungarian defiance, when the "Stars of Eger" successfully repelled a mammoth Turkish force in 1552, after Budapest fell in the 1540s. Eger rebuilt itself at the height of the baroque period and the result is stunning, making for a sensational walking tour. START: **Train from Keleti pályaudvar (Eastern railway station), Budapest.**

Practical Information

For more information on Eger, contact the Tourist Information Office at Bajcsy-Zsilinsky utca 9, ☎ 36-517-715.

❶ ★★★ kids **Eger Castle.** According to legend, the brave defenders of Eger Castle were fuelled by Bulls Blood, Eger's red wine, during the 5-week siege in 1552. Consisting of just 2,000 Magyars, and led by István Dobó, they held off Ottoman forces 40 times their size. The Turks apparently thought the heroic Hungarians were imbibing the real blood of bulls. The effects of the wine wore off by 1596 as Eger Castle fell, and so ensued a 91-year period of Ottoman rule. Meet the stars of the battle in the **Dobó István Vármúzeum** (István Dobó Museum) within the castle grounds. You'll also find the tomb of Géza Gárdony, the author of *The Stars of Eger,* also known as the "Eclipse of the Crescent Moon," which depicts the events of 1552, as well as a dungeon. ⏱ *1 hr.* ☎ *36/312-450. www.egrivar.hu/en/. 1,200 Ft adults inc. museum (700 Ft excluding museum), 650 Ft children 6–26 and seniors 62–70 (or 350 Ft excluding museum). Daily May–Aug 8am–8pm; Apr and Sep 8am–7pm; Mar and Oct 8am–6pm; Feb–Nov 8am–5pm.*

❷ ★★ kids **Dobó tér.** To this day Eger is a remarkably well-preserved tour de force in baroque architecture. This is particularly evident in and around the central square that's divided by the River Eger and has

Eger.

Eger Cathedral.

the castle rising above it. However, as with so many squares in Hungary, a Socialist-era monstrosity steps in to spoil the party. In this case, it's more of a baroque ball, and the impostor comes in the form of the mini shopping center opposite the handsome dual-spired Minorita Church. 45 min. *Dobó tér.*

3 ★★ **Minaret.** This minaret is a pointy reminder of Eger's Ottoman occupation. It was once one of many but is the only one to have survived, albeit with no mosque attached, and as such is the northernmost surviving monument from the Turkish invasion. Scale the twisting staircase of 97 steps for panoramic views of the town. *45 min. Knézich utca 250 Ft. Apr–Oct Tues–Sun 10am–6pm.*

4 ★★ kids **Eger Bazilika (Cathedral).** Seat of Eger's bishopric and the second biggest church in Hungary, this József Hild-designed, neoclassical cathedral (1836) is notable for the army of Christian statues towering above the columns at the entrance and its three cupolas. The earth-shattering tones of the biggest church organ in Hungary can be heard at regular summer concerts, during services on Sunday at 12:45pm, or from Monday to Saturday at 11:30am. *45 min. ☎ 36/515-725. Telekessy út 6.*

5 ★★★ kids **Eger's Thermal Baths.** A vast bathing complex where you can spend long summer days without getting in the least bit bored. Everything's here from a 50m (164-ft.) swimming pool to thermal pools that work against arthritis and rheumatism. There's even a thermal pond with a waterfall that you can take a plunge in, as well as pools, a "Wellness House," a water castle and slides for the children, plus restaurant and cocktail bar. The complex is also open for evening bathing every Thursday, Friday, and Saturday from 7 to 11pm. *Petőfi tér 2. Enter from the Archbishop's Garden throughout the year, while the Petőfi tér entrance is open in summer. ☎ 36/314-142. www.egertermal.hu. 1,600 Ft adults, 1,400 Ft children, 5,000 Ft family, free for under-4s. Daily 9am–7pm, open until 9pm Thurs–Sat.*

6 kids **Egerszalók Thermal Resort.** Just 6km (4 miles) outside Eger at Egerszalók, this wonderful modern bathing complex is home to 17 indoor and outdoor pools. The resort is built around the incredible natural feature of a white limestone and travertine hill that rises dramatically out of Hungary's green northern uplands. *Egerszalók. Forrás út 4. ☎ 36/688-500. www.egerszalokfurdo.hu. 2,500 Ft for 2.5 hr adults (600 Ft more for every extra half hour started), 1,500 Ft children, 11,200 Ft family (day). Mon–Sun 10am–8pm. Buses heading to Verpelétre and Gyöngyösre stop in Egerszalok.*

The
Savvy Traveler

Before You Go

Government Tourist Offices

Hungarian National Tourist Office, For the U.S.: 350 Fifth Avenue, Suite 7107, New York, NY 10118 (☎ 212/695-1221; www.gotohungary.com). **For the U.K.:** 46 Eaton Place, London, SW1X 8AL (☎ 020/7823-1055; www.gotohungary.co.uk).

Travelers from **Australia, Canada,** and **Ireland** are not served directly but can make enquiries through **www.gotohungary.com** or through Hungarian embassies.

The Best Time to Go

Budapest's peak season runs from May to September, but with July and August often verging on the oppressively hot. The city does, however, have a wealth of baths that are a godsend when temperatures soar. May, June, and early September are usually ideal temperature-wise. August is a major vacation month and so be prepared to find a fair number of restaurants, bars, and shops shut. Budapest is a good all-year destination and despite its cold winters there are plenty of indoor activities, plus outdoor novelties like skating and shopping at Christmas markets. Hotel prices are significantly cheaper in the off-season and the city is less overrun with tourists, making a strong case for an off-peak visit.

Festivals & Special Events

SPRING. The **Budapest Spring Festival** (www.btf.hu), a bevy of high culture including opera, classical, chamber music, dance, jazz, theater, and crossover, takes place during the last 2 weeks of March. It has featured many prominent international guests as well as the cream of local talent.

On the last weekend of the Spring Festival, the offbeat **Budapest Fringe Festival** (www.budapestfringe.com) is described by its organizers as one big talent show, with everything from punk bands to acrobats and belly dancers. The hip arts melting pot of Millenáris is among the main venues (p 130).

Film fanatics get square-eyed at the **Titanic Film Festival** (www.titanicfilmfest.hu), which runs for 10 days at the end of March or the beginning of April and shows many Hungarian and international films, often ahead of their release dates. It runs simultaneously in the magnificent Art Nouveau-influenced Urania and the arthouse cinemas of Toldi, Vörösmarty, and the Örökmozgó Film Museum.

SUMMER. Usually in the first week of June at Millenáris Park in most years (p 130), the **Budai Gourmet Festival** (www.sziget.hu/budaigourmet) brings together top restaurateurs, winemakers, and pálinka distillers.

Around the summer solstice **Múzeumok Éjszakája** (Night of the Museums; www.muzeumokejszakaja.hu) allows culture vultures to visit many of the city's museums until 2am at seriously discounted prices, while special buses are laid on by the Budapest transport company, BKV, to whisk participants between the museums. Tickets can be purchased at museums and some BKV ticket booths. It was extended to 2 days in 2011.

Although the main concert season runs from late September to early June, the **Budafest Summer Festival** (☎ 1/332-4816) sees the classical concerts, opera, and ballet

Previous page: The Chain Bridge.

continue throughout July at Szent István, István Basilica, the Hilton Dominican Court, and on Margaret Island, with Klezmer and folk music also included.

On weekends in the latter half of June to the second half of August, look out for **Summer on the Chain Bridge,** with stages on both sides of the bridge, and plenty of craftspeople exhibiting their wares on and around the bridge (which is closed to traffic). Lots of festival bites to eat are available, including the classic Transylvanian hollow whirly pastry known as *Kalács,* which you can witness being made.

Hungary's answer to the U.K.'s Glastonbury, while some call it the Hungarian Woodstock, the **Sziget Festival** (www.sziget.hu/festival_english) takes place for just under a week in mid-August on an island (Hajógyári-sziget) within the city limits, so there's no need to camp out. Tickets for the 6-day event cost 54,000 Ft and 46,000 Ft respectively for camping and non-camping tickets (cheaper before May 1), and 12,000 Ft per day (at the time of writing). The festival has featured many big names from The Cure, Iggy Pop, and The Killers to Iron Maiden, underground international acts, and leading world music performers, as well as many local artists, even Hari Krishna bands. There are many other typical festival attractions such as bungee jumping and abseiling. You can take a ferry from downtown Pest right into the action.

On **St. Stephen's Day** on August 20, hordes of Hungarians take to the Danube banks between Margaret Bridge and Szabadság Bridge to watch a stunning firework display.

FALL. During the first week of September, the **Jewish Summer Festival** (☎ 1/343-0420; www.jewishfestival.hu) sees a variety of concerts, including those by Israeli pop stars, at key venues in the Jewish district with the stunning Great Synagogue, also known as Dohány utca Synagogue, at the center.

Just about anyone who is anyone in the world of Hungarian wine puts in an appearance at the **Budapest International Wine Festival** (☎ 1/203-8507; www.aborfesztival.hu), which occupies the Buda Palace's grounds from Wednesday to Sunday a.round the middle of September.

In October things get seriously abstract during the **Budapest Autumn Festival** (www.bof.hu), with lots of cutting-edge performance art, modern dance, offbeat exhibitions, and all that jazz.

On **All Saint's Day,** November 1, Hungarians visit cemeteries to pay their respects to departed relatives. More beautiful than macabre, cemeteries are lit up with candles and Kerepesi Cemetery, also known as Fiumei Úti Sírkert, at Fiumei út 16 in District VIII, is the most spectacular.

WINTER. Christmas is a quiet family affair with the main celebration on the evening of December 24. The main **Christmas market** on Vörösmárty tér (p 52) is a colorful occasion. Everyone comes out to party for the New Year, some even starting before noon on New Year's Eve at the races at Kincsem Park. In early February, the **Mangalica Festival** (www.mangalicafesztival.hu) celebrates Hungary's indigenous, flavorsomely fatty pig, which is great for curing.

The Weather

Hungary has a continental climate with hot summers and cold winters where temperatures often linger below freezing point. Summers are hot and long, occasionally uncomfortable, with temperatures often hitting 90°F (32°C) as early as

AVERAGE TEMPERATURE AND RAINFALL IN BUDAPEST

	Jan	Feb	Mar	Apr	May	June
(°C)	−1	1	6	11	19	80
(°F)	30	38	43	52	66	27
Rainfall mm.	38	27	26	30	3	10
Rainfall (inches)	1.5	1.06	1.02	1.18	1.7	0.4
	July	**Aug**	**Sept**	**Oct**	**Nov**	**Dec**
(°C)	21	21	16	11	5	1
(°F)	70	70	61	52	41	38
Rainfall in mm.	71	66	66	48	53	10
Rainfall (inches)	2.8	2.6	2.6	1.9	2.08	0.4

mid-June and sometimes staying there until mid-September. The changeover to cooler temperatures at the end of September or October can leave people wondering what's happened to fall, and vice versa to spring in May. However, like many other countries in the world these days, precise temperatures are increasingly difficult to predict as the effects of climate change take hold. An extremely mild Mediterranean-type winter can be followed by a typically cold one.

Useful Websites

- **www.budapestinfo.hu:** Budapest's official tourism website that includes information on events, key sights, and the city's baths.
- **www.festivalcity.hu:** Detailed information on the Spring, Autumn, Fringe, and Summer on the Chain Bridge festivals.
- **www.budapest.com:** The city's travel and commercial portal with a hotel booking search engine that gives instant confirmation.
- **www.elvira.hu:** An interactive train timetable that's accessible in English.
- **www.bkv.hu:** Detailed information on the city's public transport system.
- **www.xpatloop.com** and **www.caboodle.hu:** English-language sites that provide lots of practical information concerning life in Hungary. The latter's sister gastronomic site **www.chew.hu** contains detailed information on Hungary's cuisine and the culinary scene.
- **www.bbj.hu** and **www.budapesttimes.hu:** The main English-language newspapers, which also come in print form.

Cell Phones

If your phone has GSM capability, your mobile will work in Budapest. Roaming rates within the European Union have been cut drastically by regulators, making it much cheaper to use your phone in Hungary. Check with your operator before you leave.

Car Rentals

With public transport still connecting the four corners of the city with relative ease, it's unlikely that you will need to rent a car. A car does come in handy though if you're looking to take excursions beyond the city limits. Prices are generally cheaper if you book online before you arrive in Budapest. **Fox Autorent** (www.fox-autorent.com) is a renowned local independent rental firm, while the likes of **AVIS** (www.avis.com) and **HERTZ** (www.hertz.com) have offices at the airport and across the city.

Getting **There**

By Plane

Budapest has one major airport, **Liszt Ferenc International Airport** (formerly Ferihegy), which is located 15km (9.5 miles) from downtown and divided into Terminals 1 and 2, with the latter subsequently split into Terminals 2A and 2B. Terminal 1 is mainly used by budget operators. The 200E bus connects both terminals and runs to Kőbánya-Kispest metro station where you can catch a metro to the downtown area. **FŐTaxi** (☎ **1/222-2222**) operates a reliable taxi service for 3,300 Ft to 5,700 Ft one way, the price depending in which of their zones your final destination lies. FŐTaxi booths are located outside the terminals, where you check in to pick up your cab. You're given a price though you pay the driver. The **Airport Shuttle** (☎ **1/296-8555;** www.airportshuttle.hu) minibus service also runs from both terminals and the booking desks are located close to arrivals. A single ticket costs 2,990 Ft and a return is 4,990 Ft. Book your return route no later than 24 hours before departure to ensure getting a return seat. Allow plenty of time for this option because other people are also being taken to their hotels and lodgings. On the return leg they pick you up at your accommodation.

By Car

All major Hungarian roads lead to Budapest and a car provides a useful way of getting to the Hungarian capital, although once in the city the driver will have the busy traffic and aggressive drivers to contend with. Try to enter or exit the city outside of rush hour (7am to 9am and 4:30pm to 6:30pm) and you'll cut significant time off your journey.

By Train

Budapest is served by three main stations, which are named after the directions they originally served and to some extent still do. As well as eastern destinations **Keleti** (Eastern) also handles most trains to Prague and Vienna. The other two are **Nuygati** (Western) and **Déli** (Southern), with the latter serving Lake Balaton as well as Ljubljana and Zagreb.

By Bus

Budapest's new modern bus station is slightly out of the center at Népliget, but it's connected to the metro system. Eurolines arrives and departs from here.

Getting **Around**

By Public Transportation

Budapest's public transport system efficiently links all corners of the city and its coverage is dense. Although getting a bit creaky and dated, as it hasn't changed radically since the 1970s when it was considered a benchmark of Socialist planning, newer buses and trams are being rolled out continuously. All parts of the city are covered in detail, whether it be by metro, tram, trolley-bus, or bus. Single tickets (320 Ft) or a book of 10 for 2,800 Ft can usually be bought at booths or ticket kiosks next to the bus stop or metro station, but it's advisable to stock up. Validate tickets at the top of the escalators before you get on the metro and as you get on trams and buses. 1-day, 3-day, and 7-day travelcards that provide unlimited travel cost 1,550 Ft, 3,850 Ft, and 4,600 Ft respectively, although you need to provide a passport-sized photo for the latter. **BKV** is the Budapest Transport Company; the website is useful (☎ 1/258-4636; www.bkv.hu) and has an English section.

On Foot

Much of the center can be covered on foot and this is also the best way of seeing beyond the city's key sights, which is where much of Budapest's charm lies.

By Taxi

Taxis are abundant and usually cheaper when you call one as opposed to flagging them down. However, the operators of many taxi firms don't speak English. Rates vary between operators but these three listed companies provide competitive rates: **City Taxi** (☎ 1/211-1111), **Tele5Taxi** (☎ 1/555-5555), **FŐTaxi** (☎ 1/222-2222).

By Car

Driving around the jammed center can be a headache to say the least and parking spaces are often hard to come by. Parking tickets are required in many central zones and are bought from coin-operated machines.

Fast **Facts**

APARTMENT RENTALS **Dunahouse** (dunahouse.hu) offers many apartments for rent and has a huge network of offices across the city. **IBUSZ** (www.ibusz.hu) has a private accommodation service at Ferenciek tere 10 (☎ **1/485-2767**), which provides a homely alternative to staying in a hotel as well as short-term rentals. A few useful websites to try are **www.budarpads.com** for shorter as well as long-term rentals and **www.apartmentsin budapest.com** offering apartments from around 20€ per night.

ATMS/CASHPOINTS The easiest and most recommended way to get cash in Budapest is via ATMs on most downtown streets. Although banks charge a fee per withdrawal, it still remains the safest option and transactions are carried out according to a generally favorable wholesale exchange rate. At larger banks you can step in off the street to use the bank machines and security cameras are operated.

B&BS Local sites **www.budapest hotels.com, www.justbookit.hu,** and the internationally popular **www.tripadvisor.com** provide online booking services for a wide range of Budapest hotels and often offer discounts compared to the regular prices you get when approaching a hotel direct. Tourist information portal **www.budapest.com** also has a hotel search and booking function.

BABYSITTING The **Babysitter Training and Agency Center** (www.babaklub.com) has a babysitter and au pair search function and uses only qualified babysitters, many of whom speak English. The renowned **Korompay Family Day Care** at Menesi út 19 in District 11 (☎ **1/466-5740** or 06/30-921-7820) also works in the English language and is run by former kindergarten teachers.

BANKING HOURS Most banks are open from Monday to Friday from 8am to 4pm, although some larger branches of major banks stay open until 5:30pm. Shops and hotels often cash travelers checks but at inferior rates to banks.

BIKE RENTALS **Budapest Bike** (☎ 06/30-944-5533; www.budapestbike.hu) at Wesselényi utca 18 in District VII rents new men's and women's bikes for 3,000 Ft per day and tandems for 5,000 Ft per day with longer and shorter rentals also available.

BUSINESS HOURS Shops tend to be open from 10am to 6pm, although many stay open until 8pm in shopping malls.

CAR RENTALS See Car Rentals earlier in this chapter on p 166.

CUSTOMS Non-E.U. citizens over the age of 16 can bring in 250ml eau de cologne and 50g perfume, 200 cigarettes, or 50 cigars, or 250g tobacco, or a combination of these, up to 250g, while citizens from EU countries can bring in 800 cigarettes.

Non-EU citizens are allowed to enter with 1 liter of distilled alcohol and 2 liters of wine, while EU citizens are permitted to carry 90 liters of wine and 110 liters of beer into Hungary.

The same numbers apply when departing Hungary. Check this website for further information: http://vam.gov.hu/.

DENTISTS (see Emergencies, below).

DINING Eating out in Budapest is generally a casual affair with no jacket required except for a few exclusive restaurants (you should enquire when making a booking).

DRINKING The legal drinking age in Hungary is 18. Drinking on public transport and on the street is illegal. Hungary has a zero-tolerance attitude to drink-driving.

ELECTRICITY Like the rest of continental Europe, Hungary uses two-pin plugs and the 230V current. Adapters can be bought in electrical stores such as **Media Markt** (http://www.mediamarkt.hu/).

EMBASSIES The **Australian Embassy** is at Királyhágó tér 8–9, District 12, ☎ **1/457 9777**; the **Embassy of Canada** at Ganz utca 12–14, District 2, ☎ **1/392-3360;** the **U.K. Embassy** at Harmincad utca 6, District 5, ☎ **1/266 2888; Ireland's Embassy** at Gránit Torony in the Bank Center at Szabadság tér 7–9 ☎ **1/302-9600;** and the **U.S. Embassy** at Szabadság tér 12, ☎ **1/475 4400.**

EMERGENCIES **SOS Dental Service** at Király utca 14 in District VI, ☎ **1/267-9602,** and **Stomatologia** at Szentkirályi utca 40 in District VIII, ☎ **1/317-6600,** offers around-the-clock dental treatment. Dial ☎ **104** for an ambulance.

EVENT LISTINGS www.funzine.hu has up-to-date information about cultural events, and look out for the print version free in hotels.

FAMILY TRAVEL The Budapest card is valid for one adult and one child up to 14 years of age and costs 8,300 Ft for 72 hours. It provides free travel and many sightseeing benefits, including free entry to numerous popular sights (see Passes, below).

GAY & LESBIAN TRAVELERS www.budapest.gayguide.net provides detailed information on accommodation, cruising, restaurants, saunas, events, etc.

INSURANCE It's always a good idea to have travel cancellation insurance, but especially so with the volatile state of some airlines. Travelers should contact their medical insurance carrier to see what their policy is for out-of-country medical expenses. U.S. travelers should note that Medicare does not provide any coverage outside of the U.S.

Travelers from the U.K. and the Republic of Ireland should carry their European Health Insurance Card (EHIC), which replaced the E111 form as proof of entitlement to free/reduced-cost medical treatment abroad. (www.ehic.org.uk/www.ehic.ie). Note that the EHIC only covers "necessary medical treatment" and for repatriation costs, lost money, baggage, or cancellation, travel insurance should always be sought.

INTERNET ACCESS Internet cafes are increasingly common and you're likely to see them around downtown. **Fougou** at Wesselényi utca 57 in District VII (☎ **1/787-4888;** fougou.uw.hu) also offers cheap calls to over 60 countries, photocopying, printing, faxing, and scanning, from 7am to 2am. The useful website www.hotspotter.hu, although in Hungarian, shows all Wi-Fi Internet hotspots on a map with the ones marked in blue representing those that are free—click on the flag and the address comes up.

LIMOS **Limousine Service Hungary** (☎ **1/220-6120;** www.limohungary.com) and **ONE Limo** (www.onelimo.com) handle suitably flash fleets.

LOST PROPERTY If your luggage is lost on arrival make a claim at the airport immediately. Police stations handle lost property. Check which district your items were lost or stolen in and go to that district's police station, although not much ends up returned.

MONEY Hungary uses the Forint (Ft or HUF). The exchange rate varies and at the time of writing US$1 was worth 189 Ft with £1 equaling 311 Ft. Hungary is far from a cashless society and the use of credit cards is slowly catching on.

ORIENTATION TOURS **City-Circle Sightseeing** (☎ **1/374-7070,** www.citytour.hu) runs a hop on/hop off city tour commencing every hour from József Nádor tér. Tickets cost Ft. 4,500 and are valid for 24 hours. It also has a hop on/hop off boat service for Ft. 2,500 from Vigadó tér.

Cityrama (☎ **1/302-4382,** www.cityrama.hu) offers an extensive range of tours in Budapest and beyond, including the **Waterbus.**

Rockhoppers runs a series of cultural tours such as Classic Budapest, Jewish Budapest and Gypsy Village, the latter taking in Pest's main Roma district as well as an authentic Roma village where you get to dance and party with the welcoming locals, www.Rockhoppers.hu.

PASSES The **Budapest Card** (www.bpcard.rombrandt.hu) costs Ft. 6,300 and Ft. 7,500 for 48 and 72 hours respectively. It's valid for one adult and one child up to 14 years of age and offers: unlimited travel on public transport; free or discounted entry to 60 museums and to several sights; reduced price tickets for cultural and folklore programs; discounts in restaurants, spas, and on car rental; travel accident insurance; and other benefits. It is available in 250 tourist and transport outlets across the city.

PASSPORTS Passports are issued by the relevant embassy who should also be contacted immediately in the case of lost or stolen passports. You are also required to report the incident to local police and request a police report. See Embassies, above.

PHARMACIES Pharmacies are plentiful in Budapest. **Teréz Patika** at Teréz körút 41 (☎ **1/311-4439**) is open around the clock and charges a small fee for an after-hours service.

SAFETY Budapest feels remarkably safe at night compared to Western cities of a similar size, although isolated incidents do occur. Be wary of taxi drivers as even those of reputable firms have been known to rip off foreigners. Refuse to take a cab ride should they neglect to run the meter. Pickpockets can be a problem on public transport. See also Tourist Traps, below.

SENIOR TRAVELERS Foreign senior citizens are entitled to the same free public transport right as Hungarians.

SMOKING Smoking was banned at public transport stops in 2011 and is to be banned in all pubs and restaurants at the beginning of 2012. Until then restaurants are required to have a non-smoking area.

STAYING HEALTHY Ticks (*kullancs*) populate woodland areas in parts of Hungary, including the Buda Hills to some extent, and pose a threat in the form of Tick brain-inflaming Borne Encephalitis (TBE) and Lyme Disease. Cover up well in wooded areas and check for the little blood suckers later, especially behind your hair line. They can be twisted out with tweezers, but go straight to a doctor if the insect doesn't come out in one piece. Mosquitoes can be a pest in summer but don't carry malaria in Hungary. Insect repellent can deter both.

TAXES VAT (Value Added Tax) is known as ÁFA in Hungary and is charged and included on most goods and services at a rate of 25%. VAT can be reclaimed at the airport on the purchase of goods.

TELEPHONES Cards can be bought at kiosks, while a few can be operated by 10, 20, 50, and 100 Ft coins, although sometimes the coin slots are blocked by fraudsters.

The prefix for Budapest is 1, followed by a seven-digit number, but you drop the prefix when calling within the city. When calling Budapest from abroad, it is necessary to dial the country code for Hungary (36) followed by the prefix and seven-digit number. When calling a Hungarian number beyond the capital, use the 06 prefix.

Mobile phones have more than 100% penetration among the population. To dial a mobile you start with 06, followed by the prefix of one of the three providers (T-Mobile (30), Telenor (20), and Vodafone (70)), which is subsequently followed by a seven-digit number. To call a Hungarian mobile from abroad, you start with the country code followed by the mobile provider's prefix and then the number.

TICKETS Central ticket offices supply tickets for the full gamut of concerts and performances: **Jegymester** (Bajcsy-Zsilinszky út 31, ☎ **1/302-4433;** www.jegymester.hu); **Ticket Express** (Andrássy út 18, ☎ **06/30-303-0999**); Ticket **Express Jókai utca** (Jókai utca 40, ☎ **1/353-0692**); and **Vigadó Ticket Service** (Vörösmarty tér 1, ☎ **1/317-6417**).

TIPPING Adding between 10 and 15% to restaurant and bar bills is the norm, but also for trips to hairdressers, beauticians, etc. Service charges are often mentioned on menus in English, but if not look out for the word *kiszolgalás*.

TOILETS Public toilets aren't in great supply but can be found at the key transport hubs. You have to pay a small fee to use them, usually around 100 Ft. Dropping into hotels discretely is often the best option.

TOURIST OFFICES The main **Budapest tourist office** is at Március 15 tér 7 (☎ **1/266-0479;** www.budapestinfo.hu) with branches around town, such as Sütő utca 2 in

District V next to Deák tér metro station and at all airport terminals.

TOURIST TRAPS The U.S. Embassy carries a black list of rip-off joints to be avoided at all costs at: http://hungary.usembassy.gov/tourist_advisory.html. For U.K. visitors, check out the Foreign Office website at www.fco.gov.uk.

TRAVELERS WITH DISABILITIES Getting on and off public transport can be a challenge, although the 4/6 trams that operate on the most important routes can be accessed by wheelchairs as increasingly on buses.

VAT See taxes.

WATER Tap water is completely safe to drink.

Budapest: **A Brief History**

106 Roman Aquincum, now part of Budapest, becomes the center of lower Pannonia.

896 Seven Magyar tribes ride in to capture the Carpathian basin, including the territory known today as Hungary.

955 The Magyars are defeated at Augsburg, marking the end of their initial expansion into Western Europe.

1000 King István (Stephen) adopts Christianity leading to the Pope recognizing Hungary as a country.

1361 Buda becomes the capital of Hungary.

1541–1686 Turkish occupation.

1703-1711 Ferenc Rákóczi II, Prince of Transylvania, and his forces enjoy some successes against the now ruling Habsburgs, but ultimately lost when French support failed to materialize.

1848 Unsuccessful revolution against Habsburg rule after a period of reform in which the Hungarian economy and culture developed significantly.

1849 The Chain Bridge becomes the first permanent bridge between Buda and Pest.

1867 Reconciliation with Austria sees a period of joint rule.

1873 Buda and Pest merge to become one city.

1920 The post-World War 1 Treaty of Trianon sees Hungary lose some two-thirds of its territory.

1956 Revolution against Soviet-backed dictatorship sees the streets of Budapest become a battlefield with the Soviets returning to suppress the short period of freedom.

1970S Free-market reforms see Hungary become the "happiest barracks in the [Warsaw Pact] camp."

1989 A velvet revolution ensues after Hungary plays a major role in helping East Germans escape to the West.

2004 Hungary enters the E.U. on May 1.

2006 Riots ensue after a speech by Prime Minister Ferenc Gyurcsány at a closed party is leaked, in which he says his party screwed up their term of office.

2010 Center-right Fidesz returns to power with a constitution changing two-thirds majority.

2011 Government's new repressive media law incurs the European Union's wrath as Hungary takes Presidency of the E.U.

Useful Phrases & Menu Terms

Useful Words & Phrases

ENGLISH	HUNGARIAN	PRONUNCIATION
Hello	Jó napot! (form.)/ Szia! (inf.)	*Your-nopot/ See-ya/*
Good morning	Jó reggelt!	*Your-reggelt*
Good afternoon	Jó napot!	*Your-nopot*
Good evening	Jó estét!	*Your-eshtate*
How are you?	Hogy vagy?	*Hodge-vodge*
Fine, thanks	Jól, köszönöm!	*Jol. cusunum*
Thank you	Köszönöm!	*Cusumum*
Good-bye	Viszontlátásra!(form.)/ Szia!(inf.)	*Visontlatasra*
Good night	Jó éjszakát!	*Yo ace-okat*
Yes	Igen	*Igen*
No	Nem	*Nem*
Excuse me	Elnézést	*Elnayzayst*
Sorry	Bocsánat	*Botch-arnot*
Do you speak English?	Beszél angolul?	*Besale ongolule*
Can you help me?	Tudna segíteni?	*Tude-na shegyteni*
Do you have…?	Van…?	*Von*
How much is it?	Mennyibe kerül?	*Men-yiber kerule*
When?	Mikor?	*Me-kore (me-core)*
What?	Mi?	*Me*
Give me	Kérek	*Kay-wreck*
Where is…?	Hol van?	*Hol-von*
the station	az állomás	*oz arllomash*
a post office	egy posta	*edge powsta*
a bank	egy bank	*edge bonk*
a hotel	egy szálloda	*edge sarl-odar*
a restaurant	egy étterem	*edge ate-erem*
a pharmacy	egy gyógyszertár	*george-sertar*
the toilet	a WC	*a vey-say*
To the right	Jobbra	*yobb-ro/a*
To the left	Balra	*bolra*
Straight ahead	Egyenesen	*edge-en-eshen*
I don't understand	Nem értem–	*nem airtem*
What time is it?	Mennyi az idő?	*Men-yee oz idur*
I would like…	Szeretnék…	*Seret-nayke*
to eat	enni	*any—but emphasize and pronounce the double n*
a room for one night	egy szobát egy éjszakára	*edge sobat edge ace-aka-ro*
a taxi	egy taxit	*edge taxeet*

ENGLISH	HUNGARIAN	PRONUNCIATION
When?	Mikor?	*Me-kore (me-core)*
Yesterday	Tegnap	*Teg-nop*
Today	Ma	*Mo*
Tomorrow	Holnap	*Hol-nop*
Men/Man	Férfi	*Fer-fee*
Women/Woman	Nől	*Nure*
Adult	Felnőtt	*Felnurt*
Student	Diák	*Dee-ak*
Senior citizen	Nyugdíjas	*Noogdee-ash*
Child	Gyermek	*Djermek*
Breakfast	Reggeli	*Regg-ily*
Lunch	Ebéd	*Ebade*
Dinner	Vacsora	*Votch-ore-a*

Numbers

NUMBER	HUNGARIAN	PRONUNCIATION
1	egy	*edge*
2	kettő	*kett-ure*
3	három	*har-um*
4	négy	*naydge*
5	öt	*urt*
6	hat	*hot*
7	hét	*hate*
8	nyolc	*knee-olce*
9	kilenc	*kee-lenc*
10	tíz	*tease*
11	tizenegy	*tease-en-edge*
12	tizenkettő	*tease-en-kett-ure*
13	tizenhárom	*tease-en-har-um*
14	tizennégy	*tease-en-naydge*
15	tizenöt	*tease-en-urt*
16	tizenhat	*tease-en-hot*
17	tizenhét	*tease-en-hate*
18	tizennyolc	*tease-en-knee-olce*
19	tizenkilenc	*tease-en-kee-lenc*
20	húsz	*huwse*
30	harminc	*har-mince*
40	negyven	*nedge-ven*
50	ötven	*urt-ven*
60	hatvan	*hot-von*
70	hetven	*het-ven*
80	nyolcvan	*knee-olce-von*
90	kilencven	*kee-lenc-ven*
100	száz	*saz*
1000	ezer	*ez-air*
2000	kétezer	*kate-ez-air*
3000	háromezer	*har-um ez-air*

Hungarian Menu

Most restaurants now have English-language menus but this list is useful in the more basic places, and for translating the daily specials list, which is often in Hungarian only.

BASICS

Reggeli	Breakfast
Ebéd	Lunch
Vacsora	Dinner
Kenyér	Bread
Vaj	Butter
Méz	Honey
Dzsem	Jam
Sajt	Cheese
Sonka	Ham
Kolbász	Sausage
Tojás	Egg
Só	Salt
Bors	Peppers
Cukor	Sugar
Tej	Milk
Olaj	Oil
Ecet	Vinegar

DRINK

Víz	Water
Ásványíz	Mineral water
Bor	Wine
Száraz	Dry
Édes	Sweet
Fehér	White
Vörös	Red
Sör	Beer
Pálinka	Fruit brandy

FISH, MEAT & ACCOMPANIMENTS

Husok	Meats
Bárány	Lamb
Csirke	Chicken
Kacsa	Duck
Liba	Goose
Marha	Beef
Nyúl	Rabbit
Pulyka	Turkey
Szarvas	Venison
Page Borjú	Veal
Comb	Leg
Mell	Breast
Máj	Liver
Sonka	Ham
Hal	Fish

Harcsa	Catfish
Kagyló	Mussels
Lazac	Salmon
Pisztráng	Trout
Rák	Crab, prawn
Ponty	Carp
Tonhal	Tuna
Burgonya	Potatoes
Hasábburgonya	French fries
Rízs	Rice
Tészta	Pasta

FRUIT & VEGETABLES

Zöldség	Vegetables
Gomba	Mushroom
Karfiol	Cauliflower
Kukorica	Maize
Lencse	Lentils
Sárgarépa	Carrot
Spárga	Asparagus
Spenót	Spinach
Hal	Fish
Zöldbab	Green beans
Borsó	Peas
Saláta	Lettuce
Uborka	Cucumber
Paradicsom	Tomato
Alma	Apple
Dinnye	Melon
Eper	Strawberry
Narancs	Orange
Őszibarack	Peach
Sárgabarack	Apricot
Szilva	Plum
Dió	Walnut
Gesztenye	Chestnut
Málna	Raspberry

HUNGARIAN SPECIALTIES

Gulyásleves	Goulash soup
Bableves	Bean soup
Halászlé	Fish soup
Töltött káposzta	Stuffed cabbage
Hortobágyi palacsinta	Pancake with minced meat
Somlói galuska	Sponge cake with chocolate sauce, nuts, raisins, and cream
Pörkölt	Stew
Harcsapaprikás	Catfish paprika with dumplings or pasta
Gundel palacsinta	Pancake with walnut, chocolate sauce, and cream

Index

See also Accommodations and Restaurant indexes, below.

D

E

F

M

N

O

P

R

S

Accommodations Index

Restaurant Index